THE BUDDHA TAROT
Companion

About the Author

Robert M. Place is an internationally known visionary artist and illustrator. He is recognized as an expert on the Western mystical tradition and the history and philosophy of the Tarot, and his work has appeared in many books and publications. Place is also the designer, illustrator, and coauthor of the highly acclaimed *Alchemical Tarot* and *The Angels Tarot*. He has appeared on the Discovery Channel and the Learning Channel and has conducted lectures and workshops throughout the country, including the Open Center and the Omega Institute in New York and the International Tarot Congress in Chicago. Place's work in precious metals has been displayed in museums such as the New York State Museum, the American Craft Museum, and the White House.

To Write to the Author

If you wish to contact the author or would like more information about this book, please write to the author in care of Llewellyn Worldwide and we will forward your request. Both the author and publisher appreciate hearing from you and learning of your enjoyment of this book and how it has helped you. Llewellyn Worldwide cannot guarantee that every letter written to the author can be answered, but all will be forwarded. Please write to:

Robert M. Place
℅ Llewellyn Worldwide
P.O. Box 64383, Dept. 1-56718-529-0
St. Paul, MN 55164-0383, U.S.A.
Please enclose a self-addressed stamped envelope for reply,
or $1.00 to cover costs. If outside U.S.A., enclose
international postal reply coupon.

Many of Llewellyn's authors have websites with additional information and resources. For more information, please visit our website at:
http://www.llewellyn.com

THE BUDDHA TAROT Companion

A Mandala of Cards

Robert M. Place

With a Foreword by Robert O'Neill

2004
Llewellyn Publications
St. Paul, Minnesota 55164-0383, U.S.A.

The Buddha Tarot Companion: A Mandala of Cards © 2004 by Robert M. Place. All rights reserved. No part of this book may be used or reproduced in any manner whatsoever, including Internet usage, without written permission from Llewellyn Publications except in the case of brief quotations embodied in critical articles and reviews.

First Edition
First Printing, 2004

Book design and editing by Joanna Willis
Cover art © 2002 by Robert M. Place
Cover design by Lisa Novak
Illustrations on pages 106, 108, 117–19, and 123 by Dover Publications
Illustrations on pages 48, 67, 69, 74–75, 110, 112–14, 133–227, and 233–308 by Robert M. Place

Library of Congress Cataloging-in-Publication Data
Place, Robert Michael.
   The Buddha tarot companion: a mandala of cards / Robert M. Place.
      p.   cm.
   Includes bibliographical references and index.
   ISBN 1-56718-529-0
   1. Tarot. 2. Buddhism—Miscellanea. I. Title.

BF1879.T2P547 2004
133.3'2424—dc22

                                                                             2003060511

Llewellyn Worldwide does not participate in, endorse, or have any authority or responsibility concerning private business transactions between our authors and the public.
   All mail addressed to the author is forwarded but the publisher cannot, unless specifically instructed by the author, give out an address or phone number.
   Any Internet references contained in this work are current at publication time, but the publisher cannot guarantee that a specific location will continue to be maintained. Please refer to the publisher's website for links to authors' websites and other sources.

Llewellyn Publications
A Division of Llewellyn Worldwide, Ltd.
P.O. Box 64383, Dept. 1-56718-529-0
St. Paul, MN 55164-0383, U.S.A.
www.llewellyn.com

 Printed in the United States of America on recycled paper

ALSO BY ROBERT M. PLACE

Tarot of the Saints
The Buddha Tarot

*I dedicate this book to
Pythagoras and to Buddha,
brothers in the One.
I also dedicate this book to my friend
Brian Williams.*

Contents

Foreword xi
Preface xiii

INTRODUCTION: THE EAST-WEST CONNECTION   1
    East-West Timeline   9

1 PAPER IMAGES   15
    The Birth of the Tarot   17
    Variations in the Order of the Trumps   20
    The Tarot's Creator   23

2 THE MYSTICAL TAROT   25
    Plato the Mystic   27
    Plotinus and His Students   33
    Hermeticism   35
    Neoplatonism and the Pythagorean Triple-Soul   40
    Neoplatonism and Romance   42
    Renaissance Platonists   59
    Renaissance Neoplatonists   68
    Neoplatonic Influences in the Tarot   72
    Interpreting the Trumps   76

3 THE LIFE OF BUDDHA   81
    The Four Noble Truths   87
    The Path Beyond Class   93

4 THE MANDALA   101
   Sacred Space   102
   Mount Meru   104
   Some Examples of Mandalas   107
   The Five Jinas   115
   Four Functions, Four Yogas   124

5 THE JOURNEY TO THE CENTER OF THE WORLD   131
      The Descent from Tusita Heaven—The Fool   133
     I. Asita—The Seer   138
     II. Maya—The Mother   143
    III. Yasodhara—The Future Empress   148
    IV. Siddhartha—The Future Emperor   152
    V. Suddhodhana—The Father   155
    VI. Siddhartha and Yasodhara—The Lovers   158
    VII. Siddhartha's Visit—The Chariot   162
   VIII. Karma—Justice   165
    IX. The Old Man and the Sadhu—The Hermit   169
    X. Reincarnation—The Wheel of Life   172
   XI. Siddhartha Cuts His Hair—Strength   179
   XII. The Invalid—The Suffering Man   183
  XIII. The Corpse—Death   187
  XIV. The Middle Path—Temperance   190
   XV. Mara—The Devil   194
  XVI. The Flaming Disk—The Tower   198
 XVII. The Chakras—The Morning Star   202
XVIII. Wesak—The Full Moon   209
  XIX. Buddha and Sakti—The Sun   213
   XX. The First Sermon—Judgement   218
  XXI. White Tara—The World   223
 XXII. Parinirvana   227

6 THE WORLD OF THE FOUR BUDDHAS   231
    Suit of Vajras   233
    Suit of Jewels   252
    Suit of Lotuses   271
    Suit of Double Vajras   290

7 DIVINATION   309
    The Three-Card Message   313
    The Relationship Spread   316
    The Chakra Reading   317
    The Mandala Meditation   323

Acknowledgments   329
Notes   331
Glossary   337
Bibliography and Recommended Reading   353
Index   359

Foreword

I finished reading *The Buddha Tarot Companion* and sat back with my eyes closed. I was expecting a vision of the Buddha with maybe a hint of a smile or frown. Instead I saw Siddhartha/Gautama/Buddha doing cartwheels on mountaintops and laughing so hard that he had to stop and catch his breath! Even the middle path allows joy.

You are about to begin a magical journey, reading what may well be the most significant book ever written about the Tarot. Grab Toto really tight because you might wake up in Moria with a glowing ring on your finger or find yourself as keeper in a game of quidditch. You will place yourself in the hands of a magus—just as Dante found himself with Virgil, Frodo with Gandalf, and Luke with Yoda. You will experience the history of human response to suffering flash by in a fascinating kaleidoscope of violet and rose. History here is scholarly but psychedelic, fascinating, and addictive.

The basic premise might strike one as strange. A fundamental parallelism between the Tarot and Buddhism? The journey of the Fool taking a path similar to the enlightenment of Siddhartha? If there is only one path, one life experience, then we must not be surprised to meet Buddha on the road. The Western and Eastern experience must necessarily converge since we are all voyaging to the top of the same sacred mountain.

Robert Place will introduce you to the legend of Siddhartha. He will instruct you painlessly in the detailed history of the Tarot. He will illustrate artistically the surprising parallels between the life of Buddha and the Tarot. He will introduce you to the Tarot trumps as stages on the mystic's journey to enlightenment. He will show you another culture that has expressed the same spiritual experience with different symbols. The symbols may seem strange at first, but they will become hauntingly familiar before you finish reading.

The scope of vision in this book has not been attempted before. Nothing like this has been written before—and you will never see the Tarot the same again, never read the cards the same again, never be the same again. I recommend some chamomile tea, maybe some incense and a candle, definitely a long bubble bath. When you emerge from *this* tunnel, you won't be the same again.

ROBERT O'NEILL
Tarot historian and author

Preface

My involvement with the Tarot started with a dream, and every one of the three decks that I have designed before this one was inspired by a dream or a vision. *The Buddha Tarot* was also inspired by a dream, however I cannot actually recall the dream. The inspiration for this deck started on Christmas in 1996. My wife and I were staying at her parents' house in New Jersey. On Christmas Eve, I had been reading *The Illustrated World's Religions* by Huston Smith and went to bed after reading the section on Buddhism. When I woke on Christmas morning, a correlation between the life of Buddha and the Tarot was all worked out. I could clearly see how the details of the story of Buddha's life fit together flawlessly with the Tarot trumps, illustrating that they are essentially the same story. I had worked on it in my sleep but I could not remember the process—only the result.

I started explaining my revelation to my wife, Rose Ann, and amazed myself with how the elements of Buddha's life fit the images in the Tarot. There were the four sights that convinced Siddhartha to leave his life of pleasure and his lover and become an ascetic: an old man, suffering, death, and a hermit. There was even the chariot that he used to ride to town to see the sights. Before this, his father had ruled his life like a Pope and had been guiding him toward the role of Emperor, another trump. Once Siddhartha realized that the ascetic life was also a dead end, he embraced the virtue temperance and had to deal with the temptations of Mara, the devil. Buddha remained undefeated and rose through various levels of enlightenment, just as the

Tarot depicts a hierarchy of celestial images leading to the mystical vision on the highest trump. The story even fit the three-part pattern that I have found in the Tarot: the first dealing with hope, the second with fear, and the third the middle path, which is beyond hope and fear and leads to mastery or enlightenment.

Armed with this new insight, I added a new lecture to my list of Tarot lectures: "Buddha and the Tarot." However, at first I found that no one wanted to hear about it. The idea of putting Buddha and the Tarot together was too much of a stretch for most of the centers that I lectured at. They all wanted something more conventional, like the development of the Tarot in the Renaissance or alchemy and the Tarot. I set up a Tarot workshop at Naropa University, a Buddhist university, but it was canceled when not enough people signed up for the class.

When I was in San Francisco on business, I visited my former professor of oriental art and explained my revelation to him just as I had explained it to my wife. He seemed impressed and encouraged me to write an article on it. So while I was in San Francisco, I pitched my idea to *Gnosis* magazine and pitched an idea for a book on the subject to my editor at HarperCollins. HarperCollins was more enthusiastic than *Gnosis,* but my editor could not get the board to agree to a contract.

I even had an agent who hated the idea, and tried to discourage me from pursuing it. "It's not Buddhism and it's not the Tarot," he said. "It's neither one nor the other. How is anyone going to package and sell it? It doesn't fit any category."

"That's the point," I replied. "It makes a connection between the two; it is about both. What I am saying is that some things don't fit neatly into one category. It's just like saying, 'Is William Blake a visual artist or a writer?'"

"He's a writer," my agent replied without any hesitation.

This is when I realized that he was not going to be able to promote my ideas. After that, our relationship came to an end.

In 1999, I finally got to deliver my lecture on Buddha and the Tarot at the World Tarot Congress in Chicago. It was there that I made contact with Llewellyn, and later received a contract to create the *Tarot of the Saints*. While I was working on the *Saints,* I pitched the idea for a Buddhist Tarot to the company and received a contract for that as well. Suddenly people seemed interested in the idea. I even gave a lecture on the subject at the New York Open Center this year (2002). It seems that its time has come.

*All that we are arises with our thoughts.
With our thoughts we make the world.*

                        Buddha

*Among the great things, which are to be
found among us, the being of nothingness
is the greatest.*

                        Leonardo da Vinci

Introduction

THE EAST-WEST CONNECTION

How could the Tarot fit so closely to the story of Buddha? First, although it is far-fetched, I examined the possibility that the creators of the Tarot were directly influenced by the legend of Buddha. It is a common misconception that ancient cultures were isolated from one another, but this is not true.

There were points of contact between Buddhists and Western culture. About two hundred years after Buddha's death in the third century BCE, the emperor Ashoka united India into one Buddhist empire and sent out missionaries to spread the religion beyond India. Because of his efforts, Buddhism spread to Sri Lanka and to Gandhara, the Greek kingdom to the north that had been part of Alexander the Great's empire. This is an area that now belongs to Pakistan and Afghanistan. It was an important link in the Silk Road, the trade route that carried goods and ideas from China to Western Europe, and it was from this area that Buddhism eventually spread to China. The Greeks of Gandhara left their influence on Buddhism by sculpting images of the Buddha in the Hellenistic style. Today, we can still see Hellenistic folds on the garments of stone Buddhas as far from Greece as Japan. However, Ashoka was not content with these victories. He set up communications with the Greek mainland and sent out missionaries across the Hellenistic world and into Egypt.[1]

The classical world maintained communications with India and the ancient Western philosophers were familiar with Indian philosophy. Clement of Alexandria exhibited knowledge of Indian religion in his writings, as did other Greek and Latin writers.[2] Having heard of the wise men of India, the third-century philosopher Plotinus tried to visit India in his youth by joining a military campaign that was headed that way, but failed to reach his goal. It is recorded that the Indian king Poros, together with learned Brahmans, participated in the Mystery at Eleusis during the reign of Emperor Augustus.[3] Literary and archeological evidence attests to the fact that during Augustus's reign there were Roman trading settlements on the coast of India, and goods and information passed between both civilizations.

After the fall of Rome, Western Europe was cut off from trade with the East, but that did not stop the Islamic Sufis from incorporating Buddha's biography into their teachings. It was the Islamic world that introduced Christians to the remarkable life of Buddha during the Middle Ages. The European Christians were enamored with the story, and they transformed him into a Christian saint. They called him St. Josaphat, a name derived from the title "Bodhisattva." Even in the early medieval period—the so-called "Dark Ages"—East-West contacts did not come to a total standstill. At an exhibit of Viking art at the Metropolitan Museum, I remember being amazed when I saw a silver Buddha that was part of a tenth-century Viking treasure hoard found in England.

In the thirteenth century, the Polo family of Venice traveled to Buddhist China for economic gain. Two of the Polos were appointed ambassadors by Kublai Khan and traveled to Rome to bring greetings from the Mongol Buddhist emperor to the Christian pope. Marco Polo went back to China with his brothers and on his return in 1295 he wrote the account of his journey. Marco Polo's book included numerous tales and legends that he had heard while in Asia. One of the stories that he included was the life of Buddha. His book became immensely popular and for Europeans it was the main source of information about the East.[4]

As we can see, there is ample evidence that the story of Buddha was available to the Renaissance creators of the Tarot. Yet although the structure and details of the trumps can be shown to fit this story, it is most likely that Buddha was not on the mind of the first Tarot artist. The Tarot is mystical and follows this same story pattern, but it does so with symbols and images that are entirely derived from the Renaissance Christian culture that created and used the cards. Although the story of Buddha may have become part of the mix of mystical ideas that were prevalent in the Renaissance, it seems more likely that the similarity between the Tarot trumps and Buddha's legend is because they both follow the same archetypal pattern, the one that scholar Joseph Campbell calls the "hero's journey." However, when we look at other manifestations of this archetype, such as the twelve labors of Hercules, a hero who actually appears in one of the earliest Tarot decks on the Strength card, we see that the fit is not as close, detail for detail, as it is with Buddha and the Tarot. It seems more likely that the similarity between the Tarot trumps and Buddha's legend is one of those magical occurrences that Jung called "synchronicity."

There is more to this synchronicity than just a correlation between Buddha and the Tarot. There is a similarity between the mystical philosophy of Buddhism and the mystical philosophy that is at the core of the Western Mystery Tradition. It is another modern misconception that the ancient Greeks set the West on a scientific, materialist path based on logic, and that there is a great gulf that separates their thinking from the mystical, intuitive way of the East. Eastern and Western cultures both are logical, intuitive, and mystical in their own way, and there are more similarities between them than most scholars, until now, have admitted. We tend to divide the past into historic and geographical divisions and act like these divisions are impenetrable boxes. We go through the past deciding into what box each individual or culture should be placed and lose sight of the continuous unity that is the true nature of time and the surface of the earth. We do the same thing with branches of knowledge. Buddhism is boxed as a religion, although it is admitted that it has philosophical aspects as well. In the Western mind, the Buddhist belief in reincarnation, which cannot be proven through scientific observation or logic, sets it apart from the philosophical tradition. However, the founders of the Western philosophical tradition, Pythagoras and Plato, also believed in reincarnation and it was an integrated part of their philosophy.

I have used this analogy of boxes separating branches of knowledge when discussing this with my students. When I have asked my students what box they would put Buddha into, they do not hesitate to say "religion." When I have asked them about Pythagoras, they put him in a box labeled "math" and sometimes "philosophy." Yet, Pythagoras was a religious leader, as well as being the first person to call himself a philosopher, and the ancient writers venerate him like a Buddha, even suggesting that he was divine.

Pythagoras lived in the sixth century BCE, the same century as Buddha. This century is at the center of the period that historians call the Axial Age. It was a pivotal time when the religious systems emerged that have continued to shape the world up to the present. Besides Buddha, it was the time of Lao Tzu, Confucius, and Zoroaster. In the West, the Axial Age was when Greek philosophy emerged from the philosophy of Thales to that of Plato. During this period, Pythagoras, after traveling and studying in Babylon and Egypt, came to a spiritual awakening and set up a community in the Greek colony at Croton, Italy, where he could guide others. In the same century, Buddha, after studying with the masters of India, also found his own way to enlightenment and gathered followers who were in need of his teachings. Pythagoras taught his followers that the soul was doomed to suffer through endless reincarnations until the individual could break loose from this pattern and reunite with a spiritual totality. This is similar to the Buddha's teaching called the Four Noble Truths, and to Buddha's vision of the Wheel of Life, which depicts as a great wheel the endless reincarnations that all humanity is doomed to suffer.

To break free of this wheel both teachers recommended a life governed by morality and the practice of contemplation in silence. In fact, those who wished to join Pythagoras's community had to refrain from speaking for five years. Once accepted, they wore white garments, adopted a vegetarian diet, and refrained from intoxicants. Pythagoras used diet and exercise for healing, but he also used music. By attuning his lyre to the music of the celestial spheres, he could use it to bring harmony to the seven soul centers located in ascending order from the base of the torso to the head. His goal was to lead his disciples to enlightenment. As his third-century biographer Iamblichus put it:

> By all these inventions, therefore, he divinely purified and healed the soul, resuscitating and saving its divine part, and directing to the intelligible its divine eye, which, as Plato says, is more worth saving than ten thousand corporeal eyes, for when it is strengthened and clarified by appropriate aids, when we look through this, we perceive the truth about all being.[5]

For this true knowledge, which Iamblichus is describing above, Plato used the term *anamnesis,* which means "to cease to forget." Likewise, the title "Buddha," which was given to Siddhartha after his enlightenment, means "one who is awake." In other words, East and West both agree that to be enlightened is to stop living in delusion and remember who one really is: the One. Western philosophers and Eastern religious leaders were both using similar methods and aiming at the same goal.

Pythagoras is one of the ancient thinkers who is credited with the development of Western consciousness. From him come the terms *philosophy, cosmos,* and *mathematics.* He developed the seven notes of the Western musical scale. He is credited with the insight that all reality can be expressed in numbers. Without this insight, all our technology could not have been developed. Yet, he used the seven notes to heal people by balancing their chakras (although he didn't call them that). He not only believed in reincarnation, but, like Buddha, remembered his past lives, and he used meditation to help him "wake up." His religious community was a major influence in the ancient world and directly influenced Plato and Aristotle, and he was venerated as a divine being. Miraculous stories circulated about him. It is said that he had a golden thigh and that he could appear in two places at the same time. In this light, Pythagoras is like a Western Buddha.

The Pythagorean community thrived in Italy for over a hundred years. Then, as has happened with other religions, it fragmented into various forms that continued the teachings but eventually died out. This is similar to what happened to Buddhism in India. If Buddhism did not have a missionary movement that carried it to other areas, it would not exist as a separate religion today. In India, Buddhism was absorbed into Hinduism. In the West, Pythagoreanism was absorbed into Platonic philosophy and then into Christianity.

Yet, it may not be true that the Pythagoreans did not have a missionary movement. The scholar Peter Kingsley has suggested that the alchemical schools of Egypt were connected to the Pythagoreans, and that alchemy is Pythagoreanism under a different name. One may wonder, did the Neopythagoreans just emerge in Egypt in the first centuries after Christ, or was this a continuing Pythagorean school that became visible to us at that time? Whatever your answer, no one can deny that there is a mystical Pythagorean current that runs through Western culture, and, like a great serpent, surfaces at times in history. One such time was the Renaissance when the Tarot was developed, and another is the present. As author Joscelyn Godwin has observed when writing about modern American culture:

> In phenomena as various as vegetarianism and the wholefoods movement; post-modernist architecture; the synthesis of religions; travels in search of Oriental wisdom; researches into ancient Egypt and Babylon; the revivals of sacred geometry, arithmology, and speculative music; reprints of Pythagorean literature; meditation; music therapy; the speculations of modern physicists; communes and spiritual com-

munities; the widespread belief in reincarnation. Pythagoras is the center toward which all of these scattered impulses point.[6]

A friend once asked me why I create different Tarot decks. He reasoned that there must be one true model for the Tarot, and that by creating decks on different themes, I am deviating from the true pattern. A study of the oldest Tarot decks will prove that even in the Renaissance there were variations in the Tarot. Considering that most modern decks follow the numbering of the Tarot of Marseilles for their trumps, and that in the Renaissance there were numerous known orders that assigned different numbers to each of the trumps, in some ways there was more variation in the Renaissance than now. I feel that each of the decks that I have created is connected to those various Renaissance decks, and that each of them delves into the philosophy and wisdom that was in the Tarot from the beginning. There was never one true Tarot. The Tarot evolved in the Renaissance and continues to evolve today. By making Tarot decks I am part of that evolution. The Tarot is an expression of a synthesis of mystical, philosophical, and religious ideas, and each of my decks picks up one or more of those threads and explores the connections.

To see the connections we have to step back from the details and perceive the pattern that is there behind the scenes. This is what the ancient philosophers and alchemists taught. The highest wisdom is to see the patterns that are timeless; to see connections between centuries, continents, and cultures. This is what happened to Buddha as he sat under the Bodhi Tree—he saw the pattern of all his incarnations like a great wheel. This wheel-like pattern is called a *mandala* in Buddhism. It is a sacred pattern of archetypal reality that emerges from the visions of enlightened masters, and when it is captured by an artist, it becomes an object of contemplation that can lead others to that wisdom.

The wheel is a circle that surrounds the hub. The hub represents the most sacred spot, the center. This center is the fifth location. This is the source of the other four directions—north, south, east, and west—which define physical reality and form a square around the circle. The Western alchemists called the sacred center the *quinta essentia,* meaning the "essential fifth." This is the source of the word *quintessence.* They pictured it as a goddess, the World Soul, who is the mother of the physical world. To uncover her and capture her essence in the philosopher's stone was the goal of their work. The work itself was described as "the squaring of the circle" and was depicted in art as a mandala-like structure. As Buddhism developed, Buddha himself was given this archetypal pattern when he ascended to Nirvana. He became not just one Buddha but five: one for the center and one for each of the four cardinal directions. This is the same pattern that runs through the entire Tarot deck with its five divisions: the four minor suits (representing the four directions and other fourfold associations) and the trumps (representing the sacred center and the hero's journey).

In traditional Tibetan culture, artists create hand-painted cards called *tsakli.* Unlike a mandala with its multiple imagery organized in geometric unity, each tsakli depicts just one sacred object, Bodhisattva, or deity. The tsakli are used in ritual and meditation to focus on the single element, but the same archetypal unity runs through the set of cards. They are a mandala broken into its separate parts; a mandala of cards. This is how I see the Tarot. The Tarot is a set of individual images that are derived from the synthesis that is Renaissance culture, but in the entire deck there is an archetypal pattern that is sacred and enlightening.

It may seem strange to write so much about Western philosophy when the theme of this Tarot deck is Buddha, but this deck is not just about Buddha. It is about us and about things in our culture that we may have forgotten. It is about how much our mystical heritage is like Buddhism. It is about why we can find Buddha in the Tarot, and a demonstration that the Tarot is a sacred tool—a mandala.

East-West Timeline

3100 BCE	Menes unites upper and lower Egypt into one kingdom.
2900 BCE	The first Egyptian hieroglyphs are created.
2600 BCE	Kufu (Cheops) builds the Great Pyramid at Giza.
2350 BCE	The Akkadian Empire is founded in the Tigris-Euphrates valley, the first empire in history.
2200–1300 BCE	The Indus valley civilization trades with Sumer in the Tigris-Euphrates valley.
2000–1000 BCE	Indo-Europeans invade Italy.
1900 BCE	Indo-Europeans invade Greece.
1700 BCE	Hammurabi establishes the Babylonian Empire.
1750–1500 BCE	The height of Minoan culture in Crete.
1500–900 BCE	The Aryans, members of the Indo-European language group, invade the Indus valley. The Vedas are written.
c. 1300–1200 BCE	Moses leads the Jews out of Egypt.
c. 972–932 BCE	The reign of King Solomon in Israel. He commissioned the building of the temple in Jerusalem.
900–500 BCE	The Epic Age in India. The caste system develops, rajahs rule city-states, and there is continuous trade with Mesopotamia.
750–700 BCE	Homer writes the *Iliad* and the *Odyssey*.
700–338 BCE	The Hellenic Age in Greece, which sees the rise of independent city-states ruled by noble families.
582–507 BCE	In Greece and Croton, Italy, Pythagoras finds enlightenment and teaches others the way off of the wheel of reincarnation. He also coins the word *philosophy* to describe his discipline.
563–483 BCE	In India and Nepal, Gautama Buddha finds enlightenment and teaches others the way off of the wheel of reincarnation.

539 BCE	Cyrus captures Babylon and establishes the Persian Empire.
525 BCE	The Persians conquer Egypt.
427–337 BCE	Plato, the most influential philosopher of all time, founds the Academy to teach philosophy. He writes about reincarnation and the soul centers.
332 BCE	Alexander the Great founds Alexandria in Egypt, the most prominent center of trade and learning in the Hellenistic world.
331 BCE	Alexander the Great conquers Persia and spreads Greek culture and philosophy through the East. This is the start of the Hellenistic period.
326 BCE	Alexander the Great spreads his empire to the Indus valley.
302–297 BCE	Megasthenes, ambassador to India for the Hellenistic Middle Eastern ruler Seleucus I Nicator (one of Alexander the Great's generals), writes *Indica,* a Greek text about Indian culture and religion.
273–232 BCE	Asoka unites India into a Buddhist empire. He spreads Buddhism to Sri Lanka and to the Hellenistic kingdom, Gandhara (in what is now Pakistan and Afghanistan), and sends Buddhist missionaries to Alexandria, Egypt. There is regular trade and the exchange of ambassadors between India and Greece. Asoka's edicts are written in the languages spoken at that time in India: Prakrit, and in the West, Aramaic and Greek.
190–167 BCE	The Bactrian-Greek king Demetrius conquers the Punjab and the Indus Valley.
c. 100 BCE	Heliodorus, the Greek ambassador to India, sets up a column in central India with a declaration of his devotion to the Hindu god Vishnu. The Greek king Menander rules the Punjab. He is mentioned in a Buddhist catechism as "Milinda," a Greek king who converted to Buddhism.

63 BCE–14 CE	Augustus Caesar becomes the first Roman emperor. He defeats Antony and Cleopatra at the battle of Actium (31 BCE), thus ending the Ptolemaic rule of Egypt and solidifying the Roman control of the Hellenistic world. During his reign, a Roman trading settlement is established on the coast of India and King Poros of India, together with learned Brahmans, attend the Mystery at Eleusis, Greece.
6 BCE–30 CE	The life of Jesus Christ, the founder of Christianity.
72 CE	St. Thomas, the disciple of Christ, is martyred in India where he spread the Christian belief.
c. 100–200 CE	The Chinese invent paper.
c. 100–300	The *Hermetica* is written.
148	The first extensive Buddhist community is established in Loyang, China.
c. 175–249	The sophist Philostratus writes *The Life of Apollonius of Tyana,* in which he makes a comparison of Indian, Greek, and Egyptian religions.
c. 185–254	The life of the Christian theologian and mystic Origen, who taught in Alexandria and championed the belief in reincarnation.
205–270	The life of Plotinus, the first Neoplatonist philosopher.
234–305	The life of Porphyry, Neoplatonist and student of Plotinus. Porphyry wrote a biography of Pythagoras.
245–325	The life of Iamblichus, the student of Porphyry who also wrote a biography of Pythagoras, in which he mentions how Pythagoras used music to influence the seven soul centers. The first written mention of the chakras in India is from the second century CE.
286	The emperor Diocletian divides the Roman Empire into two parts: east and west. This is the beginning of the Byzantine Empire.

312	Constantine becomes the emperor of both the eastern and western parts of the empire. In his reign, he makes Christianity the dominant religion in the empire.
354–430	The life of St. Augustine, who Christianized Platonic philosophy.
476	The end of the Western Roman Empire.
553	The emperor Justinian calls an ecumenical council in Constantinople. To settle the controversy that had continued since the time of Origen, the council declares that the belief in reincarnation is heretical.
618–907	The T'ang Dynasty, the golden age of Buddhism in China.
622	The Hegira, the migration of Mohammed to Medina, marks the beginning of the Islamic religion.
641	The Islamic conquest of Egypt.
700–1000	The Chinese invent playing cards.
711	The Islamic conquest of Spain. The Islamic conquests effectively isolated Christian Europe from the East.
787	The first Buddhist monastery is built in Tibet.
c. 933	The medieval Jewish scholar Saadia writes the *Book of Beliefs and Convictions,* in which he expounds on Brahman, Christian, and Islamic religions.
1100	The first Crusade captures Jerusalem.
1144	Robert of Chester makes one of the first translations of an alchemical text into Latin.
1151	The first European paper is manufactured in Xativa, Spain.
1191	The Islamic ruler Muhammad of Ghur conquers northern India. India becomes divided between the Islamic and Hindu religions.
1208–1213	The Albigensian Crusade destroys the Cathars in southern France.

1244	The Franciscan Jean du Plan de Carpin writes his *History of the Mongols* after his return from central Asia.
1272	Ramon Lull, the Spanish mystic, has an epiphany and develops his medieval Neoplatonic philosophy, influenced by Sufis and Kabbalists. Later he writes the first romance, *Blanquerna*.
1291	The Mamluks drive the Crusaders out of the Holy Land.
1298	Marco Polo writes about his travels in Buddhist China. He includes the story of Buddha in his book.
1304–1374	The life of Petrarch, the Renaissance Florentine poet and author of *I Trionfi*.
1367	A ban on card games is made in Bern, Switzerland. This is the first evidence of cards in Europe.
1410–1440	The Tarot is created in northern Italy.
1433–1495	The life of Marsilio Ficino, the Renaissance Neoplatonist.
1442	A statement about the Tarot is made in the court records in Ferrara. This is the first definite evidence of their existence.
1453	The Byzantine Empire is conquered by the Turks.
1471	Ficino translates the *Hermetica* into Latin.
1486	Botticelli paints the *Birth of Venus*, illustrating Ficino's idea of the nude as a symbol of ideal love.
1498	The Portuguese explorer Vasco da Gama anchors on the coast of India. This is the beginning of the Portuguese monopoly on trade with India.
1507	The first French Tarot is manufactured in Marseilles, France.
1781	Antoine Court de Gebelin publishes the eighth volume of *Monde Primitif*, in which he puts forth the theory that the Tarot is an ancient Egyptian book of wisdom. This is the beginning of occult interest in the Tarot.

1803–1882   The life of Ralph Waldo Emerson, Transcendental philosopher and author who introduced Hinduism and Buddhism to the West.

1831–1891   The life of Madame Helena Petrovna Blavatsky, the founder of the Theosophical Society, which mixed Hindu and Buddhist teachings with Western occultism.

1844   The German philosopher Arthur Schopenhauer publishes the revised edition of *The World as Will and Representation,* in which he compares his philosophy to Hindu and Buddhist philosophy. Schopenhauer was introduced to Eastern philosophy by the orientalist Friedrich Majer and was able to read translations of Hindu and Buddhist texts that were made available in the West at this time.

1854–1855   Eliphas Levi writes *Dogme de la haute magie* (*The Doctrine of High Magic*) and *Rituel de la haute magie* (*The Ritual of High Magic*), in which he links the Tarot with the Kabbalah and the trump cards with the letters of the Hebrew alphabet, but also makes links with Buddhist ideas, such as the balancing of yin and yang qualities.

1893   The World Parliament of Religions, held in Chicago, brings Asian Buddhist teachers to the U.S. for the first time.

1909   Pamela Colman Smith and Arthur Edward Waite create their modern occult Tarot.

Chapter 1

Paper Images

To enhance its prestige, eighteenth-century occultists claimed that the Tarot's origins were Egyptian and Kabbalistic. For over a century, these assertions have been disproved by serious historians. *The Buddha Tarot* demonstrates that the Tarot contains an archetypal mystical structure, and that it can be used as a tool to direct its user toward enlightenment. This view of the Tarot is similar to the view held by the occultists, but it is not necessary to make up a fanciful origin for the deck in the ancient past to support this view. These mystical trends have always been a part of our culture. They are woven through our culture like a golden thread, and, from time to time, the thread seems to shine more brightly. The century in which the Tarot was created was one of those times.

Cards are made of paper. Without paper they do not exist. Other materials have been used for cards at times, such as mica in India and Tibet and leather used by the Native Americans, but these are afterthoughts, an imitation of paper cards in another media. The ancient Egyptians did not have paper. They had papyrus and later developed parchment, but neither of these materials lend themselves to the creation of cards. Papyrus tends to fray at the edge and it was best to use it in a long scroll. With the development of parchment from animal skins, books could be made with individual pages, but separate unbound pieces of parchment tend to crinkle and bend and cannot easily be stacked or shuffled. The Chinese were the first people in the world to have cards because they invented paper.

In the second century CE, the Chinese began to make a pulp from the bark of the mulberry tree and press and dry it into thin sheets. This new substance could be made in varying thicknesses, it kept its edge, and it stayed flat. It could be painted or drawn on, and because it was flat and absorbent it would accept ink from a carved block. With this discovery, printing was born and the Chinese created printed books, images, money, and cards. For approximately five hundred years the art of papermaking was confined to China. Then, paper spread through Asia, and although it was introduced to Egypt by about the year 800, it was not manufactured there until about the year 900.

Historians believe that paper money was used not only as the stakes, but also as the actual cards in the first card games. One of the oldest known Chinese decks of cards has four suits based on paper money. (Scholars also report that there were Chinese money-card decks with three or five suits. Because the evidence is fragmentary, there may be some confusion in identifying the structure of early decks.) The first cards were printed on heavy paper in black ink before the twelfth century. The four-suit deck is said to have consisted of (1) coins, which shows one or more of the familiar circular Chinese coin with a square hole in the center; (2) strings of coins, which depicts one or more cylindrical stacks of coins (the hole in the center of the coin allows a string to hold the stack together); (3) myriads of strings of coins, which has groups of stacked coins on each card; and (4) tens of myriads of strings of coins, which, surprisingly, depicts a series of illustrations from "The Story of the River Banks," a Chinese legend about the heroic exploits of the emperor's emissary on a journey to the mountain of the Taoists in the center of the world. It is a hero's journey that includes a fight with a devilish dragon before the final reward is achieved. It is easy to see in this ancient Chinese deck similarities with the deck that will emerge in the fifteenth century in Italy.

As the art of papermaking spread through Asia toward the Middle East, new card games were developed. At times the cards were round or oval instead of rectangular. Besides gambling, cards were used for religious instruction, ritual, and divination. It is believed that along with the art of papermaking, the idea of creating decks of cards was introduced to Europe through contact with Islamic culture in Spain in the fourteenth century. It is also possible that the Islamic models were introduced through the port of Venice or through Sicily.

The first definite evidence of the existence of decks of cards in the West is their inclusion in a list of games of chance that were banned in Bern, Switzerland, in 1367.[1] Then, as now, there were legal restrictions on gambling and before this date, cards are conspicuously absent from any such bans. After this date, the evidence begins to multiply and we can see that the game has spread over most of western Europe. However, these fourteenth-century decks were not Tarots. They were decks with four suits, each with ten pips and three or four court cards. They are the ancestors of modern playing cards, but the original suit symbols were staves, cups, swords, and coins. These suit symbols seem to be modeled on an Islamic deck called the *Mamluk deck,* which had four suits consisting of polo sticks, cups, scimitars, and coins.

The Birth of the Tarot

The first Tarot deck was created in northern Italy between 1410 and 1430 when an unknown designer added a fifth suit containing allegorical figures to the already-existing deck of cards. Although there is some evidence for the use of the cards for divination, the main purpose of the deck was for playing a new trick-taking game in which the fifth suit acted as trump. This game is the ancestor of the modern game of bridge. However, where today's game of bridge is designed to be played with a standard four-suit deck and, therefore, requires one of the suits to be designated as the trump suit, in the Tarot there is a natural trump suit.

In fact, the English word *trump* is derived from the original Italian name for this suit, *trionfi,* which means a "triumph," a type of parade popular in the Renaissance. The entire deck was called *carte da trionfi,* meaning "a deck of cards with triumphs added." Around 1530, the name was changed to *tarocchi*. The most likely reason for the change is that apparently the game of triumphs was starting to be played with an ordinary playing-card deck, and as in bridge, the players would assign the status of trump to one of the four suits. Therefore, *triumphs* (*trumps*) became an ambiguous term, and a new name was needed for the five-suited deck.

The first evidence of the existence of the Tarot is a written statement in the court records in Ferrara in 1442. The oldest existing Tarot cards are from fifteen fragmented decks, hand-painted circa 1450 with rich, gold leaf backgrounds, for the Visconti-Sforza family, the rulers of Milan. In the Renaissance, it was unlikely that an artist would create such a work of art without it being commissioned, and evidence may suggest it was a noble patron. However, it is also logical that the first decks could have been produced for the middle class, and that the examples that we have were saved because they are rich productions made for nobles. If that is so, the original decks were not considered as valuable and they were discarded after they were well used.

The most complete of the early decks in existence is the Visconti-Sforza deck, also known as the Pierpont Morgan-Bergamo deck because the majority of its cards are now in the collections of the Pierpont Morgan Library in New York and the Accademia Carrara in Bergamo, Italy. There are seventy-four cards in existence from this hand-painted deck and it is dated circa 1450. I have examined some of these cards in person and the thickness of the cardboard that they are painted on and the fragility of the paintings, even when they were new, would make them impractical to actually use in a card game. Also, each card has a hole through the top of the card. This suggests that at one time they were hung up by a tack. Although we do not know in which century they were displayed in this manner, it is unlikely that they were used for card play. This adds evidence to the theory that the older cards were the ones commonly in use and that they no longer exist.

Northern Italy in the fifteenth century was a patchwork of city-states that had been part of the Holy Roman Empire since the time of Charlemagne. However, at this time the emperor was essentially the king of Germany and his power outside of Germany had declined. Although the pope was more influential, his power over the northern city-states was declining as well. The city-states were prosperous and fiercely independent.

The most likely city of origin for the Tarot is Milan, Ferrara, or Bologna. These cities were all centers for the manufacturing of cards, and can display the earliest documentary evidence of their existence. Later, the Tarot was also produced in Florence. It is logical to assume that the deck had to be created before the first evidence appeared. Tarot historian Michael Dummett favors Ferrara as its birthplace, based on the pleasure-loving attitude of the court. In his early books, he feels that the cards were created only shortly before the first written evidence in 1442. He admits that it is possible that they were created as early as 1420 in Bologna, but he says the evidence for this is slim, and it is unlikely.[2] In his latest book, *A History of the Occult Tarot 1870–1970,* which he coauthored with Ronald Decker, he has changed his position. Dummett and Decker now state that the Tarot was probably invented in northern Italy in the 1420s.[3]

It seems that in the time between 1986, the date of his first estimate, and 2002, when his newest book was published, Dummett has found new evidence about the origin of the Tarot that was compelling enough to cause him to change his mind. In connection with the writing of this book, I consulted Tarot historian and author of *Tarot Symbolism* Robert O'Neill about the nature of this evidence. O'Neill explained to me that there is evidence recently uncovered by Italian historians that suggests that there were earlier decks. The problem in evaluating the evidence hinges on how we define the Tarot. It seems that there were decks as early as 1420, and maybe as early as 1410, with a fifth suit used for playing a new trick-taking game, but these did not follow closely the pattern that we now think of as standard to the Tarot. Does the fifth suit have to contain the familiar mystical allegory to be considered a Tarot? Even among the fifteenth-century decks that are undisputed Tarots there are wide variations in the allegory.

Variations in the Order of the Trumps

After 1500, the French Tarot became the model for most Tarot decks outside of Italy. It had twenty-two cards in the fifth suit: an unnumbered wild card called the Fool and twenty-one trumps numbered in the order of their importance. Because the eighteenth- and nineteenth-century occultists focused on this deck as the standard deck, modern Tarot enthusiasts tend to think of this as the standard pattern and ordering. They tend to feel that modern Tarot decks have deviated from this standard with their numerous themes and special interests. However, when we look at the decks first produced in the 1400s, it can be argued that there is greater variety among them than in the modern decks. The early decks are unnumbered. From written documents and the earliest numbered decks we can determine that there were three main orders for the early decks. In these numbering systems, all of the trumps bear different numbers. The Visconti-Sforza cards mentioned above contain a Fool and all of the familiar twenty-one modern trumps except the Tower and the Devil. There is no evidence of these cards existing in any of the other hand-painted decks from Milan.

Another early hand-painted deck from the royal family of Milan is known as the Cary-Yale Visconti deck. This is the second most complete deck to survive of the fifteen hand-painted Milanese decks. Among the eleven trumps that survive from this deck we can see the Lovers, the Chariot, Death, and other familiar allegories including the virtue Strength, but we also find the three Christian virtues Faith, Hope, and Charity. This inclusion suggests that this deck contained all seven virtues instead of only three of the cardinal virtues as we find in modern decks. This deck also contains six royal cards in each of the four minor suits: a male and female Jack or Page, a male and female Knight, and the King and Queen.

The only complete engraved deck from the 1400s is the Sola-Busca deck, possibly of Ferrarese or Venetian origin. In this deck we find the Fool—titled "Mato" and in this one example bearing the number zero—and twenty-one trumps numbered with roman numerals. However, the twenty-one trumps have little in common with the mystical allegory that can be found in various forms on the other Tarots from this century. Other than the Fool, the cards of the fifth suit depict famous warriors from history and legend.

It is the nature of games to demand conformity, and the order of the trumps eventually became standardized. However, because of the independence of the Italian city-states, each city-state tended to develop its own standard order. As stated above, the cards were not numbered at first, but from lists of trumps in sermons and other literature and from the earliest numbered cards, we can determine that there were several different orders (which fell into three main groups). Each of the trumps were assigned a different number in each order (except the Death card, which was consistently number thirteen). As there were three city-states that were the primary users of the cards, this is not surprising.

At first, variation in the numbered order would seem to be disruptive to the allegory. However, although the numbers changed, whole groups of cards were still kept in the same sequence and most of the changes are minor. For example, if one card from the beginning of a sequence was moved to the end, the number of each card in the sequence would change but the sequence itself would not change significantly. What it does imply is that the number of each card has little symbolic significance. This view is reinforced by the fact that most fifteenth-century decks in existence do not have numbers on the cards. The pictorial symbol on each card is what gives it meaning in the allegorical sequence. In other words, the pictures are important, not a number or another association. The one example that deviates the most from the allegory, the Sola-Busca, is purposely numbered to avoid confusion while playing the game. Over time as the Tarot migrated to France and other countries and the significance of the allegory would be less familiar to the players, it became standard to number and label each trump.

As we look at the sequence of trumps, it becomes obvious that the allegory can be divided into three sections, each with a distinct emotional and philosophical coloring. The first section contains a hierarchy of worldly figures; the second part is darker with images of time, suffering, and death; and the final section depicts an ascent to the heavenly realms. In the different numbering systems, the characters in each section rarely migrate to another. The only exceptions are the three cardinal virtues. In two of the original orders they are sorted in the middle section, but in the third order they are each assigned to one section. I will save the discussion of this variation for later.

As a result of the French invasion of Milan in the early fifteenth century, the Tarot spread to France and Switzerland. It was the Milanese order that first left Italy.[4] The first evidence of the Tarot being in France is a record of its manufacture in Lyons in 1507. Marseilles, France, became a major production center of Tarots and introduced the Tarot to other parts of Europe. The pattern that we know from the Tarot of Marseilles, which is descended from the Milanese order, became the most popular order outside of Italy. In this form, now considered standard, the Tarot consists of four minor suits, each with ten pip cards and four royal cards, and a fifth suit containing an unnumbered Fool and the twenty-one trumps listed in order below:

1. The Magician
2. The Papesse
3. The Empress
4. The Emperor
5. The Pope
6. The Lovers
7. The Chariot
8. Justice
9. The Hermit

10. The Wheel of Fortune
11. Strength
12. The Hanged Man
13. Death
14. Temperance
15. The Devil
16. The Tower
17. The Star
18. The Moon
19. The Sun
20. Judgement
21. The World

The Buddha Tarot is based on this standard form.

The Tarot's Creator

One finds that discussions of the history of the Tarot among Tarot enthusiasts often lead to speculations as to who created the deck and what was this person thinking—as if the Tarot was created by one person: a magician, a Kabbalist, an artistic genius, or perhaps simply a commoner, a pious conservative Christian. If only we could see that deck in its entirety or if its creator had left a written record of his or her thoughts, one may complain, it would have cleared up, once and for all, the questions we have about the Tarot's symbolism and purpose. From the discussion above it should be clear that this is yet another unfounded assumption about the Tarot. This assumption stems from a fundamentalist urge for authority and certainty. Reality is not this neat and simple.

Yet, the truth can be more satisfying and empowering. Over the 1400s the Tarot evolved and many people had a hand in its development, no doubt including common men and women and geniuses. If we could find the first Tarot deck, in its entirety, the evidence suggests that we might be disappointed. We might not be certain it is a Tarot. From this humble beginning, a mystical allegory developed in the early part of the fifteenth century. This is how collective art evolves. It was with the intelligence and insight and hard work of many individuals that the Gothic cathedrals evolved from thick-walled Romanesque churches to become soaring monuments of light. Likewise, it was through the intelligence and labor of many that the Tarot, a set of paper images designed to play a game, became a vessel holding a profound and mystical story.

By the 1450s, the decade in which our oldest examples were created, the deck is definitely recognizable to us as a Tarot, with its trumps containing a three-part mystical allegory. However, it was still subject to variations in the number of cards, the order of the cards, and the symbolism associated with the individual cards. By the end of the 1400s, it had become somewhat standardized. In this process, the Tarot absorbed the mixture of mystical Christianity and pre-Christian classical philosophy that is characteristic of the Renaissance. As Renaissance Neoplatonism developed and influenced the popular culture, the Tarot, a child of popular culture, reflected this influence as well.

In Italy and Spain, we can still find decks of playing cards that use the four original suits. What makes a deck of cards a Tarot is the enigmatic fifth suit with its twenty-one symbolic figures organized in an ascending order plus an unnumbered Fool card. These are the cards that intrigue us today with their mysterious allegory. To uncover the philosophy that underlies this pictorial story, we need to examine the mystical currents of the past and follow these currents to the time of the Tarot's creation and see how they evolved over the centuries.

Chapter 2

THE MYSTICAL TAROT

The Renaissance—a name that means "rebirth"—is an era that named itself. What the people of the Renaissance believed was reborn in their era was the art, knowledge, and wisdom that had existed in the ancient classical world. Most of us remember this from our high-school history class, but what we didn't learn in high school is that the Renaissance view of the ancient world included magic and mysticism as well as the rational and scientific aspects that we focus on today. They saw Plato as a mystic, hence we call these magical and mystical philosophies *Neoplatonic*. Neoplatonic philosophies tend to combine various threads in a way that can be confusing, and even scholars disagree about who is and is not a Renaissance Neoplatonist. In this chapter, we will explore the nature of Neoplatonism and demonstrate how it influenced the Tarot.

Although we think of Neoplatonism as an ancient school of philosophy that resurfaced in the Renaissance, there was no one in the ancient world or the Renaissance who called himself or herself a Neoplatonist. The term was first coined by German scholars in the nineteenth century to make a distinction between the philosophical school stemming from Plotinus in the third century CE and the school founded by Plato in the fourth century BCE. Plotinus called himself a Platonist. The Renaissance philosopher Ficino called himself a Platonist. It is a common misconception that Neoplatonism is one coherent tradition of philosophy that stems from a revival of interest in Plato in the third century and that was again revived in the Renaissance. The name actually refers to individual philosophies, which are not necessarily consistent with one another in their details. The Neoplatonists were inspired by Plato and used that inspiration to create a synthesis of their work with other traditions that they valued.

Interest in Plato never stopped in the first five centuries after his death. Scholars label the period from the first century BCE to the time of Plotinus "Middle Platonism." In this period, we already find the trend toward synthesis, including in the mix a renewed interest in Pythagoras, which will be a part of Neoplatonism. Plato and Neoplatonic ideas continued to be revered throughout the Middle Ages.

What distinguishes the philosophies of the Neoplatonists in the modern mind is that they saw Plato not as the source, but as the transmitter of many of his ideas. He was a link in a chain that led back to the sixth-century BCE philosopher Pythagoras (at times, they are called Neopythagoreans as well), and to the origin of the Mysteries. Also, the Neoplatonists knew Plato as a mystic. The nineteenth-century scholars who coined the term *Neoplatonism,* on the other hand, saw Plato as a champion of reason who initiated a break with the magical, mythological thinking of his predecessors—a break that paved the way for his student Aristotle to initiate scientific logic. They created a new term for the mystical Platonists to suggest that the nineteenth-century understanding was more correct.

According to the Neoplatonist Olympiodorus, shortly before Plato died, he had a dream that predicted the variety of interpretations that his work would inspire. In the dream, Plato transformed into a swan and flew from tree to tree, frustrating the attempts of the bird-catchers who tried to ensnare him.[1] Modern scholars have redeemed the work of these third-century bird-catchers, and in this new light, we will look at the Neoplatonists and their holistic vision.

Plato the Mystic

From a mystic's point of view, Plato's goal was to find the answer to the eternal question that all philosophy and religion tries to answer. It is the same question that started Buddha on his quest, and that led to the creation of the mystery cults: how does one end suffering?

Plato saw that we are beings who are in possession of a divine intelligence, capable of understanding the abstract patterns that underlie reality, and capable of contemplating endless expanses of time. Yet, this intelligence is housed in an impermanent physical body. To deal with impermanence and death, he sought to find what was immortal in each human—the soul—and through purification and insight bring the soul to identification with its immortal source.

In the ancient world, this knowledge of the immortal came to be called *gnosis,* a word meaning "experiential knowledge." We find this term in early Christian writings and in the Hermetic texts from the third-century Egyptian mystics. However, Plato's term for knowledge was *anamnesis,* which means "to stop forgetting." He reasoned that if we emanated from the One, then the One was our true self; all knowledge, from mathematical logic to the highest illumination, was within us and we need only to remember. This is similar to the term *Buddha,* which means "one who has woken up."

From the earliest period of history, this quest of the soul has been expressed through myths. A hero, mourning the loss of a loved one, longs to be reunited with him or her. Ishtar descended into seven hells to find her lover Tammuz, and Isis wandered the land collecting the fragments of her lover Osiris. In Greek mythology, Psyche searched for Eros, Demeter for Persephone, and Orpheus descended into the underworld to bring back his love Eurydice. Plato recreated this myth in a philosophical form and included it in *The Republic.* In his version, we are all trapped in the underworld (a cave) living an illusion and what is missing is the sun, a symbol for the true light that emanates from the One, the Good, and the Beautiful.

Plato's heroic lover is a lover of wisdom, which is literally what it means to be a philosopher. He frees himself and ascends from the cave, drawn by his love of light and truth, symbolized by the sun. He is reunited with his missing part, but after this enlightenment he is not yet content. Like Orpheus, he enters the underworld to free the others and is frustrated in his attempt.

To the Greeks, the sun was the radiance of Apollo, the god of beauty and reason. The sun was the source of light and life, and the Pythagoreans saw it as a reflection of a divine light, the true source that was known as the *Logos*. The universe was the *Cosmos* (a word coined by Pythagoras and which implies a beautiful, harmonious unity), and the Logos was the numeric, geometric, musical impulse that underlaid it.

In Jungian terms, Plato made use of all four functions of consciousness to understand the source. With his thinking function, Plato reasoned that the source was the "Prime Mover," the cause that is before all cause. With his intuition he determined that as he approached this source, he experienced greater and greater unity. Therefore he called the source "the One." As he experienced unity, his feeling function transformed it to bliss. So, he also called the One "the Good." With his sensation function he appreciated the Good as "the Beautiful" and equated it with the brilliance of the sun.

The Threefold Platonic World

Plato perceived that because the Prime Mover was the first source, the first impulse toward expanse, the world had to emanate from this unity. The first emanation that he perceived was the world of forms or patterns—the aspect of the world that is eternal and can only be experienced by the immaterial aspect of an individual: the mind, the highest aspect of the soul. He called this the *archetypal world*. The *sensual world*, the second emanation, emerges as a reflection of the archetypes in the physical world of the four elements. The third emanation, the *physical world*, is in a constant state of flux, and the elements themselves change form through four intermediary qualities, each of which is shared between two elements. Earth is cold and dry; water is cold and wet; air is wet and warm; and fire is warm and dry. Everything in the world of the elements is impermanent. If we were able to come back after several hundred years to revisit a landscape, almost everything that we remembered of it would have vanished, but the forms would persist. Although they may not be the same trees, new trees that have emerged from the same form could be there. Plato believed that the individual was tied to this impermanent world through the lowest aspect of the soul: the *soul of desire or appetite.* At the highest, archetypal level, each person also possessed the *soul of reason.* Between these two Plato placed a third soul, an intermediary called the *soul of will.* The soul of will desired honor and prestige and pulled the spirit upward. It corresponds to the sensual world.

The creation of the world through emanation is not a creation in a biblical sense. It did not happen in the past. It is happening right now and continues to happen in every moment. The mystic in a state of contemplation can ascend this creation like a ladder and experience the bliss of the One. As stated above, in ancient Greece, this experience was called gnosis, a type of knowledge gained through spiritual initiation.

In *The Republic,* Plato describes his method of ascent toward the experience of gnosis. The book is a description of an ideal society and the ascent is necessary for the creation of the Republic's "philosopher king." To this end, Plato recommends the purification of each soul through the practice of virtue.

First, Plato addresses the soul of appetite, which he locates in the abdomen. To become a citizen of the Republic, one must develop the virtue temperance, a balance of the desires achieved through the study of music. These people become the workers that form most of the population.

From this pool, certain people will be able to purify the second soul center: the soul of will located in the heart. This soul center is associated with the desire for power and prestige. This soul is purified through the virtue strength or courage (a word derived from the root *cor,* meaning "heart"), which is developed by the study of gymnastics. These men and women can rise to the level of warrior protectors.

From this group, some will develop the virtue of prudence or wisdom through the study of math and purify the soul of reason located in the head. These men and women will become the leaders.

From this elite group one, who is equated to gold, will achieve union with the will of heaven and become the philosopher king, the embodiment of the virtue justice. This is accomplished through the study of philosophy, which unites the soul of the individual with the Logos symbolized by the sun.

For the individual, justice is defined as the harmony that reigns when the three aspects of soul are ruled by the first three virtues. By locating these aspects of the soul in centers in the body and describing their sequential purification through the practice of virtue, Plato is providing us with one of the oldest discussions of the psychic centers that we now commonly refer to by their Sanskrit name: the chakras. In the earliest lists of the chakras in Indian and Tibetan texts we also find that only three or four main centers are named.

Plato on Reincarnation

To demonstrate that the soul is immortal and to explain its fallen condition on earth, Plato ends *The Republic* with a mythic description of the soul's journey after death. Like the Buddhists and his Pythagorean predecessors, Plato believed in reincarnation. In his myth, the souls of the dead are judged and receive a reward or punishment that will last for one thousand years. When this is complete, the souls approach the physical realm where they will descend back into a body. As they approach, they can see that the whole of the cosmos is resting in the lap of the Goddess whom Plato calls Necessity.

At the center of the cosmos is the ball of the Earth with a spindle piercing it. The spindle also extends above and below to pierce eight spheres of progressively greater size, each encasing the one before it like a vessel. The eighth and largest is the rotation of the fixed stars, and on each rotation below it is one of the seven planets known to the ancients: Saturn, Venus, Mars, Mercury, Jupiter, the sun, and the moon.

It is clear from the description that Necessity is the goddess of the cosmos whom the Romans would call Fortuna. By the Renaissance, her spinning universe would come to be known as the "Wheel of Fortuna" and they would include a depiction of it on the central card in the sequence of Tarot trumps. Sitting around Necessity are her daughters, the three Fates. Lachesis sings a song of the past, Clotho of the present, and Atropos of the future. Together, they determine the length and quality of the thread that will become the life of each mortal.

According to Hesiod, the mother of the Fates is Themis, the classical goddess who is the model for our figure of Justice. Here, Plato is illustrating what he has stated earlier in the book: that Justice or Themis is the ruling principle of the cosmos, his goddess Necessity. By doing so, he is also equating Justice with Fortuna or Fate. He makes the points that as we enter life, we come into the domain of Fate, are subject to her ups and downs, and to mortality. This is the cause of suffering. The cure is to become one with the principle that is the essence of the cosmos, and by doing so to ascend past the realm of Fate back to the One. Like Buddha, Plato is suggesting that to end suffering one must get off of Fortuna's wheel of rebirth.

In *Timaeus,* Plato records a dialogue that is said to happen right after Socrates' speech in *The Republic.* In this dialogue, Plato introduces the idea that the world is one living organism possessed of a soul (a *psyche* in Greek), and that all individual souls are a fragment of this one. With this idea, he adds another level to the emanations—a life force that we are all part of—called the *World Soul,* or, as it came to be known in Latin, the *Anima Mundi.*

Plato's ideas had a direct influence on Stoicism, a popular philosophy that spread through the Hellenistic world after Plato's death. The Stoics blurred the distinction between soul and the world, seeing the spiritual and the physical as one entity. To them the physical world was permeated by a *pneuma* (a "soul breath" or "world soul") that gave matter form and purpose. As in our modern understanding of their name, the Stoics shunned any emotion, and believed that a true philosopher attained a calm state in which his or her happiness was not influenced by the whims of fate. Like Buddhists, the Stoics held that the key to happiness was wisdom, because, with wisdom, a philosopher saw the temptations and threats of fate as an illusion, realized that happiness was in one's control, and that one's happiness hinged on the practice of virtue.

The virtues that the Stoics strove to incorporate into their lives were the same four Plato recommended. However, because of the chief role that they gave to wisdom, they switched the position of prudence and justice in the hierarchy. In Plato's works, he sometimes switches the order also. In fact, the goddess Themis, who is the model for justice, was also a goddess of wisdom; an oracle goddess who, according to myth, was in possession of the Oracle of Delphi before Apollo. This order with prudence on top will have a bearing on the development of the Tarot trumps, as we will see later. Although Stoicism was immensely popular in the Hellenistic and Roman world, by the second century CE it ceased to exist as a separate discipline and lived on only through its influence on Christianity.

The influence of Stoicism on Christian art and philosophy can be seen in a fourth-century Christian painting on the walls of the Chapel of Peace in Khargeh, an ancient city located in today's Egyptian desert that was once part of the Roman Empire. Here we find a central figure of Christ, bearded and enthroned in his familiar almond-shaped aura. To his left is a woman in classical dress holding scales in her right hand. To Christ's right is a woman with a hooded robe and her hands in a gesture of prayer. This painting represents Christ enthroned with Peace and Justice as his advisors. Similarly, in pre-Christian Greece it was believed that Zeus kept Athena (the goddess of wisdom, war, and peace) and Themis (the goddess of divine justice) as his advisors. From this comparison, we can see that the figure of Peace is a Christian form of prudence or wisdom, and that the Christians valued the virtues wisdom and justice as highly as did the Stoics.

Plotinus and His Students

The first philosopher to receive the modern label *Neoplatonist* is Plotinus (205–270 CE) (although some scholars award this distinction to his teacher). Plotinus studied philosophy with Ammonius Saccas in Alexandria, Egypt, and in 243 he established a school of his own in Rome. After his death, his student Porphyry collected his discourses into six volumes with nine essays in each. This work is called *The Enneads* (*The Nines*), and today it is the most respected work created by any Neoplatonist. However, in his time, Plotinus was not as influential as his prolific student.

Plotinus idealized Plato and sought to defend his work from Aristotle's criticisms. Plotinus's view of Plato was similar to the mystical view stated above, but he stressed that the emanations were divine beings. He believed that the first, the One, is the creator who is beyond human comprehension. Plotinus stressed that the One could only be spoken of in negative terms. In other words, the One is not masculine or feminine, not dark and not light. The One could not be spoken of in any duality. This is similar to the Buddhist concept of the highest state of being: Nirvana, which literally means "to extinguish" and is spoken of as a void. Plotinus would contemplate the One by cutting away all categories and thoughts until only the inner essence of reality was left, the void from which all thought emerges. To modern readers, the similarity between his method and Buddhist meditation will be obvious. Porphyry reported that, to his knowledge, his teacher had reached the height of unity and bliss four times in his life.

Plotinus said that as the creation emanates from the One, the One becomes perceptible to human consciousness as the intelligence of the world. He called this state *Nous*. From Nous, *Psyche,* the soul, emerges; from the world intelligence comes the World Soul. Nous is a reflection of the One, the World Soul is a reflection of Nous, and the world is a reflection of the World Soul.

Iamblichus

In approximately 240 CE, the philosopher Iamblichus was born in Syria. He became the student of Porphyry and one of the most influential of all Neoplatonists and Neopythagoreans. Iamblichus lived at a time when the Pagan world was being eclipsed by Christianity. In his lifetime, the emperor Constantine would embrace the new religion and the ancient oracles would begin to fall silent. Even before these events, Iamblichus was troubled by the decline of Paganism. To stem this tide, he attempted to revive the ancient religions by creating a single philosophy that united all that he valued in the various practices. He gathered aspects of the mystery cults, Pythagorean, Platonic, Aristotelian, and Hermetic philosophy into one system. Like the Hermeticists, he filled out the ladder of emanation from the One to the physical world by adding Plato's sphere of the fixed stars and the spheres of the seven planets between the world and the World Soul.

In Iamblichus's system, every living being is animated by the soul. All souls come from the one World Soul, which is the separated feminine aspect of the One (in contrast to the masculine emanation, Nous). Each fragment of the World Soul has to enter the world through one of the twelve gates in the sphere of the fixed stars known as the *zodiac* and journey down through the seven soul centers of the cosmos, the planets. Each of the planets is ruled by a god, and each god clothes the soul in qualities—later listed by Christians as the seven virtues and seven vices—as it becomes a living individual. These soul centers are echoed within our bodies as the seven centers now commonly called *chakras*. The journey of the soul can also be conceived of as a journey through this inner space. The astrological natal chart is designed to map this process.

For the mystic, this process must be reversed because all life yearns to reunite with what is greater than itself. Iamblichus called this desire *eros*. This spiritual eroticism can also be found in Plato's *Symposium*. To Iamblichus, the spiritual motivation came from love and was love. However, he also developed a practical yet complex system of mystical practices that included chanting, breathing exercises, and visualization to help his students experience these gods on the ladder of emanation and to climb back to the One.

Hermeticism

One of the schools that influenced the Neoplatonists was Hermeticism. The Hermeticists were a group of Pagan philosophers living in Alexandria in the first centuries of the common era. It has been theorized that Plotinus's teacher, Saccas, was one of them. Alexandria was the largest most prosperous city in the ancient world until it lost its position to Rome. In this Hellenistic center of commerce and learning, Egyptian and Greek culture merged, and the mystical Egyptian god Thoth was amalgamated with the Greek Hermes to form Hermes Trismegistus ("Hermes the Thrice Great"). The mystic followers of Hermes Trismegistus believed that he was the true source of their wisdom. When they wrote, they felt that the words came from their god; we might say that they were channeling Hermes. In recognition of this fact, they signed their written works with his name.

These works—written from the first to the third centuries CE—were gathered in a collection of twenty texts and collectively called the *Hermetica*. In these texts, Hermes is presented as a man who lived long ago in the golden age when the god Ammon was pharaoh. Through mystical practices, Hermes attained gnosis and became a god. Through the attainment of gnosis, the Hermeticists believed that it was possible to join the ranks of these immortals, and the *Hermetica* was a textbook that taught this procedure—it was a guidebook to gnosis.

In the *Hermetica*, we can find the same concepts that are expressed in Neoplatonism. The One is personified as God, but it is stated that he or she is of both sexes and beyond description. The world is created by God, but this creation is an ongoing emanation.

The first book of the Hermetic collection is called the *Poimandres*. In this book, Poimandres, which means "divine mind" and is equated to an internal light, comes to Hermes while Hermes is in a trance and describes the creation of the world in erotic terms. Poimandres starts by describing how God's light, emanating into the four elements, formed the world. This world is personified as Nature. From fire and water God gives birth to a creative being, the *Demiurge* (craftsman). The Demiurge fashions the seven governors who encircle the world, the seven planets. Then, God creates Man in his own image and falls in love with his beauty. Man is allowed to descend into the realm of the seven governors who also love him, and Nature, when she first sees Man, also falls in love. To obtain the object of her desire, Nature reflects Man's image in the waters of the earth. When Man sees his image, he also is smitten, and descends to earth.

> And Nature when she had got him, with whom she was in love, wrapped him in her clasp, and they were mingled in one; for they were in love with one another.[2]

Nature gives Man a body, and from the seven governors, seven qualities, which are presented as seven vices: the force of increase, cunning, lust, arrogance, audacity, greed, and falsehood. These vices are a negative interpretation of the influences of the seven ancient planets as they are ordered in the ancient Ptolemaic system from the bottom up: the moon, Mercury, Venus, the sun, Mars, Jupiter, and Saturn, respectively. Like God, Man was bisexed, but now he is split into two separate sexes and peoples the world through sexual procreation. However, he has now fallen under the domain of Destiny, Plato's Necessity, and his body suffers death although his soul is eternal.

> And that is why Man . . . is twofold. He is mortal by reason of his body; he is immortal by reason of the Man of eternal substance.[3]

As we can see from the beginning of the story, Man's true sexual desire is for the image of God that is within him and that contains both sexes. In Buddhist art, to symbolize the highest state of enlightenment, Buddha is depicted as sitting in a sexual embrace with his female counterpart, his Sakti, the female aspect of Buddhahood. When he achieved enlightenment, Buddha's sexual desire was extinguished in the realization that he was no longer separate but contained the object of his desire within himself. To be a Buddha is to be a totality that is beyond sexual duality.

Poimandres has presented the same philosophical problem that we find in Plato. Man has an immortal soul that is trapped in a mortal body. What is the cure to this suffering? As a cure, Poimandres describes an ascent back to the One:

> If then, being made of Life and Light, you learn to know that you are made of them, you will go back into Life and Light.[4]

First, an individual must purify his or her soul throughout life by the practice of virtue and a turning away from the senses (a description of meditation). Then, when the soul is separated from the body at the moment of death, the soul may ascend the ladder of the planets and, at each level, let go of the vice associated with each governor. Beyond the sphere of the fixed stars, the soul will ascend to the light that is God. In the spiritual practices of the ancient world, mystics would attempt to take this journey up the ladder of the planets while they were in a trance (the way Hermes experienced it in the *Poimandres*) and experience gnosis in life instead of after death. Although we don't know much about Iamblichus's methods, it is likely that he also incorporated this practice.

The Symposium and Optimism

Plato also saw the mystical quest as erotic and expounded on his view in *The Symposium*. In this book, Socrates is invited to a banquet—a symposium—of respected men, many of whom are eloquent speakers.

They agree that each will speak on the subject of love. Socrates speaks last and rebukes all of the previous speakers for their lack of truth on the subject. To appease them, he explains that at one time he was as ignorant on the subject as they are. However, he was enlightened by his teacher, the wise woman Diotima. He then goes on to repeat Diotima's lecture on the nature of love.

Diotima sees love as the driving force that, at each level of soul, directs us toward beauty, and leads us from sexual desire to the highest desire for union with the One in a continuum. In the following quotation Socrates repeats Diotima's demonstration that all sexual desire in the world of nature stems from a desire for immortality:

> See you not how all animals, birds as well as beasts, in their desire of procreation, are in agony when they take the infection of love; this begins with the desire of union, to which is added the care of offspring, on behalf of whom the weakest are ready to battle against the strongest even to the uttermost, and to die for them, and will let themselves be tormented with hunger or suffer anything in order to maintain their offspring . . . "Marvel not at this," she said, "if you believe that love is of the immortal."[5]

Next Diotima explains how men can take this desire up to the next soul level and strive for immortality through fame:

> Men whose bodies only are creative, betake themselves to women and beget children—this is the character of their love; their offspring, as they hope, will preserve their memory and give them the blessedness and immortality which they desire in the future. But creative souls—for there are men who are more creative in their souls than their bodies—conceive that which is proper for the soul to conceive or retain. And what are these conceptions?—wisdom and

virtue in general. And such creators are all poets and other artists who may be said to have invention.[6]

Finally Diotima describes how love in the highest level of soul becomes a love of beauty and leads one to the source of all beauty: the Good.

> For he who would proceed rightly in this matter should begin in youth to turn to the beautiful forms . . . and [he] will become a lover of all beautiful forms; this will lead him to consider that the beauty of the mind is more honorable than the beauty of the outward form . . . looking at the abundance of beauty and drawing toward the sea of beauty, and creating and beholding many fair and noble thoughts and notions in boundless love of wisdom; until at length he grows and waxes strong, and at last the vision is revealed to him of a single science, which is the science of beauty everywhere.[7]

In this view, all creation is permeated with spirit and therefore beautiful, and all beauty leads one on the mystic quest for the source of beauty. This view is termed *optimistic*.

In contrast to this, some ancient mystics developed a pessimistic or dualistic philosophy in which the world is viewed as bad in contrast to an otherworldly good. Consider the following quotation from Clement of Alexandria, the second-century Christian philosopher:

> . . . the ancient theologians and priests testified that the soul is united to the body as though a certain punishment, and is buried in as a sepulchre.[8]

Now compare that sentiment to this quotation from Claudianus, the fourth-century Alexandrian poet, believed to be Pagan:

> The soul is introduced and associated with the body by number, and by a harmony simultaneously immortal and incorporeal . . . the soul cherishes its body, because without it the soul cannot feel.[9]

Both men believe that they are accurately expressing the ideas of the Pythagorean philosopher Philolaus (470–390 BCE). The first views the physical world and the body as an evil prison, a tomb. The second sees the world as good and the body as a vessel that is animated and made beautiful by the soul and in turn serves the soul by becoming its eyes and ears and allowing it to feel. In the Pythagorean and Platonic writings, we can find a combination of both of these views. However, later philosophers tend to favor one side or the other, with the Christian Gnostics on the pessimistic side and the Hermeticists and Neoplatonists on the optimistic side.

Neoplatonism and the Pythagorean Triple-Soul

As a Neopythagorean, Iamblichus wrote extensively about the sixth-century "father of philosophy," Pythagoras, including the most complete biography of him written by an ancient writer. It was the first book of his planned ten-volume Pythagorean encyclopedia. In the biography, Iamblichus recounts the following lesson in which Pythagoras defines the nature of a philosopher, a lover of wisdom:

> He [Pythagoras] likened the entrance of men into the present life to the progression of a crowd to some public spectacle. There assemble men of all descriptions and views. One hastens to sell his wares for money and gain; another exhibits his bodily strength for renown; but the most liberal assemble to observe the landscape, the beautiful works of art, the specimens of valor, and customary literary productions.[10]

In the story, Pythagoras goes on to point out that the first type of man is acting from the desire for wealth and luxury, the second from a desire for glory and power, and that the third is the philosopher, who acts from a love of contemplation and wisdom.

With this story, Iamblichus has traced Plato's three aspects of soul to Pythagorean teachings and to the heart of the philosophic tradition. Although Iamblichus is writing in the third century and this evidence could be a projection of Platonic ideas on to the past, Iamblichus did have ancient source materials, which he often quoted, and it has been demonstrated by modern scholars that Plato was influenced by Pythagoreans.

If we compare this triple-soul to ancient myths from all cultures, we find that it is archetypal. It is the blueprint for the journey of the hero, whom we find in all mythic traditions: the hero who leaves mundane concerns behind to enter the field of valor, face his or her challenge, and ascend to a higher state where he or she attains a magical elixir or sacred truth, the necessary medicine that heals the people. The story of Siddhartha—who leaves his pampered life as a prince to become the ascetic Gautama, and then leaves the ascetic life for the middle path and becomes the enlightened Buddha—follows the same threefold pattern.

Christian Neoplatonism

Iamblichus never achieved his hoped-for revival of Paganism. As Christianity became dominant, the old temples were closed and their rituals died out. However, in the sixth century a Syrian Christian writer known as the "Pseudo Dionysus" created a synthesis of Iamblichus's system with Christianity. He substituted the Christian God for the One and nine choirs of angels for the gods of the planets, the fixed stars, and the heaven beyond. His text was translated into Latin by the ninth-century Irish scholar Eriugena (which is Latin for "Irish-born") and became a major component in the Christian worldview.

In the Middle Ages, Neoplatonism never died out. The men who created Christian theology cherished it. The list of Christian thinkers who synthesized Neoplatonism with Christian doctrine, besides the Pseudo Dionysus and Eriugena, includes St. Basil, St. Gregory, St. Augustine, St. Thomas Aquinas, and Ramon Lull. The higher emanations of Neoplatonism were retained as the higher ideas in the mind of God, and it became a standard aspect of medieval thought that the world was a reflection of those ideas. Plato had been Christianized, and his work was continually studied—particularly *Timaeus*, with its image of the world as a living unit imbued with a World Soul. *Timaeus* was available to the West in Latin translation throughout this historic period. Most of the texts in the *Hermetica*, on the other hand, were not translated into Latin until the Renaissance—except for *Asclepius*, which did exist in Latin translation throughout the Middle Ages.

Neoplatonism and Romance

Although they respected Plato, the people in the Islamic countries during the medieval period placed a greater emphasis on the ideas of Aristotle and his empirical approach to truth. The mingling of Islamic and Christian culture in the twelfth century in Spain and Sicily was a catalyst that led to a change in consciousness in the West and paved the way for the Renaissance. So, at first, there was a moving away from Platonism as the Western scholars were inundated with Aristotelian philosophy. However, in Islamic culture, there were also two Neoplatonic and Hermetic systems that were introduced at this time.

Alchemy

Along with the *Hermetica*, the followers of Hermes wrote numerous books on alchemy and magic. The oldest known alchemical texts are papyri found in Alexandria from before the birth of Christ that contain information on metallurgy and other skills. Practical and philosophical concerns were married in the ancient world, and it has been demonstrated by modern scholars that many alchemical theories can be traced to the Pythagoreans. In the first through third centuries after Christ's birth, this ancient science became fused with Hermeticism. Because of this, later alchemists came to believe that Hermes was the first alchemist and the word *Hermetic* also referred to alchemy. The Arabs conquered Egypt in 642 and for the first time came into contact with large groups of alchemists. After this date, alchemy became a respected part of the Islamic world, and the greatest alchemists of the medieval period are Islamic.

In alchemy, the mystical ladder of the planets is related to seven metals through the Hermetic belief in correspondences between what is celestial and what is earthly. Further, it was believed that all metals were of one substance but they change their nature due to impurities. Alchemists brought the Neoplatonic ladder of the planets into their workshops by attempting to transform lead, the most impure metal and associated with Saturn, into iron (Mars), tin (Jupiter), copper (Venus), mercury (Mercury), silver (the moon), and finally into gold, the purest form of metal and associated with the sun and enlightenment. They also grouped the chemical processes of their work into seven main procedures that formed a ladder of ascent toward their ultimate goal: the formation of the Philosopher's Stone, a spiritual substance that is a universal medicine and a catalyst that provokes spiritual transformation.

Whatever practical operations involved alchemists' time, the creation of the Philosopher's Stone was considered to be their main endeavor, their magnum opus. The opus was also divided into three sections designated by color and by level of refinement, from the grossest to the most pure: the nigredo (black), the albedo (white), and the rubedo (red). In later alchemy, a fourth yellow stage was added before the red, but in the original three we again find Plato's three aspects of the soul. The stone itself was composed of an immaterial substance that the third-century alchemist Zosimus called *pneuma*. Later alchemists identified it with Plato's World Soul and symbolized it as a beautiful feminine form or as the god Eros or Hermes. Christian alchemists identified it with

Christ. Alchemists believed that this Anima Mundi was contained in all matter, and it was their job to bring this spiritual essence to the fore. To the alchemists, not just man but the entire physical world contained soul. Alchemy is definitely an optimistic philosophy that sees the world as a living organism.

In the twelfth century in Islamic Spain, alchemy was reintroduced to western Europe. One of the first of what was to become many alchemical texts was translated into Latin by Robert of Chester in 1144. In the fourteenth century alchemy was widely and openly practiced in northern Italy. By the early fifteenth century, when the Tarot was born, alchemy had become an accepted part of the culture and alchemical terms and images were part of the common vocabulary.

One aspect of alchemy in the West that exemplifies its Neoplatonic mysticism is that many texts used enigmatic—what we would call surreal—illustrations to communicate the essence of the teachings. These illustrations stem from the tradition of the memory arts, a classical study that continued into the Renaissance and made use of emotionally charged pictures to fix information in the mind. In the classical world, the memory arts were developed to help orators remember their speeches, but soon it evolved into a system that used pictures to organize and remember vast amounts of information. Finally, it was discovered that contemplation of these complex, emotionally charged images brought inner knowledge to consciousness and opened the mind to philosophical insight. Through the art of these images we are again reminded that Plato said knowledge is remembered.

Sufis

The second Neoplatonic influence comes from a group of Islamic mystics called *Sufis*. The word *Sufi* is derived from the root *suf*, which means "wool." From the time of Mohammed, there have been Islamic ascetics who wore wool garments and sought a pure spirituality in contrast to the worldliness of the Islamic rulers. These ascetics were called "those who weep" or "those who live in a hut of sorrow." They were dualistic and pessimistic—not like the optimistic mystical image that has come to be associated with Sufis today.

The Christian emperor Justinian closed the Neoplatonic school in Athens in 529 and its philosophers took refuge in Persia. Three centuries later, a new optimistic wave of mysticism swept out of Persia and transformed the Sufi ascetics into poetic, dancing mystics inflamed with divine love. One of the first leaders of this school of love was the female Sufi Rabi'ah al-Adawiyah, who died in 801. The link with the Neoplatonists from Athens is circumstantial, but it cannot be denied that at this time, the Sufi movement took on a Neoplatonic quality, one in which divine love was equated to erotic love. Later Sufis are known to have adopted Hellenistic, Neoplatonic, and Hermetic ideas, as well as influences from Gnostics, Zoroastrians, and Brahmans from India, and the greatest Islamic alchemists were Sufis.

By the twelfth century, Sufism had developed a Neoplatonic theosophical system that was well represented in Islamic Spain and freely talked of the teachings of Hermes along with the Quran. The story of Buddha was also incorporated. Avicenna, one of the greatest Sufi alchemists, based his story *Salman and Absal* on Buddha's life. This open-mindedness sometimes brought Sufis into conflict with more orthodox authorities, and some Sufis were executed as heretics. One such Sufi was the mystic Hallaj, who is credited with the mystical declaration, "I am the creative truth." He was executed for his belief in 922 and afterward came to be called the "Martyr of Love."[11]

Perhaps the greatest contribution that Sufis made to Islamic culture was through their poetry and songs. They became the masters of love poetry that expressed the longing of the soul for union with God, the beloved. In the poetic forms that they created, this longing was housed in the metaphor of a lover longing for the one he loves. Eternal beauty was symbolized by female beauty, and the loved one by a woman of a higher rank that was beyond the singer's reach. In other forms, the soul was said to be a loving wife and her husband God. The Sufis' poetry so thoroughly infiltrated Islamic culture that all Middle Eastern love poetry is influenced by it and the distinction between profane and spiritual love has become ambiguous. In the twelfth and thirteenth centuries, these mystic singers inflamed the Christians of Spain and southern France with their passion and the troubadour tradition was born.

Troubadours and Romance Literature

The troubadours were mostly nobles who composed love poems in the vernacular. These poems were performed by professional musicians called *jongleurs,* who traveled from one castle to another singing for their keep. The image of noble love that the jongleurs crafted transformed European thought. The subject of their songs was always love and beauty, which they saw as a force of spiritual transformation. The songs were of noble knights who would pledge their love to a lady of higher social status, and this love would transform the lover as he tried to prove himself worthy of her affection.

The troubadours' area of influence was at first Spain, southern France, and Italy. However, through the influence of their powerful patrons (such as Eleanor of Aquitaine, who came from the south but married first the king of France and then England), their songs soon spread to the north, where they mixed with songs of adventure and became romance literature. The term *romance* refers to the fact that the works were written in the Romance languages instead of Latin. Romances mixed love and adventure in a way that pleased men and women alike, and at the heart of the stories was the ideal lady as the spiritual motivating factor behind a great knight's exploits.

The most famous characters to come out of the romance tradition are King Arthur and his Knights of the Round Table. In Arthurian legend, we find a mixture of ancient Celtic and Christian mysticism combined with courtly love and alchemical symbolism. All of these elements converge to form the legend of the Grail, in which the ancient myth of the soul's search for its lost partner takes the form of a knight's quest for the lost chalice that Christ used at the Last Supper. When it is found, it will heal the kingdom.

Connections to the legend of the Grail can be found in some of the earliest hand-painted Tarot cards, particularly three fifteenth-century Italian cards now in collections in England and Germany. These three cards depict the Grail as a combination baptismal fount and chalice with a hexagonal bowl. (Similar connections can be found in medieval and Renaissance illustrations of the Grail, such as in van Eych's famous *Ghent Altarpiece* in which the central panel visually connects the Grail, collecting the "Blood of the Lamb," to the octagonal fount place directly in front.) From the bowls on the cards sprays of water arch to either side, and a lance or sword is suspended in the center—an allusion to the lance that drips the holy blood into the Grail.

In one card now in Germany known as one of the nine Goldschmidt cards, the chalice is surrounded by a serpent biting its tail. This mystical and alchemical symbol, called an *ouroboros,* is an ancient symbol of time that has connections with Fortuna's wheel. Placing the Grail in the center of the wheel of time is a symbol of immortality (see Figure 1). Most often these cards are thought to be Aces of Cups. However, unlike any of the pip cards associated with them, they each depict the Grail on a black-and-white checked floor. This same detail can only be found on the trump cards from these sets. This suggests that they are really trumps (perhaps the World card) from these decks.

A diet of troubadour songs and romance literature had a civilizing effect on the noble class. From their participation in the Crusades, knights had already begun to see themselves as defenders of Christianity attempting, but not always succeeding, to live by a code of ethics called chivalry. Emulating the heroes of legend, knights now saw themselves as defenders of the weak, and were admired for their skill at poetry as well as the use of arms. At the heart of chivalry was the noble lady as a symbol of beauty and goodness. Just as in the stories, a knight would pledge his love and service to a woman of higher rank, and carry a scarf or some other token from his mistress as he participated in a joust. At the highest level, the lady was a symbol of spiritual purity.

Figure 1—Fifteenth-century Goldschmidt card depicting the Grail (author's depiction)

Chivalry definitely enhanced the position and prestige of women in the eleventh, twelfth, and thirteenth centuries, especially among the noble class. During this period the word *she* was added to the English language. This addition to the language allowed English speakers to refer to women with greater sensitivity. When the game of chess was introduced from the Islamic culture, the Europeans transformed it by adding the queen as the most powerful piece on the board. Similarly, the Mamluk deck, which was the model for European cards, contained three male court cards in ascending rank. In northern Europe, the deck was transformed by the addition of a Queen as a fourth court, and this pattern was also used in the Tarot. The inclusion of the Queen in the cards is directly influenced by chivalry. The King has the highest rank, and in the original Spanish model the Knight is below and therefore serving the King, and below the Knight is the Jack or Squire who serves the Knight. With the inclusion of the Queen, the Knight now serves the Queen in chivalrous fashion instead of the King.

During this period, Eleanor of Aquitaine and her daughters Marie and Aelis exerted more influence on court life than any medieval woman before them. In the spiritual realm, the cult and veneration of the Virgin Mary was borrowed from Byzantium and quickly spread through the West. This was also the great age of cathedral building, and more of these gothic monuments were dedicated to the Virgin than all of the other saints.

The Troubadour Saint

Although love in the Sufi model (which inspired courtly poetry) was a spiritual metaphor, in the work of the troubadours it often took on a lustful worldly character. However, the spiritual transformative aspect still came through in some startling examples, including the best-loved and most-respected of all the saints. In 1181, a boy named Giovanni was born to a rich cloth merchant in Assisi. As he grew, he earned the name Francis ("Frenchman") because of his mother's French heritage and his love of French culture. He grew up to be a spoiled young man who loved drinking, womanizing, and listening to the songs of the troubadours.

Like the legendary heroes in the songs, Francis dreamed of becoming a knight himself, and with his father's encouragement, he tried several times to distinguish himself in battle. However, his attempts were continually met with frustration. He participated in the war between Assisi and Perugia, but for him it ended with a perilous bout of illness and imprisonment. Upon his release, Francis attempted to participate in the war with Apulia, but illness forced him home again. Once home, he was shocked by the sight of an important general who had been reduced to begging in the streets. Francis was already tormented by his own failures and the ridicule that he suffered, but this evidence of the cruelty of fate was more than he could bear. He entered a deep depression. Pondering the pointless suffering that he had seen, he wandered the countryside looking for solace.

In his youth, Francis had been terrified by the sight of leprosy. One day while wandering, he came across a leper coming from the opposite direction. The voice of God told Francis to kiss the leper. Although he was terrified, Francis heeded the command. With this kiss, the depression lifted and he began to see that the cure for his suffering was in the service of others.

On another occasion, Francis came across the ruins of a church in San Damian and fell to his knees in prayer at the foot of its abandoned cross. As he did, Christ spoke to him, saying, "Francis, repair my house." In later life, Francis would come to realize that Christ was asking him to repair Christianity itself. By pledging himself to poverty and service, he would be repairing the institution of the Church, which, at that time, was coming under criticism for its greed and opulence. But when Francis first heard Christ's words, he was naive enough to believe that he was only being asked to restore the ruined church at San Damian. To accomplish this, he sold some of his father's rich fabrics. This act outraged his father, causing him to disown his son. Undaunted, Francis continued to raise money for supplies by begging, and began doing the construction work himself.

Having given up his worldly position and goods, Francis accepted this new role as the true fulfillment of his chivalrous quest. He saw himself as a troubadour of Christ, and spoke of himself as being married to Lady Poverty. Francis had a gift for speaking and his sincerity, commitment, and joyous nature soon won him followers who helped in his efforts. After San Damian was successfully restored, as well as several other churches, the Franciscans wandered through the countryside begging, preaching, and administering to the sick and the poor. Francis thought of his followers as a brotherhood of spiritual knights. He patterned aspects of his order on the legend of King Arthur, such as having a yearly assembly of the wandering brothers on Pentecost.

The rules of the Franciscan order were extremely stringent. To join, one had to give away all of one's possessions to the poor and beg for one's food daily. The brothers were not allowed to own property or accept money. They often did not know where they would sleep, and at times, they were mistreated by townspeople who, when they had not seen them before, treated them with suspicion. In spite of this, the ranks of the Franciscans grew, and many young men of noble birth joined. Although he was an ascetic, Francis was a spiritual optimist. He saw poverty as a gift and cherished every aspect of God's creation as sacred. As his biographer, Omer Englebert, explains:

> Voluntarily poor one may be from philosophy or asceticism, for reasons of zeal, of charity, and others still. But Francis was poor from love. He made himself poor because his beloved Christ had been poor. He espoused poverty because she had been the inseparable companion of the Most High Son of God, and because for twelve centuries she has wandered about forsaken.[12]

In his optimism and uninhibited love for the world, Francis took on the role of a sacred fool and called himself "brother *idiota*." Of course, his actions at the time may have seemed foolish to some, but this was because he loved the world with a childlike innocence and was exhibiting an enlightened disconcern for the customs of the day. When Pope Innocent III told Francis to preach to the pigs in an effort to insult him, Francis went out and preached to the pigs. This act of humility impressed the pope and won him papal approval for his order. On other occasions he preached to the birds, and talked a wolf out of attacking sheep.

Francis remained a troubadour to the end of his life and continued to write poetry. His most famous work is "The Canticle to Brother Sun." This poem can be seen as a Neoplatonic magical invocation, designed to draw down God's blessing into all of creation. In a ladder of emanation, Francis first praises God, then the sun:

> Be praised, my Lord, with all your creatures,
> Especially Sir Brother Sun,
> Who is daylight, and by him you shed light on us.
> And he is beautiful and radiant with great splendor.
> Of You, Most High, he is a symbol.[13]

Then Francis praises the moon, and stars, then each of the four elements: wind, water, fire, and earth. In the highest trumps of the Tarot we also find the same hierarchy of celestial symbols: the sun, the moon, and the stars. (However, cards representing the four elements are only found in the Florentine variation of the deck, which is called the *Minchiate*.)

In the quotation above, it can be seen that Francis, like Plato, uses the sun as a symbol of the Highest Good. Similarly, in Buddhism, the archetypal Buddha of the sacred center is symbolized by the sun. In Buddhism we can also find magical practices and symbolic art that depict spirit descending and blessing the physical world through a ladder of progressively more dense elements. One example is the Buddhist *stupa*. The stupa is a tall monument that evolved from the tombs of ancient India to become a symbol of the axis mundi (this will be discussed in more detail later). The Buddhist stupa is a tower composed of a stack of geometric shapes, each of which symbolizes one of the elements. An illustration of a stupa can be found on the Seven of Jewels card in *The Buddha Tarot*. At the top there is a teardrop form that represents Buddha nature descending into aether, which is symbolized by the sun and moon. Below this, Buddha nature continues its descent into a half-dome representing air, a stack of cones that represents fire, a large dome that represents water and the cosmic egg, and finally a rectangular base that represents the earth.

The stringent rules that Francis created for his order were impractical, and even in his lifetime the brothers began to modify them. Francis saw that it was time to resign as the head of his order, and devoted himself to prayer and solitude in a cave at Assisi. Near the end of his life, Francis had a miraculous vision in which he received the stigmata, the five wounds that correspond to those of Christ. Francis felt that they were a gift that allowed him to identify with Christ and share his suffering. Although he was physically weak after this gift, he had the brothers help him travel through the countryside on the back of a donkey. As he came to a town, the people would stop their work and pour out of the fields and buildings to see him. The sick who touched him were said to be healed. Francis had transformed himself into a living Philosopher's Stone or Grail, the universal medicine and cure for the land.

Doctor Illuminatus

Although romance literature was developed in northern Europe, the first romance was written by the thirteenth-century Spanish Neoplatonist Ramon Lull, who was also known as Doctor Illuminatus. Ramon was born to a noble family in Palma, Majorca, circa 1235, a time when Christians were driving the Moors from Spain. As a young man, Ramon became a troubadour and a squire and was known for his rash and lustful behavior. On one occasion he is said to have followed a young woman into church while he was on horseback. Then, like Francis,

Ramon had a vision of Christ on the cross that changed his life. He left his position of power and wealth and his wife to become a hermit and a lay associate of the Franciscans.

In thirteenth-century Spain, Christians, Moors, and Jews lived together in the same towns and were constantly in contact with one another. It was customary for a wealthy noble like Ramon to have Moorish servants. Ramon came to admire many aspects of Islamic culture, particularly the mystical teaching of the Sufis. He taught himself Arabic so that he could study Sufi literature, extract what was truthful in it, and Christianize it. In this way, he hoped to show the followers of Mohammed where they had strayed and convert them to Christianity. Of course, what Ramon loved about the Sufi teaching was the Neoplatonic aspect. He took Mohammed out of this Neoplatonism and added Christ instead. Today he is considered to be one of the greatest medieval Neoplatonists and a major influence on the philosophers of the Renaissance.

In 1272, Ramon had an epiphany. He saw the workings of the whole of creation and how each part related to God through nine qualities: goodness, greatness, purity, power, wisdom, free will, strength, truth, and glory. These qualities were a tripling of the Trinity. In turn, the Trinity was expressed in man as the three powers located in the three souls: the soul of the Father, the intellect for divine reflection; the soul of the Son, the will for divine loving; and the soul of the Holy Spirit, the memory for divine recall.

This pairing of the Platonic triple-soul with the Holy Trinity is one of the ways that Neoplatonists Christianized Plato. We find aspects of this in the work of the twelfth-century monk Joachim de Fiore. Joachim also had an epiphany in which he saw all of history ascending through levels, each associated with one aspect of God. In the first age, the Age of the Father, the physical world was created, the law was given, and the Old Testament written. In the Age of the Son, Christ was born and made his heroic sacrifice to save the world, the New Testament was written, and the Church began. In the coming Age of the Holy Spirit, the Church will be dissolved. It will be the golden age that Christ promised when love will rule and individuals will communicate directly with God.

St. Dominic, who was a contemporary of St. Francis, founded the Dominican monastic order. The Dominicans are credited with the creation of the mystery of the rosary. In this practice, the rosary beads are used as a memory device to focus on a cycle of prayers and meditations that are divided into three groups with five mysteries in each. Each section is centered on one of the three main icons of Christ. The first, called the Joyful Mysteries, focuses on the Nativity and Christ's physical incarnation. The second, the Sorrowful Mysteries, focuses on the Crucifixion and the Passion of Christ. The last, the Glorious Mysteries, focuses on the Resurrection and the Ascension. In these mysteries, we find the story of Christ clearly outlined as the three-part quest of the hero.

Ramon called his system the *Ars Magna*. He related these qualities to every aspect of nature, science, and art, and created a complex system of wheels and calculating devices with these qualities and other systems of knowledge written on them. As the wheels were turned and various combinations were created, Ramon believed that the philosophical truth would be uncovered and that the Christian Trinity would be shown to be reflected in all creation. This was the logical system of truth that he was searching for—a tool that he could use to convert the Moors.

Ramon was a voluminous writer. He is known to have written 321 books. He became so famous that later writers signed his name to their works to give them more credence. There are about three thousand works attributed to him. Most of the pseudo-Lullian works are books on alchemy and the Kabbalah. Among the works that he did write is one of the most important books on chivalry; illustrated texts that combine his *Ars Magna* with memory images, showing them as a Neoplatonic ladder of ascent or as the roots of a tree with arts and sciences as the fruits; two novels; and works on logic, rhetoric, grammar, philosophy, astrology, geometry, politics, medicine, theology, and other topics.

One of the novels that Ramon wrote, which is also his most famous work, is called *Blanquerna*. Actually, this is the first European novel, the first book to be written in the common language instead of Latin, and the first romance. *Blanquerna* is named after its main character and concerns his life. It is divided into five parts, which symbolize the five wounds of Christ, but it is also structured to illustrate the three Platonic aspects of the soul.

In the first part, which concerns marriage, we are introduced to Blanquerna's father, Evast, a wealthy noble who is struggling with the choice of which path his life should take. He is drawn to the religious life of chastity, solitude, and contemplation, but he also desires to show the beauty and value of married life. He decides on marriage and finds a woman of high moral virtue to be his bride. Her name is Aloma. Evast devotes himself to commerce, but when his son, Blanquerna, is born, he gives him an education that stresses religious and philosophical pursuits. When Blanquerna becomes a man, he comes to the same crossroad that his father did. In a scene symbolically similar to the Lovers card from the Tarot of Marseilles, he is tempted by the beautiful Natana, but ultimately he decides to leave home and become a holy hermit. This chapter presents the lowest part of the soul, which desires wealth and sensuality. It ends with chapters that present the seven vices.

The next three parts concern the second part of the soul, which desires prestige and power. Here we start with chapters that present the seven virtues. Blanquerna has left home to embrace the religious life. He comes to a forest and wanders, looking for a suitable place to reside, and finds a monastery. Although he had desired to be a hermit, Blanquerna joins the monastery, and, because of his merit, he quickly rises to the role of abbot. Blanquerna is a sincere and natural leader and the monastery prospers. By the third chapter he has reached the role of pope.

All through this section, whenever Blanquerna is faced with temptation or is in need of help with a decision, a jongleur arrives to help him. As stated above, these jongleurs were performers. They were part musician, part juggler, and part jester. When Blanquerna becomes pope, the emperor sends him a jongleur named Ramon the Fool, who arrives with a dog and a hawk, an image close to the Fool card in the Tarot of Marseilles. Ramon is like a Zen master who clarifies with riddles and cuts through misconceptions with simplicity and ease. He is the model for the wise fool that will be enshrined in the Tarot's wild card.

With Ramon the Fool's help, Blanquerna sets the affairs of the Church in order, and is at last free to do what he set out to do. He resigns his office and sets out to become a hermit and seek divine illumination. His first duty as a hermit is to help his fellow hermits to defeat temptation. At their request, he composes a book of meditations to give them daily guidance. This book, called *The Book of the Lover and the Beloved,* is a book within the novel and is often published as a separate piece. In the novel, Blanquerna freely admits that it is inspired by Sufi poetry. It consists of 365 love poems, one for each day of the year, in which the devout in contemplation is the lover and sometimes a fool, and the beloved is God. This relationship and the Neoplatonic aspect of the work can be seen in the following quotation:

"Say O Fool! Wherein is the beginning of wisdom?"

He answered: "In faith and devotion, which are a ladder whereby understanding may rise to comprehension of the secrets of my Beloved."

"And wherein have faith and devotion their beginning?"

He answered: "In my Beloved, Who illumines faith and kindles devotion."[14]

After temptation has been put aside by love, Blanquerna makes the final ascent to illumination through a series of meditations. First he contemplates the nine qualities of *Ars Magna,* then the Trinity, the Incarnation, the Paternoster, the Ave Maria, the Ten Commandments, the seven sacraments, and the final ascent is accomplished by pairing the seven virtues with the seven vices so that each vice is concurred—a

Neoplatonic ladder through the seven planets that is depicted on the Marseilles Star card. In the end, Blanquerna entrusts his story to a jongleur for the benefit of humanity.

Anyone familiar with the Tarot trumps and Fool will see the similarity between them and this novel. Not only are there similar characters, but the structure and purpose are similar. One could easily use Tarot cards as illustrations for the story.

It would be difficult to overestimate Lull's influence on the Renaissance and on Western culture in general. His contribution to literature has already been illustrated above. All the founders of the Renaissance tradition created works of romance and wrote works in the vernacular. His attempts to make a philosophical calculating device influenced the creation of the calculator and this, in turn, influenced the creation of the computer. His use of the memory arts helped to make them a popular art form in the Renaissance and led to their use as Neoplatonic devices to organize the arts, sciences, virtues, and other aspects of reality into a hierarchy of images. His mystical philosophy was an influence on St. John of the Cross, Teresa of Avila, Nicholas of Cusa, Pico della Mirandola, John Dee, Cornelius Agrippa, Giordano Bruno, Paracelsus, Bacon, Descartes, and Newton, to name a few.

There is qualitative and structural similarity between the story of Blanquerna, the life of St. Francis, and the life of Buddha. No doubt the similarity between Blanquerna and St. Francis is intentional, but it is impossible to estimate how much—or if at all—the story of Buddha influenced either of them. During the Middle Ages the story of Buddha was Christianized and Buddha was transformed into St. Josaphat. This was no doubt because Christians recognized something saintly in the story. It was similar to other stories of saints, who renounced worldliness to seek illumination. Just as the stories of romance influenced knights and they sought a noble lady to whom they would pledge their service, the stories of saints became a model for those who would be a saint. As one of the saints, Buddha was one of the influences. However, it seems that at its heart the similarity is archetypal. There is a divine pattern one must follow to seek enlightenment. As we proceed, we will see that this archetype is contained in the Tarot.

Renaissance Platonists

As I stated in the beginning of this chapter, the Renaissance is a period that named itself. However, the name did not appear until 1550 in Vasrari's *The Lives of the Painters*. It is well-known that the name means "rebirth." Vasrari coined it to distinguish the artists and writers of the fourteenth century—men who looked to the golden age of the classical world for inspiration and attempted to reclaim that grandeur—from the period that separated them from the ancients. In their own century, these men would have been called humanists. *Humanism* is the historical term for the fascination and reverence for the classical arts and literature that gripped Italian society in the 1300s. The name derives from the artists' concern with the study of the humanities: grammar, rhetoric, poetry, history, moral philosophy, and politics. These artists had a reverence for nature that stemmed from an optimistic philosophy. Like the alchemists, they looked for the divine in nature, and unlike the Aristotelians of the late Middle Ages, they turned to Plato and his mystic vision for their philosophy. In painting there was Giotto, who reclaimed a sense of depth and perspective in painting. In writing there was Dante, Petrarch, and Boccaccio, who created in their work a parallel emotional realism and a consciousness of the individual. Although these artists were inspired by classicism, they were also a product of the Middle Ages and were involved in expressions of the divine feminine that are based in romanticism and ultimately in Neoplatonism.

Giotto is well-known for his frescos depicting the life of Christ, but he is also famous for his paintings of Madonnas on wood panels or on walls. These paintings of the Christian manifestation of the divine feminine had an immense influence on the artists and writers of the Renaissance. Petrarch, for example, is known to have owned a Madonna painted by Giotto, which he greatly prized.[15] The Madonna had already become a major focal point of devotion in the preceding centuries. Now,

Giotto's illusion of depth made the painting seem more miraculous and other artists soon copied him. As stories of miraculous cures and other miracles in connection with these icons circulated, they began to rival the relics of saints as the focus of pilgrimages. They also helped create the need for more and more miraculously beautiful paintings. In the 1400s, these Madonnas became an important aspect of the religious life of the ordinary people.[16]

The three most famous writers of the fourteenth century—Dante, Petrarch, and Boccaccio—while embracing the new realism and a veneration of the classical world, maintained a connection to romance. Like the knights in the songs of the troubadours, each wrote works in which he was inspired and guided by the image of a beautiful and chaste female—a personification of the soul—who led him on to the highest state of spiritual experience. Dante had Beatrice, a woman whom he fell in love with when he was nine and who died when he was twenty-five. In his *La Vita Nuova*, he revealed that his idealized love for her was the inspiration for most of his works. In his masterpiece, *The Divine Comedy*, Beatrice is his guide for the highest spiritual ascent. Petrarch was the most influential of the three in his lifetime and the most devoted to Plato. In many of his works he writes of his idealized love for Laura, who is unattainable but, because of that, inspires him to become a great poet. Scholars debate whether or not Laura was inspired by a real woman, but in his writing, Petrarch describes his love for her with a realism that goes beyond the romantic tradition. Boccaccio also wrote numerous romances, including *Fiammetta,* in which the heroine of the title is the spiritual equivalent to Dante's Beatrice and Petrarch's Laura.

The Platonic Triple-Soul in Dante and Petrarch

Two of the most influential works produced in this century were Dante's *The Divine Comedy* and Petrarch's *I Trionfi*. In both of these we again find a three-part structure that is a Christianization of Plato's three-part journey of the soul. In *The Divine Comedy*, the entire poem is divided into three sections of thirty-three cantos each. In the first, Dante finds himself lost in the wood of Error where he meets the Roman poet Virgil. Virgil represents the highest knowledge of the human mind, the virtue that is needed to complete the descent into Hell (the lowest part of the soul) and to climb the mountain of Purgatory (the middle soul). At the top of the mountain, Virgil leaves and Beatrice, who represents revelation through love, takes over as Dante's guide. She brings him through a Neoplatonic ascent through the seven planets and to the highest heaven, which is depicted as a cosmic rose, another symbol of the divine feminine.

The title of Petrarch's *I Trionfi* refers to a type of parade popular in the Renaissance. In the poem, Petrarch uses this device to structure an allegory in which each major character triumphs over its predecessor. This is the same device that is used in the Tarot trumps, and this poem is believed to have directly influenced the Tarot (Tarot historian Gertrude Moakley has written an essay that explores the influence of this work on the Tarot trumps). We will first delve more deeply into the nature of this parade and how it was used as a poetic device.

The triumph originated in ancient Rome. When a conquering general would return to the city, a triumph would be arranged down the Appian Way. The parade was organized by rank from the lowest to the highest, starting with the captives and ending with the general himself. By the Renaissance, the triumph had been Christianized and the characters in the parade became allegorical figures drawn from Pagan and Christian sources.

It was the custom that a triumph would be performed during Carnival, for weddings, and other special occasions. During the Renaissance, every major city in Italy held at least one triumph yearly, and they were elaborate affairs with beautiful chariots and costumes made by gifted artists. Even Leonardo da Vinci is known to have directed the triumph in Milan and to have designed for it an elaborate machine representing the cosmos with moving planets.[17] This was one of the principle ways in which artists of the Renaissance influenced all of the classes of society, and, in turn, the triumph influenced the arts. Because the triumph is a natural way to organize characters in a progression of ascent, it became a device used by authors and artists to present a moral allegory. Petrarch's poem *I Trionfi* is one example; the Tarot trumps are another.

In *I Trionfi*, Petrarch presents an allegorical procession in six parts or three pairs. Although Petrarch did not provide much detail in the written text about the appearance of each figure, illustrations for the poem were immensely popular and each triumph developed a specific iconography. The first pair is Love and Chastity, in which a processional car carrying Cupid is seen to triumph over numerous characters, including earthly rulers. Cupid's car is trumped by the car of Chastity, which carries Petrarch's ideal love, Laura, accompanied by the virtues. The similarity to the Tarot's four temporal rulers, the Lovers, the Chariot (which in the earliest hand-painted Milanese cards depicts a beautiful woman in the chariot), and the virtues should be obvious.

In the next section of this parade, Laura is triumphed over by Death—the "Grim Reaper"—who, like in the Tarot, is depicted in the illustrations riding over (or harvesting) the bodies of common people, kings, and popes. Death, in turn, is trumped by Fame, which in the Renaissance was usually symbolized by an angel blowing one or two horns. This angel is substituted for the Judgement trump, with Gabriel blowing his trumpet, in the Minchiate of Florence. Both angels symbolize immortality and victory over death.

In Petrarch's triumph, Fame is trumped by Time symbolized in the illustrations by a car carrying a hunched old man with wings. This figure is similar to the earliest Tarot Hermit cards in which the figure carries an hourglass instead of a lantern. In the illustrations for the final trump, a car holding the Holy Trinity being pulled by the Four Evangelists with their four creatures (the lion, bull, eagle, and man) triumphs over Time. Petrarch gives the Platonic title "Eternity" to this triumph. There is a similarity between this image and the World card in the Tarot of Marseilles, which bears a triumphal figure in the center of the symbols of the Four Evangelists.

In composing this poem, Petrarch was influenced by Dante and Plato. Although *I Trionfi* has six parts, I describe them in pairs because when we examine them closely, we can see that they comprise three groups each with a negative triumph overcome by a positive. Each of these three parts also corresponds to one aspect of the Platonic soul.

The first triumph, Love, may not seem negative to the modern reader, but Petrarch meant it as a symbol of the lowest soul when it is overcome by indiscriminate appetite.

> Who by short lived joys by anguish long obtain,
> And whom the pleasures of a rival pain.[18]

To symbolize this lack of control, Cupid, the charioteer, is depicted as blindfolded, a symbol of ignorance and self-deception.

Next, Laura, representing Chastity, with the help of the virtues and a host of virgins, takes Cupid as her captive and brings harmony to this chaos.

> And there consummate Beauty shone, combined
> With all the pureness of angel-mind[19]

The middle section addresses the soul of will and starts with the philosophical problem that both Plato and Buddha sought the answer for: how can we defeat the triumph of Death? Death, usually depicted as a corpse armed with a scythe and standing on a coffin, triumphs over Chastity and takes Laura prisoner.

> O blind of intellect! Of what avail
> Are your long toils in this sublunar vale?[20]

Just as in Pythagoras's description of the man dominated by the middle soul as one who seeks glory and fame, the positive aspect of this pair is the triumph of Fame. Fame allows one's work and reputation to outlive the body, and in this way defeats death. This is especially relevant for a poet like Petrarch who hopes that his work will live on.

> When turning around I saw the power advance
> That breaks the gloomy grave's eternal trance.[21]

The final pair begins with the triumph of Time as the negative aspect, and is represented by a Saturnian old man on crutches. Saturn was not only the god of time, but also the god of contemplation and intellectual pursuits. This triumph addresses the soul of reason. By virtue of our intellect, we can reason that although fame can overcome death, this is not true immortality. Given enough time, even our fame will die.

> What is renown?—a gleam of transient light,
> That soon an envious cloud involves in night.[22]

The final triumph in Petrarch's poem is a mystical Christian vision of God as the only true permanence called Eternity. Here Petrarch sees God as the Christian equivalent of Plato's eternal Good. In this section, Petrarch envisions himself at the end of time in the presence of God and reunited with Laura in eternal love—a vision symbolically linked to the Tantric Buddhist image of Buddha united with his Sakti.

> Then shall I see her as I first beheld,
> But lovelier far, and by herself excelled.[23]

The Platonic Triple-Soul in the Tarot

As stated above, Petrarch's *I Trionfi* was immensely popular in the Renaissance. Numerous illustrations of his triumph appeared in the form of prints, paintings, and relief sculpture. The creators of the first Tarots had to be aware of them, and were likely to have drawn on them for inspiration. When we look at the earliest hand-painted decks, we can find many similarities. Although the Tarot triumph is not identical to Petrarch's, it is composed of the same three-part Platonic structure. In the now-standard order, the twenty-one trumps can neatly be divided into three groups of seven cards. Each of these groups relates to one aspect of the Platonic soul.

In the first section, addressing the soul of appetite, we find a sequence of worldly figures each trumping the one before. The order of the four temporal rulers in this section is changed in the different variations, but all of them are always trumped by Cupid, which in the now-standard order is the sixth trump. In the earliest decks, Cupid is consistently blindfolded as in the illustrations for *I Trionfi*. The last card of this group is the Chariot, which, in the earliest hand-painted decks, contains an image of a sumptuous parade chariot carrying a beautiful woman. This Chariot is painted from the side view, as are the chariots in many of the popular illustrations for *I Trionfi*.

In the middle section, which addresses the soul of will, we find the virtues combating images of death and time. In all the earliest decks, the card that will come to be called the Hermit contains an image of a hunched old man holding an hourglass instead of a lantern; sometimes he is on crutches or has a cane. This image is close to the triumph of Time in *I Trionfi*. Also, like the triumph of Death in *I Trionfi*, the Death card in the early Tarot consistently bears the figure of a corpse with or without victims. His weapon of choice may at times be a bow as well as the scythe.

In the final seven trumps we find the soul of reason addressed. Here, the cards start with the Devil. As in Dante, they make an ascent through the celestial bodies, the stars, the moon, and the sun, and end with a vision of the end of time, the resurrection of the dead, and the highest Good. In this section, the artists have been more influenced by Bible illustrations from the book of Revelation, which were also popular in the late Middle Ages and Renaissance.

In the various orders, the final two cards switch places with each other. Among the hand-painted cards from the fifteen decks made for the Visconti-Sforza family, we find two variations of each of these cards. On the card representing the last judgement, there are two angels blowing trumpets while below, three figures rise from the grave. In one variation, God, pictured as a monarch with a long, white beard, appears above the angels. In both variations, the newly risen dead consist of a young man and woman and an older man with a beard. In both variations of the World card is a depiction of a city seen through an arch or a circular opening. This is an illustration of the mystic vision of the "New Jerusalem" that appears at the end of Revelation and represents the age after the end of time when Christ will rule on earth and abolish death. From Revelation 21:2:

> And I, John, saw the holy city, New Jerusalem, coming down from God out of heaven, prepared as a bride adorned for her husband.

In Revelation, it states that the new Jerusalem is lit by the glory of God instead of the sun and moon. Therefore, it is fitting that this card trumps the Sun and Moon cards.

In the World card that is paired with the Judgement card bearing an image of God, we find the new Jerusalem shown as a hexagonal walled city seen through a circle held aloft by two *putti,* angels depicted as nude boys with wings. The putti are angelic messengers that simply deliver the vision.

In the other variation, the new Jerusalem is depicted as a beautiful landscape with several buildings, a river and sea with boats, and in the central field is a knight on horseback. This landscape is viewed through an arch, and above the arch there is a beautiful, richly dressed woman rising out of a cloud, which in turn rises out of a crown (Figure 2).

The symbolism of this image is a complex tapestry woven of the themes that we have been discussing. In the Bible quotation above, the new Jerusalem is described as a bride, and here the image of the city and the bride have been separated and symbolically joined. The addi-

Figure 2—The Soul of the World from the Cary-Yale Visconti World card (author's depiction)

tion of the knight—who, along with the city, is crowned by the lady—clearly connects the image with romance literature. We can envision the knight and his lady, like Petrarch and Laura, being joined in ideal love in the new city at the end of time.

The image of the crown suggests sovereignty, and this theme is repeated by the smaller crown that the lady holds in her left hand. This layer adds the suggestion that the woman is the ruler and soul of this new city, and here the alchemical goal of uncovering the Anima Mundi is aligned with the romantic and Christian vision of immortality. Also, the woman holds in her right hand a trumpet. This marks her as a herald, which is related to the angels on the Judgement card. With this addition, we may wonder if the crown in her left hand is intended for the knight in the picture. This would imply that she is the Lady of Sovereignty, a mythical embodiment of the soul of the land that a man must marry to become king. In the World cards from the other known decks from the 1400s, we find variations of this second theme become the norm. However, the landscape is most often shown in a circle, and besides a beautiful woman, some of the cards depict the soul of the world as an angel, or even as the alchemical god Hermes (Figure 3).

It may seem that the Platonic structure that is present in these works is more obvious to us in this modern age, with our rich stores of historical information to draw on, than it would have been in the Renaissance. However, the artists and writers of the Renaissance were likely to have been more sophisticated in their understanding of this philosophical structure than we are today. They looked deeply into classical ideas and worked diligently to make them relevant to their time and the Christian faith. For example, the Renaissance writer Platina, in his introduction to his *Life of Christ,* states that Christ fully attained "the fourfold Platonic Mobilitas according to his genus."[24] In other words, Platina was equating Christ with Plato's philosopher king, who had risen through the three levels of the soul to the fourth level of union with the One.

As I have said above, there were three main orders of the trumps in the fifteenth-century decks. Changes in each of these, however, do not disrupt the three-part theme. With the exception of the virtues, all of the cards remain in their appropriate group. In two of the orders, the virtues are grouped, either together or intermingled with other cards, in the middle section. In the third order, one of the three virtues is assigned to each section: Temperance to the first part, Strength to the second, and Justice to the last. If we allow for the substitution of justice for prudence, this is exactly how Plato would have assigned them to the three parts of the soul.

Renaissance Neoplatonists

Although the humanists of the early Renaissance were involved in mystical Platonism and artistic and philosophical ideas that were derived from Neoplatonism, historians do not consider them Neoplatonists.

Figure 3—Fifteenth-century World card portraying Hermes (author's depiction)

They reserve the title "Renaissance Neoplatonism" for a school of philosophy that developed later in the Renaissance. The origin of this school is linked to a specific historic event.

During the Middle Ages, the Byzantine Empire, in the eastern Mediterranean, was actively involved in Neoplatonic speculations about divine ideas and their relation to the physical world. They developed the most dynamic Neoplatonic tradition of this period and continued the synthesis of Platonism with Christianity. In the fifteenth century, the most influential of these Neoplatonists was Gemistus Pletho. In 1439, the Byzantine emperor, in an effort to make alliances with the West and obtain military aid in his struggle with the Turks, sent a council to Ferrara to meet with Italian religious and political leaders. Pletho was present at that council, and so was the ruler of Florence, Cosimo de' Medici. Seeing that the resources in Ferrara were inadequate for the size of the gathering, and hoping that the exchange of ideas could continue longer in more comfortable quarters, Cosimo moved them to Florence. Of all the scholars and philosophers present, Cosimo was most taken with the ideas of Pletho.[25]

Cosimo came away from that gathering with a desire to bring these Neoplatonic teachings to Florence, and eventually, as he became more enamored with this philosophy, he desired to set up a new Platonic Academy. He found an ally in this endeavor in Marsilio Ficino, the nineteen-year-old son of his personal physician. Cosimo took charge of Ficino's education, seeing to it that he was educated in Greek as well as Latin. Then, Cosimo used his wealth and influence to obtain Greek texts for Ficino to translate. In 1462, Cosimo gave Ficino a villa outside Florence where he could complete his dream of recreating Plato's Academy.

Ficino became the most influential Neoplatonist of the Renaissance. In his Platonic Academy, he translated into Latin the complete works of Plato, Plotinus, and other ancient Neoplatonic authors. His works allowed many Europeans to read this material directly for the first time. Before this, most relied on the accounts of Augustine and other early Christian writers to learn about Plato and Plotinus. Ficino's translations were widely used and relied on for several centuries. However, one of his translations that he valued the most was the *Hermetica* of Hermes Trismegistus. Ficino took at face value the claimed antiquity of the material. In Hermes, Ficino believed he had found a common source for the mystical teachings that influenced both the Greeks and the Hebrews: a historic way to connect the teachings of Christ and Plato.

Ficino gathered around him a group of intellectuals that included the poet Poliziano and the philosopher Giovanni Pico della Mirandola.

Also, he directly influenced the artists Botticelli and Michelangelo, who studied at the Academy as youths. Because of their deliberate influence on the arts, these philosophers had an influence on the culture of the Renaissance far beyond their numbers. This influence did not stop with the high arts but included popular arts, including public festivals like the triumph.

One of Ficino's most influential books is his commentary on Plato's *Symposium*. It is this work that gave our culture the concept of "Platonic love." Ficino used Plato's text to develop his theory of love and to demonstrate that all love, including erotic love, stems from the soul's love of God. Imitating Plato, Ficino said that there were two goddesses of love, which are related and yet rule over the separate aspects of love. First there is Natural Venus, who inspires procreation and makes beauty perceptible in the natural world. Then there is Celestial Venus, who represents the soul, the highest mystical love, and the beauty that resides in the mind. Botticelli's painting *Primavera* is a portrait of Ficino's Natural Venus, and his *Birth of Venus* represents Celestial Venus. Note that the Venus of *Primavera* is clothed and that the Celestial Venus is nude. Botticelli was following Ficino's guidance in making this choice. Crafting the beautiful nude as a symbol of the soul and of the purest love was one of the major contributions that Ficino and Botticelli made to European society. Before this time, Renaissance artists had trouble reconciling their love of classical nudes with their Christian faith. Male nudes began to appear in art in the 1300s, but the female nude, with its erotic overtones, lagged behind. Before Ficino's time, we rarely find the female nude in art except in a negative connotation, such as Eve tempting Adam. After Botticelli painted his Venus and Michelangelo made the nude the focus of his work, the nude became an accepted—almost required—theme of Western art, as we can see in later Renaissance works such as the paintings of Titian, Giorgione, and Raphael.

Neoplatonic Influences in the Tarot

Considering Ficino's influence on the arts, it is not surprising that we find Renaissance Neoplatonic influences being introduced into the Tarot as it develops. By the 1600s, the variation of the trumps that we know of as the Tarot of Marseilles was developing in France and Switzerland. In this deck, which we now use as standard, we can see changes from the earlier models. Several of these reflect the ideas of the Renaissance Neoplatonists.

As noted earlier, in most of the fifteenth-century decks the figure of Cupid is blindfolded, reflecting his indiscriminate negative influence. In Renaissance symbolism, a Cupid with unobstructed sight represents the conscious application of love as a creative force that brings people together in harmony and commitment.[26] In the Tarot of Marseilles, Cupid is clear-sighted, symbolizing that carnal love is not negative, but of the same substance as the highest love depicted in the final cards and that it can inspire us to progress to the highest beauty.

In the Tarot of Marseilles, we find that the old man representing Saturn, or Time, has transformed into a Ramon Lull–like holy hermit. In the early Renaissance, Saturn had an exclusively negative connotation; one that was associated with time, aging, and death—the images that we find him associated with in the Tarot. It was the Renaissance Neoplatonist who reconnected Saturn with his positive aspects as a god of profound contemplation and religious devotion. This revival ultimately led to our association of saturnine melancholy with artistic genius.[27] The change in this card from an old man with an hourglass to a hermit with a lantern reflects this change in attitude, and again shifts the trumps to a more optimistic message in which spirit is seen to animate all aspects of life.

In the fifteenth-century Tarot decks, the Star card mostly bears a simple scene with either a lone woman or man holding a single star above her or his head. In the Minchiate of Florence, we find an image of a king on horseback following a lone star and holding a covered jar before him, a reference to the magi from the story of the Nativity. In the Tarot of Marseilles, we see a more developed allegory. The image is of a nude female pouring water from two pitchers: one onto the land and one into the sea. This is an alchemical symbol for the combining of the opposites, symbolized as the wet and the dry. Above the woman are seven stars situated around a larger eighth one. This arrangement is almost identical to alchemical images where the seven stars are clearly labeled as the seven planets. Here we find Ficino's nude representing the purified soul that has found the harmony beyond the polarity of opposition and is now ready to make a Neoplatonic ascent through the seven planets. The eighth star represents the eighth sphere, which holds the fixed stars. This is the gateway to heaven.

On the World card in the Tarot of Marseilles, we find a female nude in the center with the symbols of the Four Evangelists—the lion, bull, eagle, and man—assigned one to each corner. This image is based on the standard Christian icon called "Christ in Majesty." This image, representing Christ on his celestial throne, is based on two descriptions of God's throne in the Bible: the first is in Ezekiel, and the second is found in Revelation. The surprising thing about this image is that although it depicts Christ's throne, Christ is not in the center. Instead, in the center we find the Neoplatonic female nude representing the purified soul (Figure 4).

But why is she on God's throne? We can find the answer in Ficino's writings. One example can be found in a letter that Ficino wrote to his friend Michele Mercati. In this letter, he describes a conversation between God and the human soul, which he depicts as God's daughter. Through the course of the conversation, the soul is reconciled with her father and moves closer to him as her suffering is healed. At the end she exclaims:

> My God has come to me, the God of the Universe has embraced me. The God of Gods even now enters my inmost being. Now indeed God himself nourishes me. He who brought forth the soul, transforms it into angel, turns it into god.[28]

Figure 4—Eighteenth-century World card in the tradition of the Tarot of Marseilles (author's depiction)

By putting Ficino's nude soul on the throne of Christ, the Tarot of Marseilles has created the visual equivalent of the quotation above.

Because this image is inspired by the Christ in Majesty icon, we would expect to find Christ in the center of at least some of the decks

*Figure 5—The Jacques Vieville World card
(author's depiction)*

that follow the Marseilles tradition. However, the decks in this tradition almost unanimously prefer a female nude. There are two World cards of this type that bear ambiguous figures, and only one early example uses Christ in the center. This example is found in the Jacques Vieville Tarot printed in Paris in the early 1600s (Figure 5). The Christ on this card is related to the northern Gothic tradition in which the Christ in Majesty is depicted as nude with a cape and holding a scepter. However, even here we find Neoplatonic influences. The typical Christ in the northern icons modestly wears a loincloth and has dark hair and a beard. The Christ on the Jacques Vieville World card is distinctively blond and beardless and unashamedly nude except for his royal cape. He is closer to the Apollo-like Christ of Michelangelo's Sistine Chapel mural than to any Gothic model.

Interpreting the Trumps

With the previous discussion in mind, we are now ready to interpret the sequence of trumps as found in the Tarot of Marseilles. The Fool, of course, is not one of the trumps. Most Tarots with numbered trumps use Roman numerals. In the Roman system, there is no zero and no concept of zero. The Fool is simply unnumbered in these decks. In the known orders, he is either included at the beginning or at the end of the sequence of trumps. In the game, he is a wild card that can be played instead of any trump, and in game points he is one of the most valuable cards. It seems that the Fool can be both foolish and wise. He can be a novice who leads this parade of trumps, or one who has progressed through the sequence and been initiated. As a wild card, he is like Ramon Lull's jongleurs, who can pop up anywhere in the story and even advise a pope.

On the first numbered trump, we find dice on the table of the Magician—called the *Bateleur* in the Marseilles deck. This is true of most early printed decks from Italy or France. Dice were an ancient tool for divination as well as gambling, and this use of combinations of numbers can be related to Pythagorean mysticism. There are twenty-one possible combinations of the throws of two dice, and this number represents all the possible divinatory solutions that two dice can give. In the Renaissance, these twenty-one possibilities were represented as twenty-one allegorical figures in a book on divination titled the *Trionpho della Fortuna* by the Ferrarese astrologer Fante. This book is also notable because figures related to the Tarot trumps and expressing a related allegory appear on the frontispiece.

This connection with dice is one piece of evidence that connects the Tarot with divination in the fifteenth century. Dice are designed so that the numbers on alternate sides of the die always add up to the mystical seven. The Bateleur initiates the sequence of trumps; his two dice are a tool for divination. They can be used to predict the events of the story before it starts. The Bateleur is like the narrator of a play, and the trumps can be thought of as this three-act play, each act composed of seven cards.

The first act, which depicts couples triumphed by love, addresses the *soul of appetite*. The second act, dominated by images of time, mortality, and suffering, but also containing virtue, addresses the *soul of will*. The third act, with its celestial ascent to the soul of the World, addresses the *soul of reason*. These three acts represent the mystical ascent of the spirit. At the start of the journey, the spirit is immersed in the physical world, the world of the four elements, four directions, and four seasons represented by the other four suits in the Tarot.

In the first act, there are four ruling figures that are paired into two couples, each trumping the one before it in rank. The Papesse is outranked by the Empress; the Empress is outranked by the Emperor; and the Emperor, in turn, is trumped by the Pope. These figures also relate to the fourfold physical world with four directions, four seasons, and four elements. The theory of the four elements can be traced to the Pythagorean philosopher Empedocles (490–430 BCE). Although he was a natural philosopher—something like a physicist—he was also a mystic, and he presented his theory with the following fragment from a poem:

> Here first the four roots of all things: Dazzling Zeus, life-bearing Hera, Aidoneus, and Nestis who moistens the springs of mortals with her tears.[29]

In these lines, the four elements are presented as two divine couples who rule over the physical world and the afterlife. Zeus, the god of heaven, represents the air; Hera, his wife and the life-bearing mother, is earth; Aidoneus—an alternative name for Hades—is the god of the underworld, where there is fire in the earth; and Nestis is a Sicilian name for

Hades' wife, Persephone, who represents water with her tears. Notice how the Tarot also has two couples representing the fourfold world: the Emperor and Empress are like Zeus and Hera as the rulers of the physical world, and the Pope and Papesse are like Hades and Persephone as the rulers of the world of the soul.

In some early decks, this masculine and feminine division is reflected in the minor suits, which can be related to the four elements. In the feminine suits—cups and coins—the lowest ranking royal cards depict a woman, and in the masculine suits—staffs and swords—the lowest royal cards depict a man. In the Tarot of Marseilles, these four rulers in the trumps—the Papesse, Empress, Emperor, and Pope—can be thought of as the four elements presented in this order: water, earth, air, and fire. When looked at in reverse order, like the Buddhist stupa, they can represent the descent of spirit into matter. When they are in forward order, they represent the spirit rising back to its source.

The sixth card of this first act depicts love trumping all four of the temporal rulers. The Lovers card in the oldest decks simply shows a marriage or a betrothal with Cupid, the god of love, hovering overhead. This clearly indicates the triumph of Cupid over the fourfold world of the Emperor, Empress, Pope, and Papesse—after all, that is why they are in couples. In the Tarot of Marseilles, the Lovers card depicts a man choosing between a life of study and one of sensuality, symbolized in some of the decks in this tradition as a woman with a laurel wreath and a woman with a wreath of flowers. This is the decision that every true philosopher has to face, as did Blanquerna in the first part of Lull's novel. This image can be traced to a Pythagorean allegory that describes the Greek letter upsilon as representing two paths (this letter, which looks like our Y, is believed to have been added to the Greek alphabet by Pythagoras): the first path is easy but leads to ruin, and the second one is difficult but leads to mastery.

The final card of the first act, the Chariot, shows a young hero who has resolved to take the journey to the next level, the path that takes the sorrows of the world head-on. Even in the earlier decks that depict a beautiful woman in the chariot, she represents virtue and the strength to go beyond the confines of Cupid.

The second act contains three cards that represent the human mortal condition: the suffering to which all life leads. They are the Hermit, the Hanged Man, and Death, and they symbolize old age, suffering, and death. As we will see, these are three of the sights that Buddha had to confront to find his motivation for his mystical quest. (It is not always clear in modern decks that the Hanged Man represents suffering, but in the Renaissance, to be hung by the feet was a punishment reserved for traitors, and "Traitor" was an early name for this card. In an engraved deck produced in Bologna in 1664, we find a man hitting another man with a mallet as a substitute for this image.) Interspersed with this group are four cards representing the four cardinal virtues that were extolled by Plato as the path out of impermanence and suffering. Three of the four are clearly labeled as Justice, Strength, and Temperance. Occultists, knowing that there should be four, have tried to turn the Hanged Man into Prudence. However, to see Prudence, we have to understand the allegory.

The virtues were first called "cardinal" by St. Ambrose, the fourth-century bishop of Milan. Like St. Augustine, Ambrose was one of the early Christian scholars who worked to Christianize Greek philosophy. The word *cardinal* is derived from the Latin root *cardo,* which refers to the axis of a wheel. *Cardinal* means "that which turns the wheel." Originally, this referred to the four directions and the four constellations of the seasonal changes, which turned the wheel of time and space. This wheel was depicted in Plato's myth at the end of *The Republic.* St. Ambrose used the word to indicate that Plato's virtues were more powerful than time and space. This insight is Wisdom or Prudence and it is exactly what is illustrated on the Tarot of Marseilles's Wheel.

On this Wheel of Fortune card we see the wheel of fate or time with three foolish creatures traveling around it. They represent the three follies that cause the three aspects of suffering that are placed in this second act. Notice that in the Tarot of Marseilles the cardinal virtues are in the opposite order from the way they were presented by Plato. In the other two original orders of trumps, the labeled virtues are in the correct Platonic order: Temperance, Strength, and Justice, either grouped together or assigned one to each act. Here, they are gathered together in the second act and Justice and Temperance switch places—a deliberate reversal of their order.

In the Tarot of Marseilles, the virtues are moving against time and suffering. As we remember from Plato's myth, the symbol of the wheel of time is related to the concept of reincarnation. On the Tibetan Buddhist image of the wheel of rebirth, we can also find in its center three creatures symbolizing the folly that ties us to the material world. In this light, the virtues are leading us to the end of mortality—the immortality of mystical union.

The last act starts with two cards that can be described as dealing with evil and ends with two that can be described as achieving the Good. They are complements of each other. In the middle are the three celestial figures that we remember from St. Francis's "Canticle to Brother Sun": the Star, the Moon, and the Sun.

We start the act with the Devil in charge. The Tower breaks this power—what was crowned is toppled. Judgement allows the physical to ascend to the spiritual (or the soul to return to its source), and the final card, the World, shows the attainment of the Good. The transition is accomplished by ascending through the seven planets, depicted on the Star card as seven stars. This ascent leads to the eighth sphere, which is represented on the Star card by the large star in the center. This configuration is introduced with a nude representing the soul purified by truth and beauty. The Moon and Sun, although part of this group, are highlighted on separate cards because, as in alchemical texts, they also represent the feminine and masculine forces that form the golden relationship. Then finally, like all true philosophical quests, the cards deliver us to the mother of our soul, the Anima Mundi, who is depicted in the center of the World card sitting on the throne of God, a mandala of sacredness and spiritual attainment.

Chapter 3

THE LIFE OF BUDDHA

The legend of the life of Buddha has many variations. Even the date of his birth is disputed. In China, he is believed to have been born in 947 BCE, but elsewhere the most commonly given date is 563 BCE. At birth, he was given the name Siddhartha, and his family name was Gautama. He is also called *Sakyamuni,* which means "the sage (*-muni*) of the Sakya clan." *Buddha* is a title, not a name. It means "one who is awake." To the Buddhists, a Buddha is no longer a person. It is a different category of being—not a mere god, but a being superior to a god.

The following account is a popular version of Buddha's life, focusing, as do the Buddhist texts, on Siddhartha's early life and his heroic quest for enlightenment. The oldest Buddhist texts were written in the first century BCE in Pali (an ancient language of northern India close to the language that Siddhartha spoke), although the oldest copy of a Pali manuscript that we actually have today is about five hundred years old.[1] These stories are more concerned with symbolic significance than an accurate account of Siddhartha's life. Later a more complete biography was written in Sanskrit.

In the Pali texts and the subsequent Sanskrit texts, we learn not only of Siddhartha's life, but also of his past lives and of the twenty-four Buddhas who preceded him in other ages. At one time in a past incarnation, Siddhartha was a Brahman named Sumedha, an ascetic who came into the prescience of the first Buddha, named Dipankara. Like all Buddhas, Dipankara had the power of clairvoyance, and seeing Sumedha in the midst of the assembled crowd, he announced that one day Sumedha would also become a Buddha. This event set Siddhartha on his spiritual path, and led to his eventual Buddhahood. In the following 547 incarnations, Siddhartha experienced life as a lion, a snake, and other animals, as well as a human. During this process he purified himself and perfected the ten virtues: generosity, morality, renunciation, intelligence, energy, patience, truthfulness, determination, benevolence, and equanimity. He became a *Bodhisattva,* a title that refers to a person on his or her way to becoming a Buddha, and he incarnated in Tusita Heaven with the gods.

Tusita Heaven is a paradise above Mount Meru in the sacred center of the world. The beings that live there are gods, but in Buddhist theology, the gods are not immortal. Although their lives are so long that they seem immortal to us, they, too, will suffer death. Of the six worlds shown on the Wheel of Life mandala, Tusita is the best place in which to incarnate. Realizing that his time there was ending, Siddhartha knew that it was time to incarnate in the world of men and to take the final step that he had been preparing for throughout all of his past lives: to become a Buddha.

Siddhartha was born on the full moon in Wesak (our month of May), although the Chinese fix his date of birth on our modern calendar as April 8. He was born in Kapilavastu, a principality that no longer exists but which included an area that is now encompassed by northern India and Nepal. His father and mother were Suddhodhana and Maya, the wealthy rulers of Kapilavastu. They were members of the Ksatriya caste (the noble or warrior class).

Before Siddhartha's birth, Maya had a dream in which she was visited by a white elephant with six tusks. In the dream, the elephant impregnated Maya by piercing her side painlessly with one of his tusks. Ten lunar months later, Siddhartha was born. After his birth, it is said that he immediately stood and a white lotus rose under his feet from which he surveyed the ten directions. He then took seven steps toward each of the cardinal directions, and declared this to be his final birth. In some versions of the story, Suddhodhana and Maya had not yet consummated their marriage when Maya became pregnant. Therefore, Siddhartha's birth, like that of Jesus, was from a virgin. Seven days after Siddhartha's birth, Maya died of joy and ascended to Tusita Heaven. Maya's sister, Mahaprajapati, married Suddhodhana and raised Siddhartha.

A short time later, a seer named Asita, a saintly old man from the Himalayas, came to visit the child and confirmed that two possible destinies awaited him. If Siddhartha embraced a worldly life, he would grow to be a *chakravartin* (literally, "a wheel-turner"), a great emperor over a unified India. If he embraced asceticism, he would become a world savior—a Buddha. Asita was sure that Siddhartha would take the religious path.

As the child was growing, his father summoned a council of wise Brahmans (members of the priest class). They determined that Siddhartha's destiny hinged on whether or not he beheld the four sights: old age, sickness, death, and the life of the holy hermit. Suddhodhana wanted his son to succeed him to the throne and become a powerful ruler instead of an ascetic, so he kept Siddhartha in a beautiful palace with sumptuous gardens and delightful young women to serve as his attendants or as his courtesans. Some accounts say that the palace was surrounded by three walls; others say that it was surrounded by four gardens, one for each of the four directions. All accounts agree that the sight or even the mention of death or grief was forbidden.

The young, charismatic Siddhartha excelled in the martial arts and in his intellectual studies. He was the perfect example of his caste, even surpassing the knowledge of his teachers. When he was sixteen, his father encouraged his marriage to the beautiful princess Yasodhara. To win her, Siddhartha had to enter a competition of martial arts. He won by stringing and shooting a perfect arrow with his ancestral bow, a bow that most men could not even lift. After this, Siddhartha became enchanted by the delights of marriage, and his father felt secure that his son, having been conquered by love, would follow the worldly path.

However, this enchantment did not last. The young man grew restless; his life of sensual pleasure began to appear shallow and vain. Motivated by a desire for greater knowledge of the world, Siddhartha decided to leave the palace and prepared to visit the city in his chariot. His father, worried about what Siddhartha would find there, had the entire city swept clean of any unpleasantness. But the truth prevailed after all. Siddhartha saw an old man, bent, trembling, and leaning on a cane—the first of the four sights that had been predicted by the Brahmans. The young man had never seen someone that old before, and it taught him that decrepitude is the fate of those who live out their lives.

On his second visit to the city, Siddhartha came across a man suffering from an incurable disease. On his third visit, he saw a funeral procession carrying a corpse. Through these experiences, Siddhartha learned that all human lives eventually include suffering and death, and that it is the fate of humanity to repeat this suffering again and again during the seemingly endless rotations of the wheel of reincarnation.

On his fourth and final visit to the city, Siddhartha met a *sadhu*, a holy hermit, who wandered through the country carrying a begging bowl. Despite his poverty, this man was calm and peaceful. It seemed to Siddhartha that this man offered him a path out of the torment that the other sights had caused him. He returned to the palace with hope.

After his son Rahula was born, Siddhartha realized that his obligation to continue his royal line had been fulfilled. With great strength and determination, he prepared to leave the palace and seek enlightenment by becoming a sadhu. One night while his family slept, he rode out on his faithful horse, Kantaka, determined not to return until he reached his goal. He gave Kantaka to his equerry, cut off his hair, and exchanged his splendid robes for those of a hunter.

Siddhartha's quest for enlightenment moved through three phases. First, he wished to attain wisdom. He sought out two of the foremost Hindu masters of the day and learned all he could from their tradition, including the discipline of meditation.

In the second phase, Siddhartha decided that the desires of his body were holding him back. To crush his body's interference, he joined a band of ascetics. In that time, sadhus were known to practice severe austerity, but Siddhartha outdid his teachers in every discipline and gathered five disciples of his own. In a final effort to attain victory over his body, he went on a prolonged fast. Eventually, he turned himself into a living skeleton, but this still did not bring him to his goal. Siddhartha saw that asceticism was as futile and as egotistical as sensuality—neither would bring an end to suffering. He began to eat and build up his strength. When a village girl named Sujata offered him a bowl of rice and milk, he accepted it. After his meal, he bathed in the river. In that time, several practitioners of Jainism had fasted themselves to death in an effort to gain liberation and Siddhartha's disciples hoped that he would do the same. When he began to eat, his disciples left him in disgust.

Now Siddhartha entered the third and final stage of his quest. He was inspired to follow the Middle Way, a path of balance between the extremes of denial and indulgence. He wandered alone until one evening he sat down under a fig tree (later named the *Bodhi Tree,* which means "the tree of enlightenment"). Here, he entered into a state of deep mystic concentration and vowed not to rise until he had attained his goal.

Mara, the Evil One, king of the demons called *maras,* realized that Siddhartha was nearing his goal. If Siddhartha could find an end to suffering, this would be a threat to Mara's power, and he was determined to interfere. First, Mara sent his three voluptuous daughters, Lust, Passion, and Delight. Having overcome his attachment to sensuality in his life as a prince, Siddhartha was immune to their temptations. Next, Mara tried to frighten him by sending an army of demons equipped with an imaginative array of sadistic weapons. However, Siddhartha's life as an ascetic had made him immune to fear of bodily harm, and, as the demons approached, they found themselves halted. Siddhartha had ceased to echo emotions like fear and anger, emotions that the demons needed to feed on. In place of these emotions, they found only compassion. As the demons entered Siddhartha's aura, they became calm and peaceful and simply bowed down before him.

Mara made the final attack himself. Riding on a cloud, he hurled his terrible flaming disk at Siddhartha. Yet this weapon, which could cleave a mountain, was useless against Siddhartha. The disk transformed into a garland of flowers and hung suspended above Siddhartha's head.

Mara was beaten. In a last effort, he challenged Siddhartha's right to do what he was doing. Siddhartha merely touched the earth with a finger of his right hand, and, in a voice like thunder, the earth answered, "I bear you witness."

It was Wesak, the night of the full moon in May. During that night, Siddhartha entered into the initial stage of enlightenment. For the first time, he could see the entire wheel of rebirth, including all of his past lives. He saw the suffering of all living creatures, and then the means to end that suffering. He realized that as long as he tried to find the way to his salvation or his enlightenment, he was still trapped in his ego. It was only when he replaced all concern for himself with total compassion that he was free. When he did this, he was no longer a separate ego and he and the world became one. As the sun rose, Siddhartha was fully enlightened—but he was no longer Siddhartha. He was now Buddha, which means "the awakened one."

Buddha remained in meditation for another seven days before rising from his seat. He remained near his tree for several weeks. Then he realized that before he could proceed, he had to make a decision. Two paths were open to him: he could enter Nirvana at once, or he could renounce his own deliverance for a while in order to remain on earth and spread his message. Mara, of course, urged him to enter Nirvana. Mara argued that people are ignorant and incapable of understanding Buddha's wisdom and that Buddha should leave them to their own devices. After some initial hesitation, Buddha had a vision that helped him realize that this was the final trick of the ego. To enter Nirvana at once without thought of others who were in need of his teaching would mean letting go of the very compassion that had brought him this opportunity. There was only one answer. Without further hesitation Buddha said, "Some will understand." Buddha remained on earth to teach and to become an embodiment of wisdom and joy in the world.

Buddha's first sermon, in a place called Deer Park, was to the five disciples who had previously deserted him. They were quickly converted to his new teaching. Over the next half-century, these five disciples became the nucleus of a monastic community that grew to include both men and women from all classes of society. Buddha's parents, his wife, his son, his half-brother, and even his cousin became his disciples. Everywhere Buddha went he made converts, and his teachings reached countless individuals. This oral tradition provided the foundation for the scriptures of Buddhism, the *sutras*. It was only after reaching the age of eighty that Buddha died. He was accidentally served a poisonous meal (some say it was mushrooms; others say pork). His last words included:

> All compounds grow old.
> Work out your own salvation with diligence.[2]

After his death, Buddha passed into the bliss of Nirvana.

The Four Noble Truths

We may wish that we were at that first sermon in Deer Park when it is said that Buddha set the Dharmachakra, the Wheel of the Law, in motion. What was this teaching that has had such lasting value for over two thousand years?

By calling the teaching a "wheel," Buddhists created the symbolic equivalent to St. Ambrose labeling the four Platonic virtues "cardinal." They were saying that the teaching, like Plato's four cardinal virtues, was capable of overcoming the wheel of fate or the wheel of reincarnation. Like the virtues, this first sermon had a fourfold structure. It is called the Four Noble Truths and they are listed as follows:

I. **All life is *dukkha*,** a word usually translated as "suffering." In Buddha's time, *dukkha* described a wheel whose axle was bent or off-center. By this Buddha was not saying that life is continuously painful, but that all lives contain some pain and suffering. Buddha pinpointed four principal moments when this is true: at the trauma of birth, in illness, in the decline of old age, and at the approach of death. He also spoke of the pain of being separated from what one loves or desires, and the pain of being chained to what one does not desire. However, even at its best, there is something shallow and off-center about the pleasures of life. Buddha had lived like a playboy, having every desire granted and not burdened by anything, and yet there was something missing. Like Plato, he saw that the impermanence of life made it shallow. He longed to experience the eternal, to live in the center.

II. **The cause of dukkha is *tanha*,** which is usually translated as "desire." However, tanha is the desire for individual fulfillment. It is the desire that is ego-centered and not concerned with the good of the group. When we enslave others for our gain, this is tanha. When we pollute the earth to satisfy our desires, this is tanha. However, when we compare ourselves to others, hoping that we will feel more beautiful, smart, or important if we can see their shortcomings, or we become depressed because we did not measure up, this is also tanha. In Plato's soul of appetite we are thoroughly immersed in tanha. At this stage we need to learn the virtue of temperance, for to placate every demand of our desires without a sense of balance is not even good for us.

III. **The cure to life's suffering, or dukkha, is to let go of tanha.** This is the logical conclusion to be drawn from the second Noble Truth. This is the same cure that Plato prescribed. In his *Republic,* when we move our consciousness into the soul of will, we continue to experience personal desire, only now for fame and prestige. But at the same time, to gain prestige, we begin to work for the good of others, and this concern for others pulls us out of tanha. In Plato's *Republic*, those who could develop the soul of reason were chosen to be the leaders. This is because at this level, their desire for personal gain takes a back seat to their desire for promoting the well-being of the community. At this level, tanha is overcome by compassion. The philosopher king is one who has become the embodiment of compassion. Buddha also detailed a procedure for overcoming tanha and this is the fourth Noble Truth.

IV. **There is a method for overcoming tanha. It is called the *Eightfold Path*.** The eight steps of this path are usually associated with eight key words, which describe the recommended actions. These are the eight paths:

1. *Develop right knowledge.* For a human to create anything, the first step is to create a plan, an idea of what is to be created. This is why Plato believed that the archetypes were on a higher plane of reality—they are necessary for physical creation to proceed. The Eightfold Path is the plan for the end of suffering. The first step is to learn it.

2. *Develop right aspiration.* The way to overcome tanha is to replace it with a healthy desire. Before we start, we must be clear that we desire enlightenment more than the numerous diversions that fill our minds daily. This is how one develops the cardinal virtue temperance.

3. *Develop right speech.* Basically this means developing truthfulness, but this is not a matter of just telling the truth. It means weeding out of our speech what is hurtful, disruptive, or trivial. One old Indian proverb expresses the sentiment that some people cut off the heads of others to make themselves look

taller. To develop right speech, we must become conscious of how much of what we say falls into this category of behavior. To break people of this habit, Pythagoras required that those wishing to enter his community should remain silent for the first five years of study.

4. *Develop right behavior.* To help clarify what right behavior is, Buddha made a list called the *Five Precepts*. Each of the precepts is a negative statement, a proscription of behavior. Although it is not as widely known in the West, each proscription is paired with a positive direction, called the *Five Dharmas*.[3] The Five Precepts and Dharmas are:

a. Do not kill—develop love.
b. Do not steal—develop generosity.
c. Do not lie—develop truthfulness.
d. Do not commit sexual misconduct—develop contentment.
e. Do not take intoxicants—develop awareness.

These five proscriptions parallel the Five Wisdoms designed to help develop each of the five archetypal aspects of Buddha called Jinas (see Chart 3 on page 121). We will discuss the Jinas and their five wisdoms in more detail later in chapter 4.

The Pythagoreans, who lived in Italy in the same century as Buddha, observed these same proscriptions and directions. The first is not only a commandment not to take human life, but not to harm any life. The literal translation of the text is to abstain "from harming living beings."[4]

The Pythagoreans and many Buddhists observe the first precept by maintaining a vegetarian diet. The first Buddhists were mendicants who begged for their food. Although they were instructed not to kill an animal for meat, they did eat meat when it was given to them. Once the Buddhists settled in monasteries where they provided their own food, the monks became vegetarians.

The precept about sexual misconduct has different applications depending on one's role in life. A Buddhist monk maintains strict chastity not because sex is evil, but because to commit oneself to this level on the path to enlightenment, sexual energy must be diverted to this goal. For a married householder, this means to be true to one's marriage vows.

5. *Develop right livelihood.* Progression on the path is impossible if we undermine our practice by spending our working time in activities that are poisonous to our consciousness. Buddha considered certain occupations incompatible with a serious endeavor to seek enlightenment. In his lifetime these included poison merchant, slave trader, prostitute, butcher, brewer, arms dealer, and tax collector. At that time, most tax collectors were corrupt.

6. *Develop right effort.* One of the three poisons found depicted in the center of the wheel of reincarnation is stupidity and sluggishness represented by a pig. It is not enough to want to progress toward enlightenment, one has to work at it. This takes discipline and perseverance. This is the cardinal virtue strength.

    To develop this virtue, Plato recommended gymnastics because physical perseverance stems from mental perseverance. Similarly, in Pythagorean communities the day was divided between contemplation, study, and physical exercise. This type of lifestyle creates a natural division between physical exertion and contemplation. The communities that Buddha founded consisted of wandering mendicants who came together in encampments during the monsoon season. At first, these retreats were in caves and makeshift shelters. Later, land was donated to them and shelters were built for the monks. Unlike other mendicants at the time, the Buddhists were noted for their cheerfulness, or "dwelling with minds like wild deer."[5] Cheerfulness is the ally of perseverance.

7. *Develop right mindfulness.* Like Plato and Socrates, Buddha believed that injustice stems from ignorance, not evil intent. To overcome ignorance, one has to become self-aware. To accomplish this, Buddha recommended a rigorous process of self-examination. We must continually observe ourselves as others do and question the motivations for our actions. When looking for injustice in the world, we must first look to ourselves. It is better to spend more time concentrating on offering justice to others than demanding justice from others. When we live in this way, we not only change our behavior, but seemingly miraculous changes can happen in our lives. The Buddhist text called *The Dhammapada* opens with the line, "All we are is the result of what we have thought."[6]

8. *Develop right absorption.* This is the practice of meditation as Buddha practiced it under the Bodhi Tree. This is the most important step in the Eightfold Path. Buddhist meditation is based on the understanding that there are four parts to every human. In modern Western terms they are the physical body, the conscious mind, the unconscious mind, and, as psychologist Carl Jung titled it, the collective unconscious. As he delved into his study of the unconscious, Jung found that at a deep level the individual consciousness faded out and a group consciousness emerged. This is the level where the archetypes exist.

Archetype is a term that Jung borrowed from Plato. He used it to describe personalities or ideas that exist in all humans. They emerge in different cultures as similar patterns in myths, or as gods and goddesses that exhibit the same qualities although they may be clothed in different trappings.

At the base of all archetypes, Jung found that they were all one. They emerged from a totality that is the goal of all religious experience. He called this totality the *Self*. This is the Buddhist "Ground of Being." It is unbounded, eternally creative, and everlasting. To experience it is bliss. Plato called it the One, the Good, and the Beautiful. Plotinus said that it could not be expressed in our dualistic language. The Buddhists call it Nirvana or the void.

In meditation, we gradually draw our attention away from each of these layers of our being. While sitting, we use concentrated deep breathing or progressive relaxation (separately relaxing each part of the body by concentrating on it) to draw our awareness away from the body. When we accomplish this, the clutter of our daily thoughts comes into focus. Hindus call this clutter *monkey mind*. It is ever-active with its plans, forever wrapped up in its hopes and fears. We must learn to let go of each of these thoughts; not to try to stop them, but to not get involved in them—simply watch them drift away. If we are persistent in this process, the mind will begin to still like an undisturbed pond; the ripples caused by each thought will begin to subside. At this level, unconscious material will begin to emerge into consciousness, but we must continue to let go of each of these thoughts as well until the mind is like perfectly still water. Then we have created the right condition for our true self to emerge. If it does, we will get a taste of the bliss that is Nirvana.

THE PATH BEYOND CLASS

At its conception, Buddhism, like Jainism, could be considered a heretical form of Hinduism. This is because it ignored the social conventions of the time and set up a path to salvation outside of the class system.

Like most Indo-European cultures (a linguistic group that includes Indians, Persians, and almost all Europeans), India's people were divided into four classes. These classes were derived from the culture of the Aryan peoples who invaded in approximately 1500 BCE. In India, the classes were called *castes,* and the divisions between them were very strict.

The highest caste was called *Brahman,* the priest caste. (Today, this caste includes persons of certain trades as well, such as scribes and goldsmiths.) It was believed that the divine presence inhabited the members of this caste. The Brahmans were thought to be the incarnations of very old and advanced souls, the only ones that could achieve enlightenment. The members of the other castes hoped that, after many lifetimes, they would become Brahmans. As in many ancient cultures, it was believed in Buddha's time that the priests ascended to salvation or enlightenment through sacred acts such as rituals and sacrifices to the gods, not through personal, intellectual, or moral effort.

The next major caste was the *Ksatriya.* Ksatriyas were the warriors and the protectors of the people. In the West we would call them the landed gentry. This is the caste into which Siddhartha was born.

The third caste, *Vaisya,* was made up of commoners, which included merchants and bankers. They tended to avoid manual labor and sometimes were managers of farms.

The lowest caste was the *Sudra,* the farmers and tradesmen of low standing. The lowest members of this group were called *Untouchables.* These were laborers and their duty was to serve.

Buddha was not a member of the highest caste and he even rejected the advantages of his own caste to become a lowly beggar. As an outsider, he was able to observe how the Brahmans were abusing their authority, and he sought a way to enlightenment that was open to anyone, regardless of class. He taught that members of any caste could reach enlightenment through meditation and moral behavior. Because of this, and because he taught women as well as men, Buddha was contradicting the religion of the Brahmans. Although his teachings were eventually absorbed into Hinduism, at first his ideas were considered heretical. Buddha had created a path that existed outside of the neatly quartered social structure—a path to enlightenment that trumps the class system.

When the first decks of cards were introduced to western Europe by the Islamic cultures in Spain and Sicily, they were comprised of four suits: cups, scimitars or swords, coins, and polo sticks. At that time, the sport of polo was totally unknown to the Christian Europeans—the early polo stick was simply a pole with a bent end. When the Christians began to reproduce these decks for their own use, they straightened the ends of the polo sticks and called this fourth suit "staffs."

The four suits of these new decks must have made perfect sense to the Christian Europeans because the suit signs represented the four classes of European society. A cup in the form of a chalice holding the consecrated wine or the host was the main symbol of the Christian ritual. Therefore, in European consciousness, it stood for the priests and other members of the clergy. A sword was the sacred symbol of knighthood, and being touched with one's sword was the essence of the ritual for becoming a knight. Therefore, it symbolized the nobles. Coins were the goal and measure of worth of a merchant. Therefore, the coin was seen as an emblem for the merchant class. A staff was a tool and a weapon of the peasants, and this was their symbol.

When the fifth suit with its twenty-two cards was added to this deck to create the Tarot, this suit represented something that was outside of the class structure symbolized by the other four suits. It was called a *parade*. This parade, the triumph, was celebrated as part of the festivities for Carnival as well as at other times. Although it was a Christian celebration before Lent, Carnival was influenced by the ancient Roman *Saturnalia*. The Saturnalia was an end-of-the-year festival in which class structure was ignored for its duration—slaves could give orders to their masters and the masters would serve their slaves. This destruction of the social order is a symbolic destruction of the world common to ancient festivities at year's end. Through this destruction and cleansing, the world is ritually renewed. The renewal attained through the Saturnalia was a reclaiming of the ancient golden age over which the god Saturn was believed to rule.

The Tarot contains aspects that link it to Carnival. For example, the Fool is related to the common man who would be elected Carnival king during the festivities. The normally high-ranking rulers—the

Empress, the Emperor, and the Pope—are included in the lowest ranks of the trumps, and in some orders the common Fool is given the highest rank.

However, the trumps contain an allegory that has a religious mystical message as well. They use Christian mystical iconography, which incorporates pre-Christian symbolism, to describe the threefold path to enlightenment. Like the path that Buddha traveled, this path exists outside of the class system. As a model for this type of mystical path, the artists of the Renaissance had the life of St. Francis. St. Francis, like Buddha, rejected his wealth and position in life, and for the sake of his salvation he became a poor beggar. St. Francis embraced the role of a fool and an outcast, and through his spiritual transformation became the most honored man in all of Italy.

Enlightenment is the real renewal of the golden age. To be enlightened is to remember what we really are and what we always have been from the beginning of time. An individual who attains enlightenment destroys what he or she was before, and in doing so reclaims his or her true potential. This individual's enlightenment becomes an agent of renewal for that time and that culture. As in the legend of the Grail, when it is found, it heals the land.

As we look at the story of Siddhartha's life and attainment of Buddhahood, we can see that it is a three-part story, like a three-act play. In the first act, Siddhartha lives the life of sensuality to the extreme. Like a modern star of film or sports, he has wealth, sexual pleasure, and the admiration of his culture. He is totally immersed in Plato's soul of appetite. However, he learns temperance and he develops the best in this life.

In the second act, he sees the four sights and becomes disheartened. His old life has lost its appeal. Knowing that his and the lives of everyone that he loves will end in suffering and death makes the pleasures of this life seem shallow and short-lived. He desires to find the end to this suffering for the sake of himself and the people he loves. This is the hero's quest, and entering this path moves one into the soul of will. Siddhartha becomes an ascetic and through fasting and self-denial he tries to will himself out of his attachment to the body.

The word *ascetic* is derived from the Greek word *askesis,* which originally referred to the discipline of an athlete. This discipline was aimed at self-mastery. At times, it included chastity as well as rigorous physical training. Plato recommended athletic discipline as a means of developing strength, the virtue associated with the soul of will. As self-mastery was the goal of religion and philosophy as well, this term also came to be applied to these disciplines—especially because the philosophers of Greece, like Buddha, began to look to the perfection of individual behavior as the means to salvation instead of ritual. Like the Jains of India, some ancient Pythagoreans and Stoics were noted for the extreme asceticism of their religious practice.

In the third act, Siddhartha sees that asceticism is the opposite pole from the life of a sensualist. In both paths the individual is only concerned with his or her own desires. They are both egotistical and self-centered. In the final act, Siddhartha realizes that to attain enlightenment, he must nurture his body as his vehicle in this life and he embraces the middle path. But more than this, he has to move his consciousness to the center.

The center of the world is a universal symbol of sacredness. It is the place where the hero can make the ascent to the heavens and bring back the elixir of life that is needed to heal and renew the world. In various world myths it is symbolized as a mountain, a pole, or a tree. For example, Yggdrasill in Norse mythology is the world tree that goes through the center of our world and holds it together with the underworld and the realm of the gods above. In Greek mythology, Mount Olympus is a sacred center that connects us with the home of the gods. The Bodhi Tree in the story of Buddha is a sacred center. When Siddhartha finds this spot, he has symbolically centered himself and he is ready for the ascent. In his consciousness, to reside in the center is to reside in compassion. This is the place within where his ego dissolves and he connects with the One. It is the tree that connects our ego with Ground of Being.

The allegory in the Tarot trumps can be seen as this same story. Not only does it have the same three-part structure, but also individual cards fit the details in Buddha's story. In the first section, we find four temporal rulers. In the center of this group there is an Emperor and Empress, which relates to Siddhartha and Yasodhara who were being groomed to become the future emperor and empress. The Emperor and Empress would seem to be the masters of their realm, but they are controlled by the Pope, who trumps them. The Pope, whose name is derived from the word *papa*, is like Siddhartha's father, Suddhodhana. However, all of these characters are trumped by Cupid on the Lovers card. This represents the sensuality that rules their world.

Next we see a hero in a chariot, like Siddhartha going to town. The hero is leading us into the next section, where he is trumped by four sights: old age or time, suffering, death, and a holy hermit. These are the same four sights that Siddhartha encountered. Both the Wheel of Fortune and the original character on the Hermit card symbolize time and old age. As we discovered in the last chapter, the Hanged Man represents suffering, and the connection between the sight of death and the sadhu with the Death card and the Tarot of Marseilles's Hermit is obvious. In this section, our hero also encounters the virtues and finds the middle path, which is represented by Temperance. The woman on the Temperance card pours water from one vessel into another just as Sujata pours nourishment into Siddhartha at the end of his fast. The virtues trump the negative images and the story progresses forward.

After Temperance makes her appearance, the Devil, the ultimate image of negativity, is called up to trump her. In Buddhism, Mara is the Devil, and he shows up at this point in the story to give Siddhartha the final test. On the Tarot of Marseilles's Devil card, we even find a male and female minion in front of him. This could just as well represent Mara's two-pronged attack: the first with his daughters and the second with his male soldiers. As his final trump, the Devil, like Mara, heaves his flaming ball, and it does appear as a flaming ball on the Tarot of Marseilles's Tower. However, the trumps continue with images of a celestial ascent through seven stars or chakras found in the sky on the Star. The Star is trumped by the Moon, and the Moon is trumped by the Sun—greater and greater light. Then the series ends with images of victory over death in the Judgement card, and a mandala of the sacred center: the World.

This has been a brief overview of the story in the trumps and its connections with Siddhartha's journey. We will explore it in more detail when we discuss the individual cards.

It is hard to say how much of the story of Buddha is symbolic legend and how much is historic fact. The Jina, or Mahavira, the founder of Jainism, lived in India a century before Buddha. He also went through a personal heroic journey to relieve the suffering of humanity. His life can be divided into the same three acts: luxury, asceticism, and meditation under a tree, which led to enlightenment. It is obvious that this story influenced the legend that grew around the life of Buddha.

In his book *The Hero with a Thousand Faces*, Joseph Campbell demonstrates that all hero myths fit an archetypal structure consisting of three acts. In the first, the hero is depicted in the ordinary world. In this act, he or she will receive a call to adventure, to right a wrong, or find what is missing. In the second, the hero accepts the challenge, leaves home, and begins an adventure. Adventures may or may not be punishing and grueling, but they are usually life-threatening. The motivation for the adventure is to find the magic elixir that will heal the wrong that was introduced in the first act. In the final act, the hero faces the supreme ordeal, and, after victory, returns home with the elixir.

It is clear that both the story in the Tarot and the story of Buddha fit this archetypal pattern. This might seem like enough of an explanation for why they coincide. However, the hero's story can take different turns. Hercules had twelve challenges, only one of which can be found in the Tarot. Perseus had to decapitate the Gorgon and rescue a beauty from a monster. This would be a hard story to relate to individual trumps as well. The story of Buddha is a better fit.

The story of Buddha was included in Marco Polo's book about his journey to China (written in 1298), and, as I mentioned in the introduction, there is a history of the exchange of ideas along with goods between Europe and Asia. However, similarities in the stories are probably unintentional. The philosophy of Buddhism is very close to the Neoplatonism of the classical world, and Neoplatonism did influence the Tarot trumps. Yet, as I also mentioned in the introduction, it seems most likely that the similarity between the Tarot trumps and Buddha's legend is one of those magical occurrences called "synchronicity," especially when we consider that the fit became stronger as the Tarot evolved and changed. *The Buddha Tarot* is yet another step in the evolution.

Chapter 4

THE MANDALA

When talking about meditation in the previous chapter, we spoke of Jung's concept of archetypes, the universal patterns and personalities that are found in the unconscious. These common patterns can be found in the myths and religious symbols of all cultures, but they are also found arising spontaneously in the dreams of individuals. Underlying all of them, Jung found an archetype of unity and totality that he labeled the Self. In his investigations of the dreams of his patients, Jung found that when the archetype of the Self emerged in dreams, it often took the form of a circle or a more complex diagram based on the circle. Borrowing from the East, Jung labeled these symbols *mandalas*.

The term *mandala* is probably well known to most readers of this book. Literally, it is the Sanskrit word for "circle." However, in Hinduism and Buddhism it describes a symbolic diagram used in mysticism and magic. Often elaborately painted or carved and filled with minute detail, these works of art are organized through the use of the circle and a fourfold pattern or a square. They are diagrams of the mythic cosmology and define sacred space. To construct one is an act of magic that is related to the description of the alchemical process as "the squaring of the circle."

Mandalas are used in temples and homes, in worship, in initiation and cremation rituals, and as a focus for visualization in yogic meditation. In Buddhism, icons of individual deities, Bodhisattvas, or Buddhas are often centered within a mandala. In modern literature, we find numerous descriptions of the use of mandalas in psychophysical or meditative practices. The terms *psychophysical* and *meditative* mean "magical," but the term *magic* has negative associations in the West. So in an effort to help readers come to the material in an unbiased way, writers on this subject have found more intellectually and morally acceptable terms to use. The term *magic* is used here to make the point that magic circles and alchemical diagrams that we find in the West are mandalas. When we don't use the term *magic,* it gives the false impression that the practices of the East are unrelated to Western practices. Like all magic devices, mandalas are designed to change one's consciousness.

Sacred Space

Historian of religions Mircea Eliade observes that in all religions—in fact, in all inhabited regions—there is a place believed to be sacred above all else and that this place is considered the center of the world. This is the place where there is a connection with higher and lower worlds and where the divine can manifest. The idea of the center does not come from a logical scientific understanding of the world. There can be numerous centers within an area. Any place that manifests sacredness is the center. It is a place where the physical world coincides with a mythological cosmology, and by its structure and nature, it allows one access to the mythic realm.[1]

The center is often marked with a stone, a column, or a pole, which serves as a symbol of the axis mundi connecting the earth with the heavens. This is the function of the sacred stone in the Kaaba in Mecca, which is said to be right below the throne of Allah. It is the function of the altar stone in every Christian church, and it is the symbolic purpose of the Washington Monument in the center of the capital of the United States. From this point, the world extends in the four cardinal directions, and in this way, this symbol orients us in space. It is how we make the physical world coincide with our psychic landscape and it allows us to know where we are.

In mythology, the sacred center is often a mountain or world tree such as Yggdrasill in Norse mythology. This Germanic world tree grows through the center of the cosmic mountain. It connects our world, Middle Earth, with the realm of the gods above and with the underworld below, where fierce monsters like the frost giants are found. The pyramids of Egypt were built in imitation of the cosmic mountain. That is why they are so perfectly oriented to the four directions. In Greece, Mount Olympus was a sacred center that connected our world with the home of the gods. In the Bible, Mount Sinai, where Moses received the Ten Commandments, serves a similar function. The name *Sinai* is derived from *Sinn,* the name of the ancient Babylonian moon god who was believed to reside there. *Sinai* means "the mountain of the moon."[2]

The world tree or cosmic mountain is the destination of the hero in his archetypal myth.[3] The hero must go there to complete his adventure and obtain the sought-for elixir. The three parts of his journey are related to the three worlds that are connected by this axis mundi. The hero starts in Middle Earth immersed in ordinary life until the call to adventure causes him to journey to the center of the earth. Here he finds the cosmic mountain, or another such symbol, and makes use of this sacred portal to descend to the underworld and deal with the frightful guardians that he finds there. He does this because in many of these myths, he must go down before he can go up. The way to the heavens is really in the underworld where monsters can guard the entrance. In Norse mythology, this is where the rainbow bridge to the heavens is found. We find this same situation in Dante's *Divine Comedy* in which the road to Heaven led through Hell. The hero's encounters with the guardians leads to the trials associated with the middle section of his journey. After he passes this test, the hero can make the ascent to the realm of the gods and complete the third part of the story. In the end, he returns to Middle Earth with the elixir.

All temples and sacred buildings make use of this pattern to construct a sacred space. Religious rituals are often designed as a reenactment of the hero's journey in the sacred space of the temple. In ancient Sumer, a priest would ascend to the top of the ziggurat, a model of the cosmic mountain with seven steps representing the seven planets. Once on the summit, he could break through to the inner realm and return with information from the gods.

In the ancient world it was observed that there are seven heavenly bodies that wander in and through the constellations. In Greek, the word *planet* meant "wanderer." Therefore, these wandering bodies were called planets. The seven ancient planets are the sun, the moon, Mars, Mercury, Jupiter, Venus, and Saturn (as they believed that the earth was not moving, it was not a planet). These planets were thought of as seven gods, and our seven days of the week are named after them in the same order (although in English we substitute the names of Teutonic gods for four of them).

In classical Greece the cosmic myth was transformed in keeping with their more sophisticated understanding of the cosmos. They determined that Earth is in the center of the cosmos and that the seven planets encircle it, each at a progressively higher level, to form a ladder of ascent leading to heaven. This is the same cosmology that we find in the Platonic myth that we discussed in chapter 2.

Ancient mystics were not content to reenact the hero's journey in a ritual; they wanted to experience the reality of the myth internally and taste the bliss of knowing the One. In a trance or ecstatic state, they would travel up through the planets and enter heaven. The ancient Mithraic Mysteries codified this mystic journey into seven levels of initiation. The alchemists equated them to the transformation of the seven base metals and to seven chemical processes in their great work. In Christianity, they were incorporated as the seven sacraments.

Mount Meru

In the Indian and Buddhist sacred cosmology, Mount Meru occupies the center of the world. Mount Meru is a pyramidal mountain that is perfectly oriented to the four directions. The north slope is said to be made of gold, the east of crystal or silver, the south of sapphire or lapis lazuli, and the west of ruby. The colors of these materials are designed to relate the four sides to the four elements as well (earth, water, air, and fire, respectively), although different correlations can be found. Surrounding Mount Meru are seven concentric rings of golden mountains. The innermost, named *Yugandara* ("the Yoke"), is forty thousand miles high, and on it ride the chariots of the sun and the moon. Between the mountains are seven oceans, each of a different liquid. From the center out they are: milk, curds, butter, blood or sugarcane juice, poison or wine, fresh water, and salt water. In the last ocean are four continents, each located in one of cardinal directions and of a different color: green to the north, white to the east, blue to the south, and red to the west. Each has two satellites, which brings the number of lands to twelve. Humans live on the southern blue continent.

At the base of Mount Meru live giants, the Asura. At one time they were gods, but because of their pridefulness, they were expelled to this lowly realm. Because of their pride, they live in a constant state of war and die in futile battles against the gods.

Above the mountain live the gods in the dome of heaven, which is shaped like an Indian funeral mound. Like a giant skyscraper, the heavens are layered with numerous divisions falling into five main sections. On the first are the four guardians: the yellow guardian of the north, the white guardian of the east, the green guardian of the south, and the red guardian of the west. As we progress up through the layers, the inhabitants become more refined. At the top are found enlightened beings, or Buddhas.[4]

The ancient funeral mounds, called *stupas,* were constructed in this same sacred pattern, and over time came to be associated with Mount Meru. These dome-shaped monuments were capped with a projection at the top and had four entrances at the base, which were oriented to the four directions. Figure 6 shows a Tibetan funeral stupa of the older, more squat form.

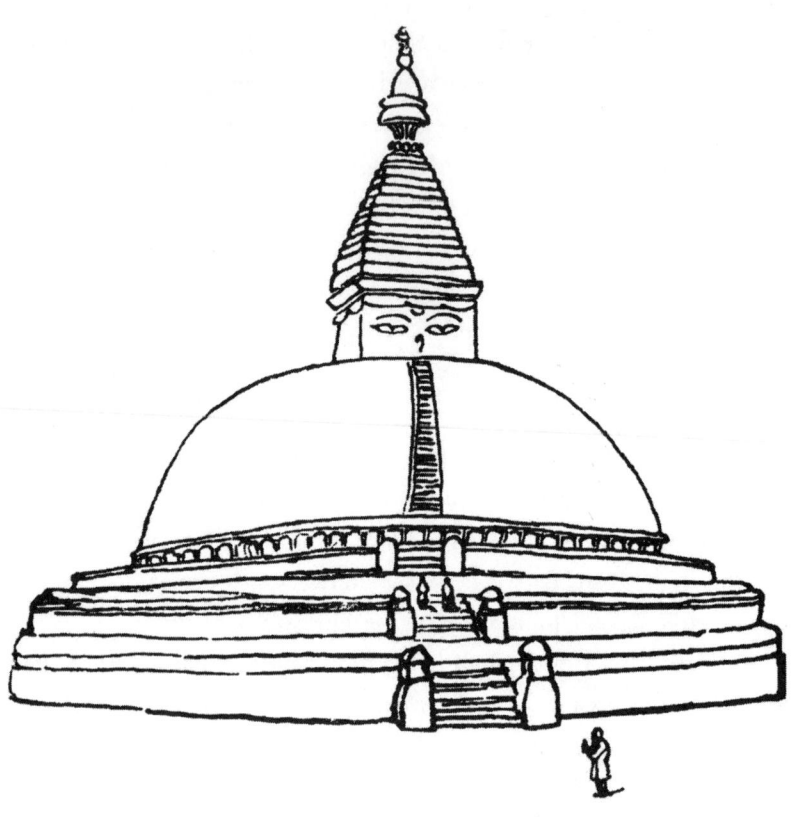

Figure 6—Tibetan funeral stupa

As Buddhism progressed, the stupa designs became taller and thinner as they incorporated more of the symbolism of the axis mundi. In China, they evolved into the pagoda. In Buddhist art we find small models of stupas made of bronze and other materials. These are magic tools used to bring Buddha presence into a dwelling. As the Buddhas were believed to reside at the highest level of the axis mundi from where their divine presence permeates the cosmos, the stupa became an illustration of this process.

An illustration of a tall stupa representing the axis mundi can be found on the Seven of Jewels card in *The Buddha Tarot* (see page 260). As you can see, the stupa is a tower composed of a stack of geometric shapes. Each of these shapes symbolizes one of the elements. At the top is a teardrop form that represents Buddha nature or Buddha mind descending into the aether. The aether is symbolized by the sun and moon. Below this, Buddha nature continues its descent into a half-dome representing air, a stack of cones that represents fire, a large dome that represents water, and at the base, a rectangular box that represents earth.

Besides making three-dimensional models of the sacred cosmos, Hindus and Buddhists created two-dimensional painted versions as well: mandalas. A mandala is a painting that represents the plan of the sacred cosmos. It is like looking at a stupa from directly above the center. As I said above, Hindus and Buddhists place deities, Bodhisattvas, and Buddhas in the center of mandalas. These figures may also be placed within a stupa, as can be seen in the stupa on the Seven of Jewels card. The center of the mandala or stupa recreates the sacred space, and placing a figure there energizes it in the psyche of the viewer. It is a demonstration that the being in the painting or sculpture is a manifestation of an archetype.

Some Examples of Mandalas

Many Buddhist mandalas are complex compositions organizing numerous Bodhisattvas and Buddhist deities around a central figure. They are too complex to be simplified and reduced for an illustration in this book. Instead, we will examine a well-known Tantric Hindu mandala that is composed of simple geometric forms. This is called the *Shri Yantra* and it can be seen in Figure 7.

Yantras are Tantric diagrams used as magical meditative devices to focus and magnify the energies of the meditator. Most yantras are mandalas. The Shri Yantra is considered the most important. It represents the creative force progressing through various geometric emanations to create reality. In this Tantric Hindu mandala, the creative force is a goddess, not a Buddha. Instead of looking down on the plan of the cosmos as we explained above, this drawing is of the view looking up. It is a representation of what we would see if we stood in the center of the

Figure 7—The Shri Yantra

sacred plan and looked up to the summit as the divine force radiated down, filling us with its compassion.

The theory of emanations that this mandala illustrates is similar to the emanations that we find in the writings of the Neoplatonists. In the center, the first emanation of the One into the physical world appears as a small dot—a one-dimensional point. Then as it progresses, it divides into a duality of opposing forces, symbolized by triangles pointing up and down. In a more elaborate version of the Shri Yantra, each of the smaller triangles that are created would contain the image of a deity. The interlocking emanations are contained within concentric circles, which have been transformed into a stylized lotus flower, and this lotus is contained within a square. The square has four projections facing the four directions. These, as in a stupa, are called the *four doors.* In a color version of the mandala, the square would be divided into four triangles, each of a different color that relates to one of the four elements. The lotus design in itself can be considered the essence of the mandala. All sacred beings in Buddhist art are depicted sitting on a lotus to demonstrate that they reside in the center.

As we look at the Shri Yantra, we may find that the abstract forms that it contains remind us of symbols from Western religion. The interlocking triangles are a more complex form of the Star of David, the symbol of Judaism. And the four doors take the form of a Greek cross. In Byzantine crosses we often find a square form overlapping the center. In Celtic crosses we find a circle relating to the center of the cross in the same way as the circle relates to the cross in the Shri Yantra. These religious emblems are designed to connect us with this same sacred space.

In Christianity, the two most prevalent forms that this sacred diagram takes are called the *cross* and the *quincunx.* The cross is used as an illustration of the martyrdom of Christ, but medieval artists abstracted it and turned it into a symbol of the sacred cosmos with Christ in the center. This symbolic connection was elaborated on at times by the inclusion of the four rivers of Eden, the Four Evangelists, or other fourfold symbols being related to the four points of the cross.

A quincunx is a diagram in which five objects are arranged in a square, with one in the center and the other four placed in the four corners, like the five dots representing the five on a die. The Christ in Majesty icon is a quincunx.

Figure 8 is a drawing of a thirteenth-century French champlevé enamel on gilded copper. It was created to be nailed to the cover of a Bible and depicts the Christ in Majesty icon. From the Middle Ages on, this image appears painted in manuscripts or on church walls and ceilings, or carved on the covers of Bibles or in the tympanums over

THE MANDALA | 109

Figure 8—Christ in Majesty icon (author's depiction)

church doors. In this icon, Christ, dressed in white and enthroned, is encircled by an almond-shaped aura. Surrounding him, one to each corner, are the four symbols of the evangelists. These four creatures represent the Four Evangelists of the Gospels: St. Mark is represented by the lion, St. Luke by the bull, St. John by the eagle, and St. Matthew by the man. These images stem from two descriptions in the Bible. In Ezekiel, four "living creatures" surround the throne of God, and each has four faces, one of each of these creatures. Reference to these four is made again in Revelation, where St. John sees them in a mystical vision surrounding the throne of Christ. Because of their association with the four fixed signs of the zodiac, these symbols came to represent the four directions and the four elements. They represent the limits of the physical world animated by the presence of Christ.

Like Buddha mind, Christ's word is seen animating the world. Notice that to either side of Christ's head are the Greek letters alpha and omega. These are the first and last letters of the Greek alphabet. In this icon, omega, the last letter, is first, suggesting that the end comes before the beginning (Christ's death came before his resurrection and everlasting life). To be in the sacred space is to be beyond time—beyond the beginning and the end.

In Figure 9, we see an early sixteenth-century woodcut in which the evangelists have been replaced by the four elements of alchemy. In alchemy, the four physical elements are said to be animated by a divine presence, which was thought of as a fifth element. In this way, the divine essence permeates the entire physical world. This was called the *quinta essentia* (the "essential fifth"). This is the origin of the word *quintessence*. As in this woodcut, Christian alchemists sometimes identified Christ as the quinta essentia. More often, however, the quinta essentia was identified as a divine female presence called the *Anima Mundi*, the soul of the world.

Figure 10 is a drawing depicting a painted illustration of the Anima Mundi that is found in an eighteenth-century French alchemical illuminated manuscript. We can see that, like the woodcut of Christ, it is a

*Figure 9—Sixteenth-century woodcut
of Christ with the elements (author's depiction)*

quincunx with the four elements neatly designated to the four corners. In the center is the Anima Mundi as the quinta essentia, pictured as a beautiful nude woman.

In this version, the Anima Mundi has aspects that depict her ability to transcend the elements. Like a mermaid, the upper part of her body allows her to exist on land and the lower part in the water, but she also has wings to allow her to transcend air. In her right hand she holds a chalice with a serpent. This image is borrowed from the symbol for St. John. In his legend, St. John was given poisoned wine to drink, but when he blessed it, the poison departed in the form of a serpent and he was able to drink it unharmed. The alchemists used this as a symbol of the alchemical transformation, which was believed to change harmful substances into a healing elixir. By holding this vessel, the Anima Mundi demonstrates the power of her secret fire.

Figure 10—Eighteenth-century French alchemical illustration of the Anima Mundi (author's depiction)

To symbolize that she is the harmony of opposites, the Anima Mundi has one eye open and one eye closed. One of her wings is black and the other is red in the original painting. These represent the first and last stages of the alchemical process. Like Christ, she is between the beginning and the end, outside of the process and outside of time.

*Figure 11—The World card from the
Tarot of Marseilles (author's depiction)*

In Figure 11 is a depiction of the World card from the modern version of the Tarot of Marseilles. This deck was first published in 1748. This card depicts the familiar icon that we find in all Tarot decks that are in the Tarot of Marseilles tradition from the seventeenth century to the present. In the Christ in Majesty icon in Figure 8, Christ is in the center of the four creatures representing the evangelists. In the woodcut in Figure 9, we still have Christ, but the symbols of the evangelists have been replaced by the four elements. In Figure 10, Christ was replaced with the Anima Mundi. Here we have the Anima Mundi, but the four elements have been replaced by the symbols of the evangelists. If we were to continue this another step, we would be back to Christ in Majesty. These are all related icons; there is symbolic continuity between the orthodox Christian symbol, the alchemical symbol, and the final card of the trumps. The World card is a mandala. It represents the divine presence that animates the world. This is the visual expression of the love that brings life to the entire cosmos.

This same pattern can be seen in the structure of the Tarot. The four minor suits are a division of the physical world into four classes, four elements, and four directions. By their existence, they define the center, the fifth suit of trumps where the hero's journey of death and rebirth is pictured. The final and culminating trump is the World card. This is a symbolic picture of the Anima Mundi that unites the world through compassion. It is the elixir that the hero seeks, and when he finds it he brings it back to heal the world. This card is a mandala. The Tarot is a mandala.

The Five Jinas

In Mahayana Buddhism, which is the most widespread form of Buddhism, there are numerous Buddhas. It is often confusing for an outsider to understand this point. The statues that one sees of Buddhas from China, Japan, Tibet, Sri Lanka, Thailand, or other countries are not necessarily representations of Siddhartha Gautama. When I was doing research for this project, I went to the Karma Triyana Dharmachakra Monastery, which is a Tibetan monastery near to where I live. I went into the monastery bookstore and asked the clerk if they had any books with pictures of the life of Buddha. "Which Buddha?" the clerk replied. I said that I was doing research on Siddhartha Gautama. "Oh, the historic Buddha," she continued. "I doubt that we have anything on him." And yet, the store was filled with books on Buddhism, many of which were illustrated with images of Buddhas. To many Buddhists, the historic Buddha is not the main image of devotion the way the historic Christ is in Christianity. Buddhists, particularly in Mahayana, are more concerned with the archetypal quality of Buddhahood.

When Siddhartha became the Buddha, he ceased to be a man in the normal sense. A Buddha is one with the entire cosmos. In the sacred cosmology, this aspect of Buddha is pictured at the highest point in the center, but Buddha is also the entire diagram—the entire cosmos. When Buddha was a man, he was also this totality. When the man died, the totality was the living Buddha. This archetypal aspect of Buddha as a totality is called the *Adi Buddha,* meaning "the primordial Buddha."

The Adi Buddha is the Buddha that has existed from the beginning of time and is eternal. Everything there emanates from the Adi Buddha. The Adi Buddha existed before Siddhartha was born, before his first incarnation, and he will always exist. He is the Buddhist equivalent of the Platonic Prime Mover and Jung's Self. The Adi Buddha is pictured at the pinnacle of the heavens above Mount Meru.

Because Buddha is the entire cosmos and the cosmos has a sacred pattern with a center and four cardinal directions, the Buddha has to embody the same pattern. Therefore, on the plane just below the Adi Buddha there are five great Buddhas called the Five *Jinas,* the Sanskrit word for "conquerors" (Figure 12). It refers to one who has conquered spiritual knowledge and overcome time—in other words, the final trump. Because the Buddha has become one with the sacred cosmos, and the mandala is the plan for the sacred cosmos, Buddha has become the mandala.

The Jinas are the personification of the five principal aspects of the mandala. In a complex tapestry of symbolism, they are related to all of the sacred fivefold patterns we find in Buddhism. Each Jina represents a direction, a color, an element, and one of the Five Precepts and Five Dharmas; they embody the Five Wisdoms and cure the Five Poisons.

Figure 12—The Five Jinas

Their names are Vairocana (the illuminator), Aksobhya (the unshakeable), Amitabha (infinite light), Ratnasambhava (jewel-born), and Amoghasiddhi (infallible success).

Buddhas are both masculine and feminine. However, they are usually depicted as male. Therefore, the female aspect is depicted as a separate Buddha, called a *Sakti* (Figure 13). Each of the Jinas has a Sakti.

Figure 13—The Sakti Tara

They are often depicted together face-to-face in a sexual embrace, as on the Sun card in *The Buddha Tarot* (see page 213). This position is called *yab-yum,* which means "father-mother." It represents the bliss of enlightenment as the fulfillment of sexual desire found within one's self instead of externally. The Saktis are also found depicted separately. Their names are Vajradharisvari, Locana, Pandara, Mamaki, and Tara.

Because the Jinas are blissful, their wrathful aspects are considered to be separate entities as well. These are called the *Herukas,* and each Heruka has his own Sakti—a wrathful Heruka Sakti (Figure 14). Each Jina also has a symbolic magic tool, a symbolic hand gesture (called a

Figure 14—Heruka with his Sakti in yab-yum

mudra), a guardian animal, and a goddess called a *Dakini,* who represents his particular wisdom when it is active in the world.

Chart 1 lists the Five Jinas and their corresponding direction, color, element, and symbol. In *The Buddha Tarot,* each suit represents one of the Jinas, and the borders of the cards are colored with the corresponding color. The mandala on the World card acts as a key to the colors and their direction. The trump suit represents Vairocana, the Buddha of the center. He and his Sakti are pictured on the Sun card, and his symbol is on the back of all of the cards. The symbols of the other four Jinas, which relate to the four cardinal directions, serve as the suit symbols for the four minor suits. They have been related to the traditional Tarot suit symbols through the element associated with each in both systems.

Chart 2 lists the Five Jinas and their corresponding Sakti, animal, and Dakini. In *The Buddha Tarot,* the Jinas, or Buddhas, are equivalent to the Tarot's Kings, the Saktis are equivalent to the Queens, the Animal Guardians are equivalent to the Knights, and their servants, the Dakinis, are equivalent to the Pages. Vairocana and his Sakti can be seen on the Sun card and his lion is on the Strength card. His Dakini, who represents his wisdom, permeates the entire deck.

Chart 3 lists the Five Jinas and their corresponding wisdom. Each of the Five Wisdoms is related to one of the Five Dharmas, which, as mentioned in the previous chapter, is a list of positive qualities designed to help one overcome the negative behaviors that the Five Precepts advise one to avoid. Similarly, each of the Five Wisdoms is thought of as a cure for one of the Five Poisons. In the center of the Wheel of Life mandala, we find three animals representing three poisons that chain one to this wheel of endless incarnations: the pig of ignorance, the cock of greed, and the snake of anger. But the mandala of the Jinas is fivefold, and as the wisdom of each Jina is a cure for a poison, Buddhists expanded the list of poisons to five: ignorance, greed, distraction, conceit, and anger. The reality of oneness overcomes ignorance, nonattachment overcomes greed, nondiscriminating compassion overcomes distraction, the reality

Chart 1

Jina	Direction	Color	Element	Tarot Suit
Vairocana	Center	White	Aether	Wheel = Trumps
Aksobhya	East	Blue	Air	Vajras = Swords
Ratnasambhava	South	Yellow	Earth	Jewels = Coins
Amitabha	West	Red	Fire	Lotuses = Staffs
Amoghasiddhi	North	Green	Water	Double Vajras = Cups

Chart 2

Jina	Sakti	Animal	Dakini
Vairocana	Vajradharisvari	Lion	Buddha Dakini
Aksobhya	Locana	Elephant	Vajradakini
Ratnasambhava	Mamaki	Horse	Ratnadakini
Amitabha	Pandara	Peacock	Padmadakini
Amoghasiddhi	Tara	Garuda	Visvadakini

Chart 3

Jina	Wisdom	Dharma
Vairocana	The reality of oneness	Awareness
Aksobhya	Nonattachment	Generosity
Ratnasambhava	Nondiscriminating compassion	Contentment
Amitabha	The reality of plurality and oneness together	Truthfulness
Amoghasiddhi	Devotion to the welfare of all living beings	Love

of plurality and oneness together overcomes conceit, and devotion to the welfare of all living beings overcomes anger.

In Buddhist art, the images of Buddha have distinctive symbolic hand gestures called mudras. Each mudra is designed to evoke a particular mood, and each is associated with a specific Buddha or a specific aspect of a Buddha. In rituals, monks imitate the mudra of a Buddha to evoke his presence. As can be seen in Figure 12, each Jina has a mudra that helps identify him and speaks of his character. As you look through the Buddha cards among the royal cards in *The Buddha Tarot,* you can see the various mudras. Close-ups of all five mudras are also included on pip cards where these gestures convey the meaning of the card.

The Five Jinas and the symbols associated with them permeate Buddhist culture, and they are not only used for strictly religious purposes. Figure 15 shows a Tibetan talisman for good fortune that would be printed on cloth and hung from a pole. It is called the *Vast Luck Flag* and it is meant to draw down luck from the great Jinas. In this square banner, we find a quincunx with the four animals of the four Jinas of the cardinal directions each in a corner of the square. A double vajra holds the sacred center. The double vajra is sometimes substituted for the wheel that is the symbol of Vairocana, the Buddha of the center. Clockwise from the upper left, the animals are: the mythical garuda bird of the north, the peacock of the west, the horse of the south, and the elephant of the east. Each has a lotus yantra forming its body with a magic inscription encircling it. For example, in the circle on the body of the garuda it says, "May the life of this charm-holder be raised sublimely."[5]

Midway between the animals in the center of each side we find two small symbols, making a total of eight on the whole flag. These are the *Eight Glorious Emblems of Buddha.* Clockwise from the top they are: the Umbrella and the Golden Fish, the Conch Shell Trumpet and the Victory Banner, the Golden Wheel and the Lucky Knot, and the Treasure Vase and the Lotus. These are also known as the *luck-bringing symbols.* They are Buddhist good-luck charms—equivalent to the

Figure 15—The Tibetan Vast Luck Flag

Western horseshoe, four-leaf clover, and rabbit's foot. The Eight Glorious Emblems represent gifts of the gods that were given to Siddhartha at his birth and at his enlightenment. Like the gifts of the fairies in *Sleeping Beauty,* each of these symbols is associated with a quality, such as beauty, long life, or joyousness. Commonly they are joined together in one figure to create a good-luck talisman. Here they have been joined with the symbols of the Jinas to make the flag more powerful. All eight of the Glorious Emblems can be found in the pip cards in *The Buddha Tarot* where their meaning coincides with the meaning of the card.

Four Functions, Four Yogas

The sacred cosmos bears little relation to the physical cosmos as we know it today. The ancient Greeks and Romans attempted to combine the spiritual model found in myths with what they knew of astronomy. The Egyptian astronomer Ptolemy perfected this system with Earth in the center and the planets revolving around it, and his was the accepted model in Europe until Copernicus placed the sun in the center of our solar system. To the scientific mind, after Copernicus's theory was accepted as fact, the sacred model became an embarrassment at best, a curiosity of the past. However, although the sacred model does not describe the physical universe, it does describe the inner universe of the psyche. The modern scientific exploration of the inner universe was accomplished by the famous psychologist Carl Jung.

Jung is known for his pioneering work exploring the unconscious. However, he also succeeded in mapping the conscious mind, and in doing so, uncovered the landscape that we find in myth. Like the division of the world into four directions and four elements, Jung discovered four divisions of consciousness. He developed a theory of four personality types, in each of which one of the four functions is dominant. Because these psychological functions and personality types are a map of the sacred landscape within the psyche, and the Tarot is a tool constructed from this same pattern, the functions and types can be related to the four suits and are a valuable aid to interpreting the cards for divination.

The four functions represent abilities or talents that each person has in varying degrees. At birth we are each dealt strengths in one or more function and are therefore weak in the others. Everyone tends to use their strong suit to solve problems and are at a disadvantage when their weak suit is what the situation demands. Each function can be expressed in an introverted (looking within for direction) or extraverted (looking to others for direction) way. Throughout life, if an individual matures, he or she will develop more functions and become more versatile in his or her capabilities. This maturing is what Jung calls the process of *individuation*, a progression toward psychic wholeness that he equates to the hero's journey.

In dreams this process of wholeness is symbolized as a journey to the center. The center is the place where the unconscious archetypes emerge into consciousness, the place where we communicate with the gods. If an individual can develop all four functions and bring the entire landscape into consciousness, then the fifth element of the true Self is attained, which is likened to the experience of the Anima Mundi or the Buddha within. The following is a list of each function, the element it is associated with, and a description of the personality type in which it is dominant.[6] Although Jung speaks of the sacred model of the four elements in his book on the four functions, he makes no correlation between the two. The correlations below are my own.

Thinking—Air is intellectual. It asks why or what is reality. This is a decision-making function. Thinking is forceful, yet intangible, like air. The introvert may tend toward the role of a philosopher or research scientist, and the extravert toward economist, judge, or statesman or stateswoman.

Sensation—Earth simply asks does a thing exist and displays a talent for manipulating it. This is an investigation of the physical world, symbolized by earth. The introvert may tend to be an artist, connoisseur, or technician, and the extravert an engineer, accountant, builder, or investigator.

Feeling—Fire is often misunderstood. To Jung, feelings are not emotions. He calls emotions "effects" and they can arise from any function. Feelings do not create effects in the face or body. They are a decision-making function that determines if something is good or bad and motivates one to action, symbolized by fire. Crying is an emotion, fear is a feeling; laughter is an emotion, joy is a feeling. An introvert may display talent as a healer, nurturer, musician, or monk/nun; an extravert may become a singer or social organizer, or a politician.

Intuition—Water is a talent for determining how a situation developed and where it is headed in the future. It is investigation directed toward the unconscious, which is often symbolized by water. The introvert would tend toward roles like poet, mystic, or psychic. The extravert would be more comfortable investigating society's unconscious and may become an adventurer or entrepreneur.

Notice that intuition and sensation are used to investigate reality but not to make decisions. Because of this, they are called "irrational." These are equated to the feminine, passive elements of water and earth. The other two, thinking and feeling, are decision-making functions. They are called "rational," and are equated to the masculine, active elements of fire and air. The irrational and the rational functions are polarities of each other. A person who is a thinking type will have the hardest time developing the opposite pole, feeling, and feeling types will have difficulty with thinking. Intuition types and sensation types will have this same relationship with their opposite pole. Therefore, a person dominant in thinking, for example, will be likely to develop both irrational functions before developing feeling. The same relationship applies for the other three functions.

Although Jung took most of a lifetime to work out his theory, once he discovered this pattern, he found that people had been working with it for centuries. For example, ancient Hindu and Buddhist adepts of the East had developed spiritual techniques called *yoga* to help individuals to proceed on the path to enlightenment. Understanding that there are four different types of people with different abilities and weaknesses, and wishing to find a yoga that made use of each type's talents for his or her spiritual practice, they developed four principal types of yoga. Each is discussed below:[7]

Jnana yoga is for thinking types, people who are reflective and philosophical. It is cool and aloof like air. This is the path through knowledge. Although this is an intellectual path and involves reading and study, the ultimate goal of oneness is beyond reason. Therefore, yogis developed a four-part yoga for leading thinking types beyond thinking. The first involves studying the words of sages in person or through books. The second involves reflection on the meaning of the lessons. The jnana yogi is particularly instructed to ponder the meaning of words like *I* and *my*. By not taking these words for granted, the yogi begins to see a deeper aspect of the self underneath the daily persona. Philosophical people tend to find satisfaction in this truth that the divine can be found within. In the third stage, the yogi is given exercises to help transfer personal identification from the persona to the underlying self. In the fourth stage, this duality is resolved in the realization that we are all the One.

Karma yoga is for sensation types. These are energetic people who need to be involved in activity. Karma yoga is the yoga of work, and through work we manipulate the physical world, symbolized by earth. Many people think that to be on a spiritual path, one has to retreat from the activities of the marketplace and live in a monastery or alone in a cave. But karma yoga is the yoga of the workplace. The trick is to be involved in commerce but not lose one's way in the self-centered desires that the workplace can engender. To accomplish this, one can combine karma yoga with a jnana yoga approach by detaching oneself from the outcome of the work—to work for the sake of the activity with no thought of reward. This is often the way an artist works, although even in art one can get lost in ambition.

The other method involves combining karma and bhakti yoga. Every action that is performed for personal gain thickens the ego. Therefore the karma-bhakti yogi dedicates the rewards of his or her work to a deity. This is the path of St. Francis, who dedicated himself to poverty yet worked continually for the benefit of others. When asked, he said that he did this for the love of Christ. Francis realized that this is how Christ would receive his love: through acts of kindness to those in need.

Bhakti yoga is for feeling types. This is the path of love and the fire of devotion. This is the simplest and most popular path. It involves transferring the love that one normally feels for a mate or another loved one to a god or goddess. For this to work, the deity has to be conceived of as separate from oneself. The object of desire is desired because it is other than us.

Bhakti yoga is the source of much religious art and music. The bhakti yogi often needs a statue or other object to make what is imperceptible to the senses perceptible. In bhakti rituals, the yogi lights candles and incense to the deity and loses his- or herself in prayer and song. And this is the point: through love we cease to think of ourselves and let go of the ego. The path of the Sufi and of the troubadour is bhakti yoga, but here the statue is replaced by an unattainable lover. Most Christian worship is bhakti. In his *Symposium,* Plato starts by describing the central problem of bhakti: that the object of desire is always the other, and therefore desire can never truly be satisfied. As a cure, he describes a path that is a synthesis of bhakti and jnana yoga.

Raja yoga is for intuitive types. This is for people who have the will to experiment directly with their psyche. *Raja* means "royal," and this path is called royal because it is the principal path to enlightenment. This is the path that Buddha took when he sat under the Bodhi Tree. This is the method that Buddha recommended in the final part of his Eightfold Path, which is described in chapter 3. It involves progressively taking attention away from the body, the ego, and the unconscious until the mind is like still water. In this stillness, the Ground of Being can be experienced. Raja yoga can be and, according to Buddha, should be combined with the other forms.

CHART 4			
Function	*Yoga*	*Element*	*Tarot Suit*
Thinking	Jnana	Air	Vajras
Sensation	Karma	Earth	Jewels
Feeling	Bhakti	Fire	Lotuses
Intuition	Raja	Water	Double Vajras

Through its association with an element, each of the four functions can be equated to one of the four minor suits in the Tarot. These associations for *The Buddha Tarot* are shown in Chart 4. These associations will help when using the deck therapeutically or for divination.

Ultimately, *The Buddha Tarot* is a mandala. As Buddha consciousness radiates through a mandala, Buddha consciousness radiates through *The Buddha Tarot*.

Chapter 5

THE JOURNEY TO THE CENTER OF THE WORLD

The fifth suit in *The Buddha Tarot* can be appreciated on several levels. At one level it is a story in pictures, something like the medieval paintings in churches that illustrate the life of Christ. Similarly, in the Gupta period in India (fourth to sixth centuries CE), the life of Buddha was codified into a series of icons and carved in relief on temple walls. Of the images from his life, there were eight icons that were considered essential to the story. Later the number was reduced to four: Buddha's birth, his victory over Mara, his first sermon in Deer Park, and the final attainment of Nirvana at his death, called *Parinirvana*. Each of these four took on an importance as separate symbolic images outside of the story, and each came to be associated with one of the Jinas. This is similar to the role of the images of the Madonna with child, the Crucifixion, and the Christ in Majesty icons in Christianity. Each is an illustration of one stage in the story of Christ, but separated from the story, they have a symbolic significance outside of the sequence of events, which includes ritual or magical use. Because I wanted to include all of the four major Buddhist icons in the trumps, and the Parinirvana was an event that happens after the point at which the trumps usually stop, I added a twenty-third card, trump number twenty-two.

All of the images that I have drawn for these cards are based on Buddhist icons from India, southeast Asia, China, and Tibet. However, to unify them and maintain the esthetic standard that I have set for myself, I have reinterpreted them in my own style. They are drawn as if they were woodcuts that were hand-painted—similar to Tibetan icons and early Italian and French Tarots. In fact, I have included details from early French and Italian woodcut decks. My style is not Eastern or Western, but a synthesis of the two. That the two styles merge in such a satisfying way is part of the message of the deck. Please enjoy them as works of art.

The main use of Tarot at this time is for divination, and this deck is meant to be used for that purpose also. Understanding the story in the cards should give the user a deeper understanding of the Tarot. In all ancient cultures, to know the story of the origin of something gives one magical power over that object or being. This is why I have been thorough in delving into the history of the Tarot. The story of Buddha is the story in the Tarot and to understand that is to have power. One can only understand that by knowing the origins. This knowledge connects the user with the ancient wisdom of our ancestors. When we use the cards, that wisdom comes through and guides us. To use the Tarot is to receive advice from our ancestors and from our higher self.

For each card in this suit, I have provided an opening quote that echoes the meaning of the image. Although this is the story of Buddha, all of these quotations are from Western sources—most of which are discussed in chapter 2. The written descriptions of each card after the quotes are divided into three sections. The first describes the scene depicted in the illustration. Each of these comprises part of the legend of Buddha's life. Besides adding depth to the reader's understanding of the individual image, they are designed so that each of these parts can be read consecutively and form a continuous story. Next, there is a commentary for each card. As I stated above, to know the origins of something allows one to make magical use of it. This section is designed to enhance that power. Both of these sections are designed to help one to develop a familiarity with these cards, and this knowledge is applicable to divination. The last section is a more concise discussion of the meaning of the card in a divination spread.

The Descent from Tusita Heaven - The Fool

"Say, O Fool! Which thing was in being first, thy heart or thy love?" He answered and said: "Both my heart and love came into being together; for were it not so, the heart had not been made for love, nor love for reflection."

Ramon Lull, *The Book of the Lover and the Beloved*

Tusita Heaven is a paradise in the sky above Mount Meru in the sacred center of the world. In the Buddhist cosmology, the heavens contain numerous individual heavens, each on its own layer, grouped into five sections. There are six heavens in the first section; sixteen in the second section; four in the third; five in the fourth, the heaven of the Five Jinas (the archetypal Buddhas); and the heaven of the Adi Buddha, the Buddha that is the One—the totality—is the top layer. Tusita is the fourth heaven in the first section above the mountain. The beings who live there are gods and Bodhisattvas, and they live in a constant state of joy.

In Buddhist theology, the gods and Bodhisattvas enjoy exceptionally long lives, but they are not immortal. After over 547 lifetimes, Siddhartha had become a Bodhisattva and incarnated in Tusita Heaven. Realizing that his time there was ending, Siddhartha knew that it was time to incarnate in the world of men and take the final step that he had been preparing for throughout all of his past lives: to become a Buddha. There had been twenty-four Buddhas before him, each coming in a different age. Siddhartha was destined to become the Buddha of our age.

Before he left, Siddhartha gave a lecture on the eight hundred doors of the law for the benefit of the gods of Tusita. Then he introduced them to Maitreya, the Buddha of the age to come. Having introduced his replacement, Siddhartha was ready to descend into our physical world.

For this, the last of his incarnations, Siddhartha chose to be born to beautiful and saintly Queen Maya and her husband, King Suddhodhana, the rulers of Kapilavastu, a small kingdom in the area that is now northern India and Nepal. As Siddhartha stepped down from Tusita Heaven, he transformed into a white elephant and came to Maya in her dream. Some accounts say that the elephant had six tusks, but in the icons it is usually shown with two. Using one of his tusks, the elephant painlessly pierced Maya's side and entered her womb. When she woke from her night's sleep, Maya was pregnant. In some accounts, it is said that Maya and Suddhodhana had not yet consummated their marriage and that this was a miraculous conception.

Commentary

The first card of the fifth suit in the Tarot of Marseilles depicts a jester called the "Fool." It is unnumbered. The other twenty-one cards in the suit are clearly labeled with Roman numerals. In the Roman system of numbering, there is no zero (the concept was brought to Europe from

India by the Arabs). All numbers were thought of as emerging out of the fullness of the number one. Therefore, the Fool is not zero; he is simply outside of the series.

Technically, the Fool is not a trump but a wild card, called the *excuse* in the known variations of the game for which the carte da trionfi was designed. In some known orders, he is counted last instead of first. He starts the story, but he can also be found at the end. In the card game, the Fool can be played instead of a trump. He did not have enough value to win a trick during play, but at the end of the game, he was of the most valued in points. Like the fools in Ramon Lull's romance novel *Blanquerna,* he can appear anywhere in the story. As a character of no rank, the Fool can talk with popes and common people alike and interject his wisdom.

In the Tarot of Marseilles, the seat of the Fool's pants is being torn by a dog. This is meant to be comical, but it also signifies that the dog is treating him as a stranger. This assumption is also supported by the fact that he is carrying a bag of belongings on the end of the stick resting on his shoulder. Before they had developed a reputation among the people, the early Franciscans, who wandered through the countryside preaching and begging, found that they were treated with suspicion at first and, like our Fool, they had to fend off the attacks of dogs.

The Fool is facing into the series of trumps, about to enter our story—a story that is often called "the Fool's Journey." In the Waite-Smith Tarot, the Fool is on the edge of a precipice walking ahead, unaware of the drop. When we think of this as Buddha's story, the Fool is the Bodhisattva who will become Siddhartha taking on the fresh incarnation. Like all who are reborn, he will fall into a naive or foolish state.

In Plato's myth of the journey of the soul (described in chapter 2), all those who incarnate are first required to drink from the river Lethe ("forgetfulness"). In life, knowledge is gained through the struggle to undo the effects of Lethe's waters. We have to remember what we have already known. Siddhartha seems to have remembered who he was when he was first born, but he soon fell into the same state of foolishness as others do at the beginning of life. In Buddhist philosophy, just as in Plato's philosophy, to be born is to fall into ignorance. All life is an illusion that is only possible because we have forgotten who we are.

The image on this card combines two separate Buddhist icons. When the Bodhisattva left Tusita Heaven to incarnate as Siddhartha, we only know from the texts that he changed into the white elephant of his mother's dream. After his enlightenment, Buddha went to visit his mother, who was living in Tusita Heaven. On his return to our world, he descended a marvelous ladder with three sections: one of gold, one of silver, and one of crystal. The second event is extremely popular in Buddhist art, but the first is rarely shown in icons outside of India. Of course, the ladder between heaven and earth is an archetypal symbol that is related to the Neoplatonic ladder of the planets that we discussed in chapter 2. This card's image depicts the future Buddha coming down this same ladder on his first descent from Tusita Heaven and transforming into the elephant on the way down.

Divination

The Fool has many seemingly contradictory meanings. It is the most worthless card, as well as the most valuable; it is the first and the last. It can represent poverty and misfortune as well as joy and freedom, a novice, a trusting beginner, and an enlightened master.

It can also be a reminder of things that have been forgotten. We have all drunk from the river Lethe. In Plato's *Apology*, Socrates complains that the Oracle of Delphi proclaimed him the wisest of Athenians. This seemed unlikely to him because he could see how ignorant he was. After many years of investigation, he determined that he was the wisest because he was the only Athenian who knew that he did not know anything. This understanding of his own foolishness has given him a reputation for wisdom that has lasted to the present. Similarly, Siddhartha began to wake up when he began to see the shortcomings of his life.

In a reading, pay attention to what the Fool is facing to determine which meaning is being suggested. Are his actions indeed foolish, is he wisely trusting, or is he helping us to remember? The Fool is a reminder that it is better to criticize ourselves than to look for faults in others.

I. Asita - The Seer

Instead of divining by the entrails of beasts, he revealed to him the art of prognosticating by the numbers, conceiving this to be purer, more divine, and more kindred to the celestial numbers of the Gods.

Iamblichus, speaking of Pythagoras
from his *The Life of Pythagoras*

After having such an astounding dream, Maya summoned sixty-four Brahmans who were skilled in divination and asked them to determine its meaning. They agreed that she was pregnant and that her child would surpass all others. If he embraced the worldly life, he would be the emperor of all of India, called a *chakravartin*. If he embraced the spiritual path, he would become a world savior, called a *Buddha*.

After Siddhartha's birth, his father, Suddhodhana, summoned seers to cast the child's horoscope. They confirmed the earlier prediction. This news reached the elderly seer Asita. He came down from his retreat in the mountains to see Siddhartha, and after examining the child's body, he found on him the thirty-two marks and eighty signs that proved that he was a great man. These marks and signs include the point on his head and the mark between his eyes, as well as the wheel patterns on the soles of his feet that are depicted in icons of his footprints. Afterward, Asita began to weep. This worried Suddhodhana, but Asita explained that he was not weeping for Siddhartha, but for himself. Surely the boy would grow to become a Buddha, and Asita was saddened that he would not live to hear this Buddha's teaching.

Suddhodhana was delighted that his son would be a great man, but being from an ambitious warrior clan, he preferred that Siddhartha would take the worldly path and become an emperor. He summoned a council of Brahmans to help him determine how to steer Siddhartha's destiny in that direction. The council determined that Siddhartha's destiny hinged on a series of experiences. The child would stay on the worldly path as long as he did not encounter four specific sights. The first was the sight of an extremely aged man, the second was the sight of a deathly sick man, the third was the sight of a corpse, and the last was the sight of a holy hermit, called a *sadhu*.

Commentary

The Magician in the Tarot of Marseilles deck is not the ceremonial magician of later occult decks, but he is a roadside trickster often thought of as juggling or performing a shell game. He is dressed in a festive tunic with alternating colors called *motley*. In his hands are a small wand and a ball or coin. On the table before him is a bag with a strap from which he seems to have removed his knife and, in turn, removed his knife from its sheath. We also find two cups, several small round objects (possibly coins and balls), and a prominent pair of dice. The inclusion of dice and coins in the picture suggests that he is a gambler, but these dice are also a tool for divination. We can find dice on the Magician's table in one of the earliest woodcut Tarots from Italy and on the earliest decks made in France. In the Magician cards made in the French tradition throughout the seventeenth and eighteenth centuries, we cannot always determine if dice are among the objects on his table because at times they are not well drawn. However, in many cases, dice are the most clearly drawn objects on the table, and sometimes he has three dice instead of two. The modern standard Tarot of Marseilles image that was established in the eighteenth century always has two dice.

From the classical world through the Renaissance, dice were the most popular tool for both gambling and divination. The quotation above suggests that this method of divination was taught by Pythagoras. In the Renaissance, dice began to be replaced with cards, and gambling and divination techniques that were developed for dice became the models for gambling and divination with cards.

There is a direct connection between the structure of the Tarot deck and the numerical possibilities that emerge from the throws of dice. In games that use three dice there are fifty-six possible combinations that can be thrown, the same number as the cards in the four minor suits. In the classical world, when four-sided knucklebones were used instead of dice, the combinations of five knucklebones also added up to fifty-six. In ancient divination techniques, the fifty-six throws of the knucklebones were divided into four suits that were each listed on one of the sides of a four-sided pillar. In the minor suits, the card names *ace* and *deuce* were originally the names of the one and the two on a die. When we throw two dice, there are twenty-one possible combinations, the same number as the trumps.[1]

Evidence that cards were used for divination in the Renaissance can be found in the *Mainz Fortune-Telling Book* published circa 1487 and in Marcolino's *Le Sorti* published in Venice in 1540.[2] However, in both of these cases, the techniques described only use the cards of the minor suits, which are the same as in decks without added trumps. The best evidence for the use of the trumps in divination are the poems and accounts of games from the Renaissance that give allegorical meaning to the trumps and use them to describe the personalities of individuals, such as the ladies of a court.

Then, there is the *Trionpho della Fortuna* by the astrologer Fante. This fortunetelling device was published in Venice in 1527 and is believed to have influenced *Le Sorti*. In Fante's system, after the querent picks a question, he or she is directed to a series of wheels, each with twenty-one divisions. One has the choice of using the hour in which the question was asked or the throw of two dice to find one's way through the book and find the correct answer on the appropriate wheel. Throughout the book, there are woodcuts of figures from astrology and allegory. However, the allegorical illustration on the title page is the book's strongest link with the Tarot trumps.

On Fante's title page we see a large figure of Atlas supporting a globe on his back. Around the globe is a vertical belt with the signs of the zodiac on it and, at the central point of this wheel, there is an axle that pierces the globe and extends out to the left and right. The ends of this axle are bent to form crank handles. On our left there is an angel, representing good fortune and turning the handle clockwise. On our right there is a devil, representing bad fortune and turning the handle counterclockwise. This is one of numerous Renaissance illustrations that demonstrate that Fortuna's wheel was considered to be the wheel of the cosmos.

At the top of this Wheel of Fortune sits a pope as master of this world. On either side of him sit one of two women with their names written above their heads. On our left is Virtue and on our right, the same side as the devil, sits Sensuality. The pope's fate hangs on his choice of a mate. In the foreground there is an athletic male nude holding a die—possibly Hermes, who was the god of divination with dice. Also in the foreground is an astrologer, who is holding calipers and an astronomical device; he is similar to the astrologers found on early hand-painted Moon cards. In the landscape that dominates the lower portion of the scene there is a river with smaller figures rowing their boats on a journey that leads through an arched gate, a large tower, and into a celestial city. From our discussion in the earlier chapters, the connection between this allegory and the Tarot trumps should be obviousness.

If we were to take the Tarot Magician's two dice and roll them to see how many different combinations can be achieved, we would find that there are twenty-one, the same amount as the trump cards. Our Magician, like the saintly old man in Buddha's story, has the means to foretell the outcome of this play. He makes the prediction of the Buddha/Fool's eventual greatness. In the illustration for this card, Asita is depicted holding a book. This is because his wisdom and abilities come from his scholarship. He has not yet attained the spiritual wisdom that a Buddha can provide.

Divination

On a mundane level, this Seer represents skill, scholarship, initiations, and divination. The Magician of the Tarot of Marseilles points simultaneously to the sky and to the earth, a gesture that communicates Hermes' famous axiom, "As above, so below," meaning that the way of heaven should be manifested on earth. In keeping with this, the Hermetic texts tell us that it is our purpose, given to us by God, to complete his creation by making the world beautiful. Like the Magician, Asita the Seer is pointing the way to the improvement and healing of the world. Pay attention to the direction that this card is facing. This is what Asita is pointing out to us. Follow his advice.

II. Maya - The Mother

Mnesarchus . . . inquired of the oracle . . . and was informed . . . that his wife . . . would present him with a son who would surpass all others who had ever lived in beauty and wisdom . . . . he immediately changed his wife's former name Parthenis to . . . Pythais, and the infant [became] Pythagoras, by this name commemorating . . . the Pythian Apollo.

Iamblichus, The Life of Pythagoras

Ten lunar months after the conception, Maya went on a trip with her sister, Mahaprajapati, for the purpose of visiting their parents. On the way there she realized that the time for Siddhartha's birth was near. She retired to a park called Lumbini. As she stood there in contemplation of this event, she reached overhead to hold the branch of the Sala Tree. Siddhartha emerged from her side. He emerged from the same spot that had been pierced by the elephant in Maya's dream, and just as painlessly.

Brahma, Indra, and other gods came to bathe the infant and bring him gifts. The newborn Siddhartha immediately stood, and as he touched the ground, a lotus sprang up under his feet. From this center, he took seven steps in each of the cardinal directions and declared this was his last incarnation. In a voice like a lion, he declared that he would conquer sickness and death.

In the lunar calendar of the time, each month was determined by the day of the full moon. The full moon was the magical center of the month. Siddhartha was born on the full moon of Wesak, which is equivalent to our month of May. On the day of his birth, his wife, Yasodhara, was born; his horse, Kantaka, was born; his squire, Chandaka, was born; and his closest disciple, Ananda, was born. Also on that day the Bodhi Tree sprouted.

Maya was speechless with joy. Her joy was so great that after seven days, she died and was reborn in Tusita Heaven, the land of joy. Her sister, Mahaprajapati, became Siddhartha's stepmother and raised him with legendary devotion.

Commentary

On the Papesse card in the Tarot of Marseilles there is a woman in a triple papal tiara sitting on a throne. In her lap, she holds an open book; this book is closed in the hand-painted Milanese decks. A sixteenth-century deck from Lyon awards her one of the pope's keys. Her purpose in the deck is to serve as a balance to the Pope card. This need for masculine and feminine balance is a major aspect of alchemical and Hermetic philosophy, and exemplifies the Neoplatonic message that underlies the Tarot. In addition, these early personages in the sequence of trumps are under the domination of Love, the sixth card. Therefore, it is natural that they are paired.

The Papesse is one of the most controversial cards in the Tarot. Catholicism is extremely patriarchal, and the idea that a woman could become pope was considered heretical. In fact, in 1300, there was a heretical group called the *Guglielmites* who elected a woman pope. The Inquisition destroyed the sect, and although when they found this new papesse she was already dead, they burned her body at the stake. It could be that this card is a reference to the Papesse of the Guglielmites. That it comes first and then is triumphed over by the Empress, the Emperor, and then the Pope fits the facts because the Papesse attempted to rise to the highest throne, but in the end fell to the lowest.

The Papesse could also be a reference to the legend of Pope Joan, the ninth-century woman who disguised herself as a man to join the clergy and eventually rose to the rank of pope. In her legend Pope Joan was found out and stoned to death, therefore she was also triumphed over by the male Pope. Those who are looking for a more orthodox interpretation compare the Papesse to allegorical images of a woman wearing the papal triple-crown. She is a symbol of the Church. This association leads to the view that the Papesse represents the Church, and that the Pope is married to the Church, just as the Emperor is married to the Empress. The interpretation is based on a logical attempt to find a precedence for the Papesse in Renaissance art, but it is not as true to the triumphal structure of the fifth suit.

A better fit with Renaissance art can be found in a mystical romance written in Venice in 1467 (close to the time that the earliest examples of Tarot cards that we have were created) and first published in 1499. The title of the book can be translated as *The Dream of Poliphilo*. The story recounts a dream in which Poliphilo (whose name means "the lover of Polia") is led by the search for his lover into the ruins of an ancient city—into classical culture and erotic wisdom—and out of his obsession with courtly love and alchemy. Near the end of the story, the lovers are united and appear before the priestess of Venus. In the woodcut that illustrates the scene, the priestess is sitting on a throne wearing a long robe and a triple-crown, and bears a remarkable resemblance to the Papesse in the Tarot. The woodcuts in *Poliphilo* are considered some of the most beautiful and influential illustrations produced in the early Renaissance.

If the Papesse is the priestess of Venus as this Renaissance use of the image suggests, then she represents classical Paganism and the Pope represents the triumph of Christianity over Paganism. The Empress and Emperor are seen going away from Paganism and submitting themselves to the authority of the Pope. However, the next card, the Lovers, which is dominated by the classical god Cupid, triumphs over all of them. This represents the triumph of sensuality, the theme of this first of the three parts of the trumps. Cupid is Venus's son, and although the Pope has trumped her priestess, she has the last laugh because even he cannot free himself from the desires that the classical gods represent.

Whether she is a representation of a legendary or historic female pope, the Church, or a priestess of Venus, the Papesse of the Tarot is the female counterpart of the Pope. The title *pope* means "father," therefore the Papesse is equivalent to "mother." The Pope represents the highest triumph of all the worldly figures, and the Papesse is the lowest, yet, like Maya, her son trumps the Pope.

The icon that this card is based on is one of the four principal icons of Buddhism. It is the Buddhist equivalent of the Madonna and child or the Nativity in the manger. Siddhartha is said to have emerged from Maya's side at the level of her heart because it is only through the chakra of love that he could enter the world, not the lower chakras. The whiteness of the elephant that impregnated Maya, and its crescent-shaped tusk that allowed it to enter, allies it to the archetype of the moon god. In ancient myths, heroes are often borne of a virgin who was impregnated by the moon instead of a mortal man.

We can see parallels between Siddhartha's birth and the birth of Jesus. Like Maya, Mary is a virgin who was impregnated by a white animal coming to her from above. Both are away from home at the time of delivery and make do in humble surroundings. After the child is born, important personages miraculously appear and bring gifts to the child.

The name *Maya* means "illusion." The month of May (our equivalent to the month of Wesak, in which Siddhartha was born) is named after the nymph Maia, a name that is pronounced the same as Queen

Maya's. Maia is the mother of Hermes, another hero whose father was divine and who was born in humble circumstances in a cave. In Hermes' myth he is also given gifts on his day of birth and exhibits miraculously adult behavior. As an adult he brings wisdom to humanity. Later, he is accredited the authorship of the Hermetic texts, which present a Western equivalent to Buddhist philosophy. The Romans called Hermes "Mercury" or "Mercurius" and they appointed the ides of May as the day of his celebration. The ides of May now fall on May 15, but in the original lunar calendar the ides were the day of the full moon.

Divination

Maya represents inner, esoteric religious experience, or mystery. A true mystery is something that the more we learn about it, the more we know that we cannot know it. We understand mystery when we accept that we cannot know it. The development of a fetus in the womb is such a mystery, and that is why the image of a woman is used to symbolize it. Maya also stands for intuition, knowledge that is hidden or knowledge that cannot be expressed in words, birth, and joy. She can represent something great that has a humble beginning.

III. Yasodhara - The Future Empress

It is pointless for you to praise a maiden to the ears of a young man and describe her in words in order to inflict upon him pangs of love, when you can bring her beautiful form before his eyes.

from a letter by Marsilio Ficino

Suddhodhana took the predictions about his son quite seriously. To assure that Siddhartha would be the future emperor, he created a beautiful palace for his son with a triple wall that was well guarded. Even the mention of sickness or death was forbidden there. In the palace there were gardens designed for beauty and comfort in each of the seasons. Some accounts say that the gardens were actually outside of the palace, one in each of the four directions. Here the young prince grew to manhood surrounded by fruits and flowers, beautiful dancing girls, and concubines.

However, Siddhartha's father knew that to solidify his son's commitment to the worldly life, Siddhartha needed to have one woman whom he loved above all else. Under the ruse of solidifying relations with the neighboring kingdoms, Suddhodhana summoned all of the available princesses to his palace and gave Siddhartha the task of distributing marvelous gems to each of them. The beautiful Yasodhara was the last to arrive, and Siddhartha had already given away all of the gems that his father had provided. As Yasodhara approached, Siddhartha removed his own ring to give it to her. When Suddhodhana saw how his son looked at Yasodhara, he knew that he had found his future empress.

Commentary

In the Tarot of Marseilles, the Empress card depicts a woman with a crown and a scepter sitting on a throne. In her right hand she holds a shield with an emblem of an eagle with its head looking over its left shoulder—the viewer's right. This is a clear reference to the wife of the Holy Roman Emperor. After the fall of the Roman Empire in the West, the Catholic Church began to view itself as a continuation of the empire in spiritual form as it attempted to unite the West into one religious body instead of a political body. With the rise of the powerful monarch Charlemagne, the Church saw a way to reclaim the political aspect of its empire. On Christmas day in the year 800, the pope crowned Charlemagne emperor. Although at times this Holy Roman Empire was more of a symbol than a reality, it was strengthened by Otto the Great in 936, and existed in various forms for approximately one thousand years. The city-states of northern Italy, where the Tarot originated, were part of the empire from the time of Charlemagne.

To create a symbol for his new title, Charlemagne combined the Roman eagle, which faces left, with the German eagle, which faces right, into one two-headed eagle facing in both directions. This two-headed eagle became the coat of arms of all the emperors. Sometimes the German emperors preferred to use the German eagle with one head, but in the 1400s the two-headed eagle was the official heraldic device of the emperors. In early printed cards, we can see this two-headed eagle on the Empress and Emperor cards in some decks. In the hand-painted Milanese decks and the Tarot of Marseilles and many of the decks based on it, we find a single-headed eagle on each card instead. Some historians attribute this to the fact that many rulers of Italian city-states adopted the German eagle as their emblem in an attempt to give the legitimacy of imperial approval to a position of power that they had seized and that this caused some confusion about which eagle was the imperial emblem. However, by the rules of heraldry, the Emperor and the Empress should have the same emblem. The Visconti-Sforza Tarot gives the Roman eagle (facing left) to the Empress and the German eagle to the Emperor, and the Tarot of Marseilles does the opposite.

To the ancient Greeks, Delphi was the sacred center of the world. In the myth of its origin, this fact was determined by Zeus. In the myth, he sets two eagles free to fly in opposite directions around the world until they meet face-to-face in the sacred center. In ancient art, the common way of depicting the sacred center was to create an image of two animals face-to-face; often they were birds. In the Renaissance, alchemists made use of this myth as a symbol of their quest for gnosis, as can be seen in an illustration in the famous alchemical text *Atalanta Fugiens*. The eagles facing in opposite directions on the Empress and Emperor cards at the beginning of the Tarot trumps may be a reference to this mystical quest, especially when we consider that their goal—the sacred center—is illustrated on the last trump.

In Buddhist icons, Yasodhara is pictured as the embodiment of everything beautiful and good about sensuality. Although Siddhartha eventually leaves her, he does so out of love. Because he loves her, he has to find the cure for life's suffering. This suffering will affect Yasodhara and all the people that Siddhartha loves. There is a connection between the romantic love Siddhartha has for Yasodhara and the love and compassion that allows him to enter the highest mystical state. Yasodhara helps to open Siddhartha's heart. Giving her his ring was an unselfish act engendered by this love, and it shows that love triumphs over the ego.

Divination

Yasodhara, the Future Empress, represents the feminine principle; the principle that is attractive and attracts what it desires. She is the fertility of the earth, the embodiment of beauty, and she opens our heart to love. She represents our hopes or the object of desire. She can be a beautiful woman and an ideal mate.

IV. Siddhartha - The Future Emperor

Picture a man endowed with the most vigorous and acute faculties, a strong body, good health, a handsome form, well-proportioned limbs, and a noble stature . . . For the body is the shadow of the soul; the form of the body, as best it can, represents the form of the soul.

from a letter by Marsilio Ficino

Although we might think that his father's pampering would spoil him, Siddhartha grew to be a thoughtful, intelligent, and good-looking young man. He excelled at his studies, even surpassing his teachers in his knowledge. Siddhartha was a natural at every type of athletic event and martial art. He quickly mastered all of the sixty-four arts required of a prince. His involvement in sports helped him to develop a tall, well-proportioned, strong body. In every way he was the ideal prince.

In the warrior tradition of his clan, Siddhartha was required to win his bride through a competition of martial arts. Therefore, although Suddhodhana had his doubts about his son's ability to compete (he, too, was worried that he had spoiled his son), Suddhodhana arranged a competition with Yasodhara's hand in marriage as the prize. Siddhartha won every event, including riding, fencing, and wrestling, but the highlight of the events was the bow competition. Siddhartha decided to use his ancestral bow, a massive weapon that no one else could even lift. Siddhartha strung it and released a perfect shot to the center of his target. This assured his victory, and soon he was married to Yasodhara and on his way to becoming the future emperor.

Commentary

In the Tarot of Marseilles we find the Holy Roman Emperor sitting on his throne, facing the viewer's left. He looks backwards, not ahead. His legs are crossed, he is holding a scepter, and at his feet there is a shield with a heraldic eagle looking over its right shoulder. As explained in the discussion of the Future Empress card above, the imperial eagle was two-headed, but this was not always the case in the Tarot. In some decks the Emperor's eagle may appear on his hat or become a sculptural side to his throne. In some nineteenth-century decks his heraldic device becomes a cross. This card is one of the most consistent in its meaning and imagery from the fifteenth century to the present.

The Buddhist icons that depict Siddhartha's competition for the hand of Yasodhara always show him shooting his ancestral bow. In the archetypal myth of the hero, it is common for the hero to exhibit a feat of great strength or ability at an early age. As an infant, Hercules strangled two serpents that were sent by Hera to kill him and his mother. The young Jesus went to the temple and successfully debated the learned doctors. The strength and ability that Siddhartha exhibited with a bow are proof that he could have taken the path of a world conqueror instead of a Buddha. I have pictured him having shot his arrow in the direction of Yasodhara. Like Cupid, he is using his arrow to stir love in the heart of his future empress.

Divination

Usually the Emperor represents a powerful person or our own power and intelligence. But in Siddhartha's case, he represents future potential that is developing and is being misdirected by his father. The Future Emperor can represent talent or ability that point to future success, or a heroic accomplishment. Unlike the Future Empress, who draws to her what she desires, the Future Emperor is active and takes steps to obtain what he wants. This card can also represent desire, and Siddhartha's bow can be pointing to the object of desire on another card.

V. Suddhodhana - The Father

Ramon the Fool made question to the Pope and the Cardinals, as to how and why it could be that the Popes who had been poor in temporal possessions had been praised more greatly than the Popes who were richer, after they had acquired the Empire of Rome.

Ramon Lull, *Blanquerna*

It would seem that Suddhodhana's plan had succeeded. Siddhartha's love for Yasodhara filled his consciousness, and he only wished to please her and to become a perfect ruler for his people. They were married when they were both sixteen years old and lived in bliss for many years. However, Suddhodhana was worried. He knew that as his son grew older, his control over him was diminishing, and he began to have troubling dreams. He doubled the guards at the palace gates, and tried to keep Siddhartha's mind occupied with delightful amusements that he invented to please all of the five senses.

Commentary

In the Tarot of Marseilles, the Pope sits on a throne facing us. He is wearing a triple-crown and holding a scepter with a triple-cross on top. With his right hand, he is making the sign of benediction, or "blessing," a Christian mudra. In front of him are two priests with their backs to us. They are obviously there to serve him. Their lesser status is symbolized by the fact that although they are in the foreground, they are drawn smaller than the Pope is. The Pope in the Visconti-Sforza deck is essentially the same, except the priests are missing. In later decks, such as the modern Swiss Tarot, the Pope and Papesse have been replaced with Jupiter and Juno. In the Waite-Smith deck, they are called the Hierophant and the High Priestess.

Of all the cards in the first section of the trumps, the Pope represents the highest-ranking worldly figure. The Protestant Reformation had not yet occurred when the Tarot was created. In the centuries before, the Vatican had ruthlessly destroyed the Cathars, who presented a religious alternative, and set up the Inquisition to assure that its authority in Europe would remain unchallenged. With no one to challenge him, the Pope card was considered the highest of the temporal rulers—the highest worldly authority. As in the example of the title page of the *Trionpho della Fortuna* discussed above under the Seer, the pope is sitting on top of the world. He is the ultimate authority. As exemplified by the Church's reaction to heretical doctrine, he is conservative and maintains the status quo. The title *pope* means "father" and, in the story of Buddha, Siddhartha's father, Suddhodhana, is his Pope.

There are very few depictions of Suddhodhana in Buddhist art. Here he is pictured as a sumptuously dressed ancient ruler sitting in the midst of sensuality and in the prime of his strength and manhood. Like the wall that he constructed around his son, Suddhodhana sits ahead of

Siddhartha in the sequence of trumps, looking out to the future and blocking Siddhartha from his destiny.

Divination

Suddhodhana's attempt to keep his son in a state of ignorance about the unpleasant realities of life may seem naive to us. But we all have a Suddhodhana inside of us. Many people cope with what is unpleasant by ignoring it, by living in denial. They feel that bad things happen to other people but not to them. They prefer to avoid the sight of death or illness. When death or illness breaks into their life, it comes as a great shock. "How could this happen to me?" they complain. Suddhodhana represents this conservative action. He tries to hold on to the past and block change. In doing that, he blocks the creative energy that is health and vitality.

VI. SIDDHARTHA AND YASODHARA - THE LOVERS

How in one so fair as thou can be so foolish a thought as this of thine which councils me to forsake the love of my sovereign Lord for the love of thee.

Blanquerna, speaking to the beautiful Natana
in Ramon Lull's *Blanquerna*

Siddhartha and Yasodhara were the perfect royal couple, and after many years of marriage, they had a son named Rahula. However, the constant amusement that Suddhodhana arranged only convinced Siddhartha that his life was shallow and vain, and he could not help but be curious about the outside world. In the following cards we will see that his curiosity and destiny won out, and that the four sights that were predicted early in his life manifested. Because of his sheltered existence, the shock of these realities was even greater than if he had been accustomed to these sights from his youth.

It would seem that the theme of this icon should be the perfect contentment of love, but although Siddhartha loves his wife and son dearly, he is preparing to leave. Once Siddhartha became aware of the suffering in life, all of his pleasures lost their glimmer. Everywhere he looked, he could see that everything and everyone was doomed to fade away and die. His strongest desire was to find a cure for the suffering in life, and to do this he had to leave this life of endless diversion. His only regret was that he had to leave his wife and son. He dared not kiss them goodbye for fear of losing his resolve. Without waking anyone else, he summoned his squire Chandaka, and had him ready his horse Kantaka. It was his twenty-ninth birthday, the night of the full moon of Wesak.

Commentary

In the Tarot of Marseilles, the Lovers card depicts a young man standing between two figures. Above, a clear-sighted Cupid draws his bow and prepares to fire an arrow. Originally in the Italian decks, this card was called simply "Love," and depicted a man and woman with a blindfolded Cupid above. These images were based on Renaissance betrothal portraits and represented a betrothal or a marriage. In these images, the blindfolded, and therefore undirected and disruptive, force of love is being safely contained by the vows of marriage.

In France, the tradition changed. The title was changed to "The Lovers" and a third figure was added. At first, in the Jacques Vieville Tarot, the third figure was possibly a priest performing the marriage of the lovers, but quickly he transformed in other decks into another woman, a second choice for the central man. Now the theme became choice or temptation. The man had to choose between virtue represented by a woman crowned with a laurel wreath, and sensuality crowned with flowers. In this tradition, Cupid is not blindfolded. Love is an aid in making this choice. This is the same choice that the Pope is presented with in the illustration from the *Trionpho della Fortuna* discussed above under the Seer.

This theme can be traced to teachings of the philosopher Pythagoras. Pythagoras is said to have added the letter upsilon, which is equivalent to our letter Y, to the Greek alphabet. He used this letter to illustrate the choice that every philosopher faces, as described in the following rhyme from the ancient writer Maximinus:

> The Pythagoric Letter two ways spread,
> Shows the two paths in which Man's life is led.
> The right hand tract to sacred Virtue tends,
> Though steep and rough at first, in rest it ends;
> The other broad and smooth, but from its Crown
> On the rocks the Traveler is tumbled down.
> He who to Virtue by harsh toils aspires,
> Subduing pains, worth and renown acquires:
> But who seeks slothful luxury, and flies,
> The labor of great acts, dishonored dies.[3]

The icon that this card is based on is popular in Buddhist art. Sometimes numerous couples are shown asleep on the floor, like the aftermath of an orgy. This is a reference to a description in the texts of the beautiful dancers who, when they fell asleep that night, lay about chaotically with their mouths open. The sight of the dancers looking so unglamorous was like a vision of the grave to Siddhartha. It showed him that all beauty in the physical world is transient.

Siddhartha's son Rahula was born shortly before he left. It seems that with the birth of his son, Siddhartha felt that his obligation to provide an heir was complete, and that his duties as a prince were over. It is said that Rahula means "fetter," but this has recently been debated by some scholars. "Fetter" would seem to be a cruel name for a child, and Rahula actually represented to Siddhartha freedom to leave since his role as prince was over.

Divination

The Lovers card is usually said to mean choice. However, both choices presented to the lover are equally ones of love. When we follow love's lead, love in any form can deliver us to the highest good. As Plato said in his *Symposium,* from sexual attraction to unconditional love, love is one continuum. This was the theme of romance literature, and the artists who created the Renaissance continued this theme. The Lovers card urges us to follow what we love. When a choice is to be made, it urges us to look deep and discover where our true love lies. This is not always the path of ease. We often must do things that we would prefer not to do for the sake of love.

VII. Siddhartha's Visit - The Chariot

The life which is unexamined is not worth living.

Socrates, in Plato's *Apology*

This card begins to explain what led Siddhartha to the decisive move illustrated in the previous card, the Lovers. Siddhartha was an intelligent man, and he reasoned that there was more to life than the hothouse existence that his father was providing for him. He wondered why he was wealthier and more privileged than others, and tried to earn his position by being a wise and kind ruler. But still he needed to know more about his people. Siddhartha realized that he had never been to the city, and he resolved to go there and learn more about how common people live. He announced to his father that he was going to take his chariot to town.

This was the day that Suddhodhana had feared. He stalled Siddhartha for a few days while he had his men clean up the town and remove the aged and sick. Siddhartha made four visits to the city. As each started, there were flowers thrown in his path and smiling people waving to him as he passed. But he was persistent in his exploration and attempted to uncover what lied beneath this facade.

Commentary

The Chariot in the Tarot of Marseilles depicts a young prince with a crown, a scepter, and classical armor standing in a chariot that is facing the viewer. The chariot's two horses, drawn in a crude perspective, trot directly at the viewer. Like the hero of a triumphal parade, the charioteer is trumping over all of the cards that came before. He is like the lover who in the previous trump has made the decision to take the road of hardship in hopes of winning a greater reward, and now he is setting out on that journey and triumphing over Cupid.

The triumphal car often found in allegorical triumphs in Renaissance art is also called a chariot. In the Italian decks, this card was sometimes called *"Il Carro Triumphale"* ("The Triumphal Chariot"). The hand-painted Italian decks from Milan depict a chariot in profile with a beautiful young woman as driver. In the Visconti-Sforza, her two horses are winged. This female charioteer seems to be influenced by the image of Laura, as the triumph of virtue, in Petrarch's *I Trionphi*.

However, the wings on the horses allow another association. In his *Phaedrus,* Plato creates the mythic image of the soul as a charioteer driving a chariot with two winged horses. As the word for *soul* in Greek is feminine, the charioteer is female. The horses represent the two lower parts of the soul, the soul of desire and the soul of will, and the woman at the reins is the soul of reason. Her job is to keep the lower parts in check so that they will work as a unit and carry the chariot to heaven. The feathers on the horses' wings represent virtue, and through unvirtuous behavior they are lost, causing the chariot to descend.

Everyone has a chariot that travels during one's numerous incarnations. As we strengthen the wings of our horses through the practice of virtue, our chariot can ascend to its ultimate goal. This myth could equally be applied to the progression that Siddhartha went through in his previous lives—a progression that has earned him the destiny that he is now setting in motion.

In the Buddhist icons, Siddhartha's chariot has two horses and two or four wheels. He is often accompanied by an entourage of servants holding an umbrella over his head, guiding his horses, and clearing the way. In later images in China, he is sometimes shown simply riding a horse. Here, Siddhartha's chariot is pictured from the side like the Milanese Chariots. He is heading into the next part of the story.

Divination

The Chariot is usually said to represent travel, safety, protection, and discipline. In Siddhartha's story, we see that it also represents curiosity, investigation, and the triumph of virtue. As expressed in the quotation from Socrates above, investigation and the desire to improve gives meaning to life. In its simplest interpretation, this card represents movement. The card or cards to the right will depict the destination.

VIII. Karma - Justice

I adore and bless thee, O divine virtue of justice, because thou chastisest me, and yet sparest me in that thou chastisest me not according to the multitude of my sins . . . Do with me that which is pleasing to thy will: my will be one with thine.

Ramon Lull, Blanquerna

Here we return to the night of Siddhartha's twenty-ninth birthday. It was the full moon of Wesak. Siddhartha has asked his trusted squire Chandaka to ready his horse Kantaka, and he was preparing to leave his pampered existence for good. Siddhartha noticed that a mysterious calm had fallen over the palace, and even the normally vigilant guards had fallen asleep. His only fear was that the sound of his horse's hooves would wake the guards or someone else who would stop him.

Later, he would come to realize that no one could have stopped him. It was his destiny to leave the palace on that day. As he left, the gods lifted Kantaka's hooves above the ground and he rode away in silence.

Through many lifetimes, Siddhartha had readied himself for this moment. In a past life, Siddhartha was an ascetic named Sumedha. In that life he sat in the presence of the first Buddha and vowed that one day he would also become a Buddha. Over 547 lifetimes he purified himself and perfected the ten virtues: generosity, morality, renunciation, intelligence, energy, patience, truthfulness, determination, benevolence, and equanimity. We often think of spiritual virtues as being passive, like love and patience, but as you look at the list of ten above you will notice that some of the virtues—like renunciation, energy, and determination—are dynamic and active. These are called the *heroic virtues* and these were the virtues that Siddhartha was expressing on this day and would use in this stage of his life.

Karma is the Buddhist and Hindu equivalent of justice. *Karma* means that one's past actions will determine the conditions of each incarnation. If one falls into ignorant, unskillful actions dominated by greed, hatred, and confusion, the karma one has earned will lead to a life of hardship. If one overcomes ignorance and begins to act skillfully motivated by generosity, love, and awareness, this will earn the karma that brings rebirth in a life of ease. Siddhartha had earned himself a life of ease. However, Siddhartha realized that both good incarnations and bad incarnations were equally states of ignorance. His goal was to wake up and stop this endless cycle of births and deaths. To accomplish his goal, he wished to burn up all karma. In this stage of his life, he believed that he could do that by leaving the life of ease that he had earned and willingly taking on the hardships of an ascetic life. Of course, it was his karma that had earned him the privilege of doing that.

Commentary

In the Tarot of Marseilles, Justice sits on her throne, crowned and facing us, holding a sword in her right hand and scales in her left. She is like our modern image of Justice except that she does not have her eyes covered. She is conscious of her activity and what she creates. As I explained in chapter 2, justice is the virtue that can be equated to Plato's soul of reason, which can also be symbolized by the charioteer in his myth about the chariot of the soul. Having the virtue that relates to the highest of the three parts of the soul come first puts them in reverse order, a situation that we only find in one out of the three basic patterns exhibited in early decks. This suggests that the virtues are working against the forces of time and death that dominate the middle section of the trumps.

The image of Justice is based on the Greek goddess Themis, who was Zeus's second wife and who stood at his side even after he married Hera. Themis represents justice as a force of good in the universe. She is divine law personified, like the Tao in the Chinese religion. Themis forsook the earth after the Golden Age, but her daughter Dike, or Asteraea, who represents earthly justice, stayed on until the Bronze Age. It is Dike who entered the zodiac as Virgo with her scales next to her in Libra.

In the earliest known Justice card found in the hand-painted Visconti-Sforza deck, the figure of justice is similar in its details to the one in the Marseilles deck. The only exception is that above the head of Justice there is a smaller figure of a knight on horseback galloping off to our right with his sword drawn. The knight's horse fits so closely to the triform arch in which Justice sits that this champion seems to be supported by this divine embodiment of goodness and righteousness. Similarly, Siddhartha on our card sets out as the champion of justice to end suffering, and finds divine support for his endeavor.

The image of Siddhartha and his horse can easily be found in Buddhist art. Often his squire is walking behind. That his horse and squire are born on the same day as Siddhartha, and that this event falls on their coinciding birthdays, demonstrates the importance of the event.

Divination

Justice represents truth, fairness, protection, and dealings with the law. In Siddhartha's story, it means that we get what we have earned. Our destiny is ours because we have earned it. When we are one with our destiny, divine forces are working in our favor. This card may refer to a journey or a break with the past. It can also mean freedom.

IX. The Old Man and the Sadhu - The Hermit

For a long time have I desired to be the servant and contemplator of God in the life of a hermit.

Pope Blanquerna, in Ramon Lull's *Blanquerna*

On the day that Siddhartha went to the city in his chariot, the festive decorations and activities that his father had arranged for him did not fool him. He knew that there were things there that he needed to learn and he was not disappointed. On one of the side streets Siddhartha saw an extremely old man hunched over and walking with a cane. The sight of this man was a shock to his consciousness. He had never seen anyone this old before. Now he realized that age did not just bring maturity, but eventually brought decline and decrepitude and that this was the fate of all who live out their life.

Siddhartha visited the city three more times. On the next two visits to the city, he uncovered sights that taught him about sickness and death and that upset him even more than the sight of the old man had. The shock of the harsh realities of life had plunged him into melancholy. Deep down he knew that he needed to find a cure for the suffering of the world, but as yet, he did not know where to look.

On his last visit to the city, Siddhartha saw a poor man in a saffron-colored robe. The man's only possessions were his staff and his bowl that he used when begging for food. Yet there was a look of serenity on the man's face. As Siddhartha came closer, he felt peaceful for the first time in days. Later Siddhartha asked about this man and found that he was a holy hermit, a sadhu, one who had renounced all of his possessions in a quest for spiritual treasure. Now, for the first time, Siddhartha had a model for how he would proceed. He knew that he also would become a sadhu.

Commentary

On this card in the Tarot of Marseilles there is a wandering mendicant in a hooded robe walking with a cane and holding a lantern at eye level. There is one early Italian printed card that depicts the same holy hermit holding a lantern and a staff, but the other Italian cards depict an old man on crutches or holding an hourglass. This original image of an old man is a personification of time related to the classical god Saturn. We can find models for him in the illustrations for Petrarch's triumph of time.

It is fitting that Father Time should be guiding us toward the images of fate, suffering, and death that are coming up in this section. All of these images are part of the negative associations that are part of the early Renaissance view of time. It was the Neoplatonists that added to Saturn's negative associations the positive qualities of wisdom and contemplation and symbolized them with the image of a hermit. The Hermit illustrates a spiritual path that can lead out of the trap of time, and that is how Siddhartha saw the sadhu.

The sadhu was the solution to the problem presented by the old man. A life of virtue can mean that with old age comes wisdom and spiritual advance. Once again, as the Tarot develops and changes, the fit with the story of Buddha is strengthened. In Buddhist art, the four sights are often pictured together in one image. On the card, the old man leans on his cane and looks in the direction of the past. The sadhu is wearing a saffron robe and holding a begging bowl and a staff. He looks to the future. The sadhu's staff continues out of the picture frame. In India, the staff would have a metal ring on top with smaller rings hanging from it. As he walks, it would jingle and tell the people that a holy man has arrived and he is in need of food.

Divination

At the mundane level, the Hermit card can simply express the need to be alone or the situation of being alone. There are two figures on the card, but each is alone and looking in opposite directions. It can also refer to something that is old. It may seem unbelievable to us that Siddhartha did not realize before this sight that people grow old. Yet, many young people act as if they will be young forever, and often adults express surprise when they see that they or their friends have aged. This card is a reminder that things age. At its highest level, it represents meditation and wisdom. If this card is in the center of three, the card to the left will represent aspects related to the old man, and the card to the right will represent aspects related to the sadhu.

X. Reincarnation - The Wheel of Life

Why it is that fortune often hates and indeed casts down a man whom the people deservedly love and, conversely, even more often loves and raises up one whom they justly hate? Is it perhaps because fortune is not only opposed to reason but . . . has also been hostile to the people?

from a letter by Marsilio Ficino

It was in this period of his life that Siddhartha began to wake up. In some accounts of Siddhartha's encounters with the four sights that were predicted from the time of his infancy, he does not experience the sights in the city. Instead, each one of the encounters happens on the way to one of the four pleasure gardens that Siddhartha's father built surrounding the palace, each in one of the four cardinal directions. In this version, Siddhartha meets the old man outside of the east garden, the sick man outside of the south garden, the corpse outside of the west garden, and the sadhu in front of the north garden. It may be that Siddhartha's four visits to the city were also each to a different quarter. This fourfold pattern allowed him to develop a complete picture of the world. Like many heroes, Siddhartha had to make a journey around the circumference of the world before he could go to the center. In doing this, he discovered that life was like a great wheel in which everyone is born only to suffer sickness, old age, and death. After death, we are reborn and repeat the process. To many readers today the idea that we are reborn may seem comforting, but to Siddhartha it was a curse. It meant that death would triumph over life again and again, and his goal was to defeat death.

When Siddhartha was born, it was predicted that he would become a world savior in either a physical way or a spiritual way. The first is called a *chakravartin* and the second a *Buddha*. However, the two paths have much in common. The chakravartin is first mentioned in the Indian sacred writings called the Vedas, which were written starting in the ninth century BCE. The Vedas tell us that when the first Aryan invaders came into India in their war chariots from the north, their leader was called the chakravartin, the "wheel turner." On the leader's chariot was the symbol of the wheel, a symbol of the sun and of its path through the sky. This symbol was evidence of his connection to the sun god, and in this context it can be found in other Indo-European cultures, including the Celts and Vikings. In the popular legends of Buddha's time, it was predicted that the chakravartin would return in a divine chariot with four wheels, each of which rolled toward one of the four directions. The chakravartin would walk the heavens and "turn the Wheel of Righteousness."[4] He would take his rightful place as ruler of the world and establish justice throughout the cosmos.

When Siddhartha sat under the Bodhi Tree and became Buddha, he had a vision of this great Wheel of Life and he remembered clearly all of his past incarnations. Later, he set out to save the world with his teaching, and his teachings are described as a wheel: the *Dharmachakra,* which means the "Wheel of the Law." Buddha saw that the Wheel of Life was a wheel of injustice driven by the three poisons greed, hate, and ignorance. Like a chakravartin, he replaced it with a wheel of justice. Therefore his teaching was called the *Wheel of the Law.* The purpose of the teaching was to help others to defeat suffering and death, and the Dharmachakra became the symbol of Vairocana, the Buddha of the center of the world. Vairocana is the archetypal Buddha that is present in the entire creation. The fifth suit in *The Buddha Tarot* represents him, and his symbol is on the back of every card.

In this part of his story, the four sights helped Siddhartha to see the wheel of suffering, but he did not yet know how to escape it. To accomplish that, he left his home and set out on another fourfold journey through the four yogas that were discussed in chapter 4: jnana, raja, karma, and bhakti. This journey is an internal circumvention of the wheel that is analogous to the fourfold development of consciousness that Jung observed. Siddhartha developed and spiritualized each of these four functions of consciousness through the four yogas, and replaced the wheel of fate with the mandala of the Self.

Commentary

The belief in reincarnation has most likely been present since before recorded history. The monthly death and rebirth of the moon and the yearly cycle of the sun are natural allies of the doctrine. In Hinduism, ideas about it were formulated in the writings of the Vedas in the ninth century BCE, and worked out in detail in the Upanishads in the seventh to fifth centuries BCE. By Siddhartha's time, it was an accepted part of the Hindu religion and considered an undisputed fact of life. In the West, belief in reincarnation was central to the religious philosophy of the Orphics and Pythagoreans and incorporated into Plato's worldview. The Neoplatonists focused on this aspect of Platonic thought and developed a theory of reincarnation that is similar to that of the Buddhists. Later, this influenced Neoplatonists within Judaism and Islam.

The famous sixteenth-century Kabbalist Isaac Luria made the belief in reincarnation a permanent part of the Kabbalah and of Orthodox Judaism. Although Islam officially does not believe in reincarnation, the mystic Sufis were open to the belief and carried the doctrine to medieval Spain.

In Christianity, we find the belief in reincarnation prevalent among the Gnostics and Christian mystics. Origen, the third-century theologian, made reincarnation a central part of his Christian mysticism, and his influence made reincarnation an accepted belief of many Orthodox Christians for the next three centuries. Controversy on this issue continued until the year 553, when a council called by the Byzantine emperor Justinian declared the belief heretical.

This should have settled the issue for good, but the Western Church found it necessary to restate that Christians did not believe in the reincarnation of the soul at the Council of Lyons in 1274 and the Council of Florence in 1439. In the beginning of the thirteenth century, the doctrine of reincarnation was preached by the Cathars of southern France, and although the Church thoroughly crushed this competitor, it still had to speak out against this heretical belief. The decree from the Council of Florence in 1439 shows that at the time of the origin of the Tarot, the belief in reincarnation was still prevalent enough to be considered a threat. Even today surveyors reveal that many people in the West believe in reincarnation.

In ancient Greece, there were several goddesses associated with fortune and fate. Chief among them were Tyche, the goddess of good fortune and the chance aspect of fate, and Nemesis, the goddess of divine punishment, a concept closer to the Buddhist idea of karma. In ancient art, Tyche's symbols were the rudder with which she steered men's lives, the horn of plenty representing good fortune, and a globe. Each city was believed to have its individual Tyche who protected the city. Nemesis's symbols were a gryphon, a lash, scales, and a wheel. Another goddess associated with fortune was Necessity, called *Ananke* in Greek, who was also associated with the globe. All of these goddesses are associated with aspects of the Roman Fortuna. As we saw in Plato's myth of the afterlife in *The Republic,* Fortuna's globe and wheel are all related to the spindle of the cosmos. Plato related this wheel to rebirth and fate. Since ancient times, the cyclical wheel-like aspect of the cosmos has been a prominent symbol used to support the idea of reincarnation.

Although the medieval Christian Church did not officially believe in reincarnation, it found that Fortuna's wheel was a useful symbol because of its moralistic message. Fortuna was now pictured sitting in the center of her wheel, blindfolded, to show that the fate she deals out is based on chance and not merit. The wheel of the year that her symbol derives from is divided into four cardinal points that corresponded to the journey of the sun. In the classical world, the word *cardinalis* referred to the principal turning points on the wheel of the year, and to the four directions and the four winds. In Medieval Latin, *cardinalis* came to mean "chief" or "principal." It was used to refer to prominent bishops, particularly the ones that elected the pope. St. Ambrose used this term to refer to the four chief moral virtues that had been expounded on by Plato and Aristotle: temperance, justice, fortitude, and prudence. These were called the *cardinal virtues* and later were added to the three theological or Christian virtues—faith, hope, and charity—to create the mystical seven. In doing this, St. Ambrose was saying that the practice of virtue is like a wheel of our making that can replace the irrational wheel of fate. This is similar to the message of Buddha's Wheel of the Law. This connection between the virtues and the Wheel of Fortune helps explain why they are grouped together in the Tarot.

On Visconti-Sforza Wheel of Fortune card, Fortuna stands blindfolded in the center of her wheel surrounded by four male figures. These figures can be seen as a satirical, microcosmic version of the sun's cardinal quest. The man on the left climbs the wheel. He is sprouting ass's ears, and a ribbon issuing from his mouth can be translated as "I will reign." On top of the wheel a man sits holding a mace and an orb. He is crowned with full-grown ass's ears and declares, "I do reign." Descending the wheel headfirst, a man with an ass's tail but no ears bemoans, "I have reigned." Finally, at the bottom, a crawling man simply says, "I am without reign."

These four figures are related to the four male figures on the cards that surround the Wheel in this section of the trumps. The Chariot is a young man looking forward to his destiny and heading up the wheel, the Hermit has achieved the top position through his age or merit, the Hanged Man is heading down headfirst, and the Corpse is on the bottom. It is a short step to picture this cycle continuing to rebirth and repeating the process for another turn of the wheel.

In the Tarot of Marseilles, Fortuna has been dropped from the image and her wheel supports three foolish creatures that are chasing each other's tails around the rim of the wheel. They appear to be three monkeys, symbols of human folly. The one on the right wearing donkey's ears is ascending the wheel in a foolish desire to be like (to ape) the monkey on top. The one on top rules the day with his symbols of power: a crown, sword, and cape flaring like a pair of wings. But what goes up must come down, and the third monkey demonstrates this by plunging headfirst with a forlorn look on his face. That the figure on top is crowned and has the suggestion of wings, and that the figures below do not have these attributes, connects this image with the alchemical symbol called the *double ouroboros*. In this alchemical symbol, a circle is formed of two serpents biting each other's tails. The serpent on top is winged and crowned and represents the volatile or active principle, and the serpent on the bottom is not winged or crowned and represents the fixed or passive principle. This is a Western form of the Chinese yin-yang symbol.

The Buddhist Wheel of Life icon is based on Buddha's vision on the night of his enlightenment. It is one of the most prevalent images in Buddhism because to see it is to share in Buddha's enlightenment—to see his vision. This card focuses on the central part of the image, and spokes have been added to the wheel to help make the connection with the Tarot image. In the center, we find the three foolish animals that keep the wheel turning. These are called the *three poisons*. The cock represents greed, the snake anger, and the pig ignorance and sloth. As in the alchemical symbol, each animal bites the tail of the one in front. The background is divided into dark and light halves. On the light side, a yogi is showing a man the way to the top, and on the dark side, an Asura, a titan, who represents anger and pride, is dragging a man down. In the full image, a larger circle would surround this core. It would be divided into six sections, each of which would contain scenes representing one of the six worlds that one can be reborn into: from the heaven of the gods on top to the hell of suffering on the bottom. Around this there would be a ring with twelve divisions containing representations of the stages of an individual life from birth to death.

Divination

In the quotation above, Ficino bemoans the irrational quality of fate. He repeats the age-old question: why do bad things happen to good people and good things to bad people? The belief in reincarnation and karma is the Buddhist answer to that question and this was Plato's answer as well. The Wheel of Life tells us that we have earned our fate and that we can improve our fate through the practice of virtue. The fact that all things change most often works in our favor; stagnation would be its opposite. Therefore, this card can be viewed as an omen of good fortune. However, it also instructs us that we have earned our good fortune and may continue to earn it through the practice of virtue. To practice virtue, we must examine ourselves truthfully and see clearly when our actions are driven by the three poisons. When we are achieving success, we must not grow complacent. An Asura is always ready to drag us down.

XI. Siddhartha Cuts His Hair - Strength

I am in utter poverty by reason of my devotion to god.

Socrates, in Plato's *Apology*

Here we take up the story from the point where we left it at the last virtue, Justice. On Siddhartha's twenty-ninth birthday after he rode out of the palace on his horse Kantaka, he stopped just outside the gates of the city, dismounted, and gave his horse to his squire Chandaka, who had followed behind him. As Chandaka and Kantaka returned to the palace, they were overcome with sadness. Some accounts say that Kantaka died of sadness, but as a reward for the part that he played in Siddhartha's departure, he was instantly reborn as a god in Tusita Heaven.

Once he was outside of his kingdom, Siddhartha encountered for the first time the king of the demons, Mara. Mara was the god of evil and death and he realized that if he did not do something to stop him, Siddhartha might become a Buddha and lead people out of the marvelous traps that Mara had devised to keep them as his slaves. He tried to reason with Siddhartha. He told him that if only he would return to the palace he would guarantee that Siddhartha would become a chakravartin. "Just think of the benefit to the world your reign of justice would accomplish," he pleaded. But Siddhartha knew that although as a chakravartin he could bring beauty and justice to the world, his accomplishment would not be permanent, and eventually the people of the world would fall back into greed, anger, and ignorance. Siddhartha knew that as a Buddha he could find a permanent solution to suffering and death.

Siddhartha continued on foot, but realized that he had to cut all ties between him and his life as a prince. As a symbol of the strength of his resolve and of his new life of discipline and self-denial, he drew his sword and cut his long princely hair. He tossed the locks into the air where they were gathered by the gods. Later when he came across a hunter, he exchanged his silk clothing and jewels for the man's rough clothing. Now his transformation was complete. He was no longer Siddhartha. From now on he would call himself by his family name, Gautama. He had become a sadhu, a seeker of enlightenment.

For the first part of his quest, he sought out the guru Alara Kalama, who taught him to rise above the emotions through cultivation of the intellect. This is called *jnana yoga*. When Siddhartha had mastered these teachings, his guru taught him the yoga of meditation, called *raja yoga*. Raja yoga gave Siddhartha the ability to rise above the intellect and master the unconscious. He was able to rise to the highest plane of consciousness that his guru knew of: the plane of nothingness. However, after experiencing this state of bliss, Siddhartha was still not satisfied. He noticed that when he came out of this deep meditative state, he still returned to his normal state immersed in the illusions of life. He reasoned that if he had attained Nirvana, then he should not be able to fall back into ignorance. Siddhartha left Alara Kalama and sought out another guru: Uddaka Ramaputta. Uddaka helped Siddhartha to reach an even higher state of consciousness, called "neither perception nor nonperception," but this state also proved to be transitory.

Gautama's strength and discipline would not let him take any teaching on faith. He had tried the teachings of the gurus and the results were not satisfactory. He had learned a great deal and he would eventually incorporate what he had learned into his own teaching, but for now, he was determined to find out what was missing in this approach.

Commentary

On the Strength card in the Tarot of Marseilles, we find a woman wearing a long gown and a broad-brimmed hat gently subduing a lion by grabbing hold of its mouth. The figures representing the virtues in Renaissance art are typically allegorical women. They represent a quality that is often attributed to a male hero. They are like the Buddhist Sakti, the female aspect of a Buddha. The figure in the Marseilles deck performs an action that is based on the story of Hercules subduing the Nemean lion, the first of his twelve labors, or possibly to Samson and his struggle with the lion of Timnath. In the Visconti-Sforza deck, Hercules himself, identifiable because of his club, is shown on the Strength card. In other decks, we sometimes find a woman breaking a column. This is a reference to the story of Samson destroying the temple of the Philistines. Perhaps because of its connection to both legendary heroes, the lion is the most prevalent symbol on this card.

In spite of being associated with legendary strong men, Strength represents more than muscular strength. Physical strength is the outcome of self-discipline and resolve. In the legends of these heroes, they demonstrate courage and self-sacrifice as well as power. These qualities are also strength and they are the outcome of training the will as well as the body.

The word *ascetic* is derived from the ancient Greek word *askesis,* which referred to the labor or exercise necessary to become an athlete. Ancient athletes were also known for their self-denial. They placed strict limits on their diets and on their sexual activity. This was also called *askesis*. As this discipline led to self-mastery, the term came to be used for spiritual discipline as well. In the ancient world, *askesis* was used to distinguish the spiritual practices of philosophers, which included fasting and silent meditation, from the ritual practices of the priests.[5]

In Buddhist art, the icon of Siddhartha cutting his hair is the standard symbol representing his break with his undisciplined life and his acceptance of asceticism. This would seem to be a reversal of the story of Samson, who lost his strength when his hair was cut, but in Samson's case this act was done to him against his will through trickery. Siddhartha is demonstrating self-mastery by cutting his own hair.

On the card, Siddhartha has replaced his horse with a snow lion. This is not part of the standard icon. However, it strengthens the connection between the Buddhist icon and the symbolism on the Tarot card. In Buddhist art, lions in general are a symbol of strength. Although Siddhartha is not usually shown sitting on a lion, we do find images of Bodhisattvas sitting on lions in this way. The lion is also a symbol of Vairocana, the Jina of the center of the world who is associated with this suit. The snow lion is a mythical form of the lion found in Tibetan art. Its milk is believed to be the universal cure for all sickness. It is fitting that Siddhartha should be sitting on a lion at this juncture in his quest.

Divination

In classical philosophy, strength is the virtue associated with the heart. It is the source of both love and courage; the root of the word *courage* is *cor*, which means "heart." The Strength card represents discipline, courage, love, and sacrifice. It can represent self-denial and self-mastery. However, even discipline itself must be disciplined. Too much denial can lead to weakness instead of strength.

XII. The Invalid - The Suffering Man

When I was yet in my sins, it seemed to me unbearably bitter to look at victims of leprosy, and the Lord Himself led me among them, and I showed kindness toward them. . . . that which had at first seemed bitter to me was now changed for me into sweetness . . .

St. Francis

On his second visit to the city, Siddhartha had seen a man with sores and a fever. The man was dying. This sight was more upsetting than the sight of the old man. This man had not lived to old age and yet death was robbing him of his life before it was complete. This sight plunged Siddhartha into a deep depression. He realized that death could come to anyone at any time, and the fear and uncertainty that accompanied this realization took all the joy out of life's pleasures. Fate seemed unfair, and yet this realization helped him to better understand the process of reincarnation. In his life as a sadhu, Gautama would make use of this knowledge. This experience also strengthened his determination to end suffering. In his new insight, he saw the world as sick and he knew that he had to find the cure. As it says in the Buddhist sutras:

> Noble one, think of yourself as someone who is sick,
> Of the Dharma as the remedy,
> Of your spiritual friend as a skilful doctor,
> And of diligent practice as the way to recover.[6]

Central to the belief in reincarnation is the belief that it is one's karma that chains one to the cycles of redeath. All worldly activity leads to new activity through a cause-and-effect relationship. These effects that are engendered by our past actions are called our *karma*. As long as we create karma, we are stuck in the cycles of life and death where the karma needs to be played out. All karma leads to new karma and continues to entrap us. Karma yoga is designed to address this problem by teaching one to engage in activity without any desire for personal gain or attachment to the results. After Gautama left his gurus, he decided to experiment with the most severe form of karma yoga. He attempted to burn away all of his karma by denying every desire. He denied himself clothing, warmth, and food. He wandered naked in the forest, avoiding contact with other humans except for five disciples who admired his extreme asceticism.

Commentary

In the Tarot of Marseilles, this card is called *Le Pendu,* "The Hanged Man." It depicts a man hung upside down from a beam supported by two rough-cut posts. He is tied to the beam by his left foot and his right leg and his arms are folded behind him. Occultists have sometimes assumed that this figure was originally the missing cardinal virtue prudence, and that as the cards were reproduced by inexperienced printers, the figure was turned on its head. However, this figure is essentially the same on the cards from the earliest decks. In fact, in some later French decks, the figure is mistakenly turned right-side up. In Renaissance Italy, this figure would have been easily recognized as a traitor—the Minchiate even labels the card "The Traitor." In Italy, the punishment for a traitor was to be hung by the feet (or foot), possibly after execution. It was also the practice to label a person a traitor by having a picture printed of him or her hanging by the foot and posting it in public. These were called *shame pictures*.

Often we find money falling out of the pockets of the Hanged Man in the Tarot. This detail strengthens the sense of loss symbolized by this card. In modern decks, this card is usually thought of as representing a willing sacrifice, but the original meaning is simply suffering and loss. It is connected with the images of time and fate found in this section of the trumps. This is the Nemesis aspect of Fortuna. Through unvirtuous behavior, the traitor has lost his position and wealth and is suffering from being hung. In a deck from Bologna printed in 1664, we find the image of a man preparing to hit another man in the head with a large mallet substituted on this card. The modern Sicilian deck has a man hung by the neck. Of course, through the fickleness of fate, someone may unjustly be labeled a traitor and this suffering may not be deserved.

In Buddhist art, the sick man is most often depicted in a group of the four sights that awakened Siddhartha to his quest. Illness strikes us in the same way as the traitor is stricken by fate. Often we bring illness on ourselves through our imbalanced diet and lifestyle, but it may also come through no apparent fault of our own. The Buddhists attribute this to past karma. After Siddhartha saw the suffering of the sick man, he was willing to take on suffering himself in an effort to burn up his karma. The sight of suffering is in harmony with the original meaning of this card. Gautama the ascetic is in harmony with the modern meaning.

Divination

The Suffering Man can represent illness, suffering, or simply an uncomfortable situation. Often the situation is of our own making, or perhaps, like Buddha, we are taking on an uncomfortable job to better ourselves in the future. At its highest level, this card represents sacrifice. This card shows that ordinary life always contains dukkha.

XIII. THE CORPSE - DEATH

"Which did you prefer in him, the body, or the soul?"
"Alas it was the body, for I had threatened to curse him if he ever became a Friar Minor."
"Then go to the cemetery, and find his body you loved so much, and you will see what has become of it."

Brother Giles, a follower of St. Francis,
speaking to a mother on the death of her son

On his third visit to the city, Siddhartha saw some men carrying a corpse to the cremation grounds. The sight of death confirmed all of his fears, and yet it gave clarity to his thoughts. He now knew the truth. As unpleasant as that truth was, the knowledge gave him a new power. He saw that all physical things, including the body, are temporary. He was determined to find the part of himself that was permanent, and by accomplishing that, he could defeat death.

After his departure, when he became Gautama the ascetic, he attempted to burn up all of his karma by working against his desires, including the desire to avoid death. Gautama slept in the open, even on freezing nights, lying on a bed of spikes. He wore rough hemp rags, or no clothing at all. He went without food, or consumed his own urine and feces. When he practiced breathing exercises, he held his breath for so long that he felt as if he would faint. Eventually he went on such a prolonged fast that his flesh shrunk and clung to his protruding bones, his hair fell out, and his skin blackened. He had transformed himself into a living corpse and he hung on the verge of death. His five disciples were sure that he would obtain liberation at any moment.

Commentary

In the Tarot of Marseilles, Death is depicted as a skeletal corpse using a scythe to mow a field littered with heads, hands, and feet. There is no box for his name on the bottom. Originally he was unlabeled out of fear of repeating his name. All the early decks depict various forms of this same theme. The Grim Reaper is sometimes on horseback, and he may use a bow instead of a scythe. This image is borrowed from the popular Dance of Death, an allegorical dance or work of art in which death is seen to triumph over individuals of every age and class. But in all the known orders, Death is consistently number thirteen. In the Tarot, Death is always in the middle; it is never the final trump. Unlike the Dance of Death, the Tarot's story is about the defeat of death.

As mentioned earlier, the four sights are usually depicted together in Buddhist art. The skeleton, however, becomes a symbol in itself in Tibetan art, along with human skull cups and human thighbone trumpets. In Buddhist meditation, contemplation of the human corpse was recommended for the development of detachment and awakening to a deeper reality. The skeletons of Buddhist art are designed as substitutes for actual corpses. When one accepts these images into one's consciousness, a person can overcome the need to evade the unpleasant aspects of life and reclaim the energy that is wasted in blocking these thoughts.

Divination

The simplest meaning of the Death card is that it represents the end of something. All things end and this is their death. When you finish reading this book, you will have come to the death of this reading. You will put the book down and look for something new to begin. All death points to a new beginning. Ultimately, there is no death, including the death of the body. Death is just one aspect of the eternally changing reality. The Tibetan spiritual teacher Sogal Rinpoche said:

> Life and death are in the mind and nowhere else. Mind is . . . the creator of happiness and the creator of suffering, the creator of what we call life and what we call death.[7]

Tibetans consider skeletons a wholesome reminder of the truth under appearances—the bare bones of a situation. The skeleton can help us overcome fear and tap our creativity. This is its function in the American Halloween celebration.

Often people are fearful of the Death card. They are afraid that it will predict the death of someone during a reading. In all of the years that I have been doing readings, I have never seen that happen. If one is in tune with the Tarot as a tool for connecting with the higher self, this will not happen. Our higher selves are more considerate than that. This fear can be totally avoided if we use the Tarot for true divination. Divination is not a method of predicting the future, but a way of connecting with inner wisdom and helping one make informed decisions.

XIV. The Middle Path - Temperance

Our brother the body, needs a certain ration of food and sleep. If you refuse him this, he will also refuse to serve you, and discouraged, reply, "How can you expect me to give myself up to vigils, prayer, and good works, when because of you I am too weak to stand?"

St. Francis

As a result of his lengthy fast, Gautama was on the verge of death. His body had withered and he had lost the thirty-two marks and eighty signs of the great man. All the gods, except Mara, were concerned. They sent word to Suddhodhana, Gautama's father, hoping that he would put a stop to this fast. Suddhodhana knew that it was predicted that his son would succeed in becoming a Buddha and refused to believe that Gautama was in danger.

At this point, the god Indra appeared before Gautama and began to play a three-stringed lute. However, on this lute it was only possible to make music on the middle string, which was perfectly tuned and made a harmonious sound. The lower string was too loose, and when Indra played it, an unpleasant thump was produced. The upper string was too tight, and when Indra plucked it, the string broke. The message of this vision was clear to Gautama. He realized that as a prince he was like the string that was too loose. He needed discipline to bring himself into tune. However, too much discipline would also put one out of tune. Like the tight string, he was now ready to break. He would die without achieving his goal of liberation. Instead of overcoming his desires, his asceticism had only made his cravings stronger. He had failed because his desire for liberation was at its root selfish, and all it created was more selfish desires. To proceed, one had to embrace the middle path, nurture the body, and find motivation that was deeper than the ego.

After this realization, Gautama fashioned a robe from the shroud of a corpse and obtained a begging bowl. Now properly equipped, he was able to beg for his food and began to build up his strength. He regained the marks and signs of the great man. However, his five disciples were discouraged by his new behavior and, believing that he had given up his quest, they left him in disgust.

One day while he was meditating, Sujata, a beautiful young woman from the village, appeared at Gautama's side offering him rice and milk in a golden bowl. Gautama divided the food into forty-nine parts, for he knew from his dreams that he would need to sustain himself without begging for the next forty-nine days. After this, he bathed in the river and threw the golden bowl away. It is said that it floated up the river to the very spot where the bowls of the previous three Buddhas rested after they, too, had thrown them away. With his strength totally recovered, Gautama traveled through the forest. He was heading for Bodhimanda, the sacred center of the world, because he knew that only there was the earth capable of supporting him during his attainment of enlightenment.

When Gautama arrived, he found a beautiful fig tree called the *Bodhi Tree*. He made a pillow from a bundle of grass. Then, while circling the tree looking for a spot to sit, he found that "the broad earth heaved and sunk, as though it was a huge cartwheel lying on its hub, and someone was treading on its rim."[8] Only on the eastern side was the ground solid and still. He placed his pillow under the tree and sat down on the pillow, facing east, with his legs crossed. This seat is called the *Vajrasana*, which means the "Diamond Throne." As he sat, he vowed that he would not leave that spot until he reached his goal and that death would take him if he broke this vow. When his vow was completed, the earth quaked six times.

Commentary

The word *temperance* is derived from the Latin word *temperare*, which means "to mix or blend," and that is just what the angelic figure on the Temperance card in the Tarot of Marseilles is doing: mixing liquid contained in two vessels. The figure of a woman in a long dress pouring water from one vessel to another is consistent on this card in all early decks. In the early seventeenth-century Jacques Vieville Tarot, she is also holding a winged staff, an addition that may be related to Hermes' staff, and therefore may add an alchemical association to this card. In the French decks after this, the wings are depicted on her back, transforming her into an angel.

In the ancient world, temperance was the virtue associated with Aphrodite, the goddess of beauty and art. Plato said that the temperance of desire was the primary virtue that was necessary to develop in all the workers in his ideal republic. To learn temperance, Plato recommended learning music, which demonstrated that he, too, connected temperance with the arts.

In the Renaissance mind, the balancing of desires was closely connected to the physical balance of the four humors. The humors were part of Renaissance medicine, and they consisted of four bodily liquids—phlegm, blood, and black and yellow bile—that were related to the four elements (water, air, earth, and fire, respectively). A balance of the humors was believed to be necessary for mental and physical health. When these liquids were in proper balance, one was said to be in "good humor" or able to "hold one's temper." In India and Tibet, we find a similar theory of medicine. Here the humors are called the *doshas,* and there are three of them: *vata, pitta,* and *kapha,* which are related to the three active elements—air, fire, and water.

The image on the Temperance card in *The Buddha Tarot* is based on icons from southeast Asia. Here we find Sujata playing the part of Temperance pouring her life-giving milk and rice from her vessel into the human vessel that will become the Buddha. In Indian medicine, rice and milk are believed to be a tonic for restoring strength and balancing the humors. Like the classical Temperance, Sujata is creating balance and health. Along with physical balance, Gautama has learned that to proceed toward his goal, it is best to balance his approach to the quest for enlightenment and find the middle path.

Divination

Temperance means "balance," "beauty," and "health." It is how an artist achieves beauty when he or she creates a balanced composition. It is how a healer creates health when he or she helps an individual achieve a balanced diet and life choices. It represents finding peace and not being driven by our emotions. This card represents patience and the middle path. It can also symbolize the need to accept help and to nurture ourselves to create health. A card to the right of this card may give us more insight into who is playing the part of Sujata and what is the nature of the help that is offered.

XV. Mara - The Devil

By some foolish, or rather, unhappy fate . . . most mortals make more perverse use of prosperity than adversity . . . Let us remember that the nature of evil is to offer itself to us daily under the guise of good.

from a letter by Marsilio Ficino

Mara is one of the gods, but he is also the king of the demons called *maras*. He is the Buddhist equivalent of the Christian Devil. His name means "delusion." Mara is dedicated to maintaining his power over humanity. From our hopes and fears, he fashions two families of demons and uses them to keep our minds occupied with endless distraction. Through our own ignorance, anger, and desire, he chains us to the wheel of fate.

Mara first appeared to Gautama on the day that he left home, and he continued to harass him during the six years of his spiritual search. But now Mara himself was overcome with fear. When he saw Gautama sitting on the Diamond Throne in the center of the world, he knew that Gautama was nearing the achievement of his goal. Gautama's goal was the defeat of suffering and death, and Mara was the lord of suffering and death. Mara launched an all-out defense of his domain.

For his first attack, Mara summoned his three lovely daughters. His daughters were more sensual and voluptuous than any human female, but in reality they were the three poisons greed, anger, and ignorance wrapped in a beautiful and appealing form. Their names were Lust, Passion, and Delight. Mara's daughters attempted to seduce Gautama away from his seat but, as prince Siddhartha, he had already lived a life of sensual satisfaction and knew its rewards would not satisfy his inner thirst. Gautama remained unmoved.

Mara reasoned that if Gautama was not vulnerable to desire, perhaps he was vulnerable to fear. He summoned his demonic army, which was equipped with a fantastic array of horrifying weapons. Mounted on horses and elephants like a great conquering army, his men surrounded Gautama and launched their attack. At first, Gautama used the virtues that he had acquired as shields. However, as the attack proceeded, he realized that he was sitting in the invulnerable center and did not need to shield himself. During his six years as an ascetic, Gautama had learned to let go of fear, anger, and other emotions, and now he made use of that knowledge. As the army entered Gautama's aura, they found no negative emotions to exploit. They were overcome with peace. They laid down their weapons and bowed at his feet. Gautama had not moved from the sacred spot and Mara was unhappy.

Commentary

The Devil in the Tarot is based on the horned demon that is the Christian personification of evil and who is common in medieval and Renaissance art. He is absent in the early hand-painted decks, but in the printed decks we find him depicted as a horned humanoid figure, sometimes with bird feet and a face in place of his genitals and holding a pitchfork. In the Tarot of Marseilles, he has antlers and bat wings and is holding a torch. That his weapon is a torch is more obvious in older copies of the deck when it was hand painted. In the modern printed deck, the flame of his torch is not distinguished in color from the blue of his wings. He seems to have the breasts of a woman and the genitals of a man and sometimes a face on his abdomen. Also on the Marseilles card there is the addition of two smaller minions chained to his pedestal. They are crudely drawn, but one has the body and face of a female and the other a male. Once again, as the symbolism developed in the French decks, the image is a closer fit to the story of Buddha.

To the Christian Gnostics, the Devil was the creator and ruler of the physical world. Although Mara is not credited as its creator, his role as ruler of the world is similar. To both Gnostics and Buddhists, the job of the evil one is to keep us from achieving the freedom of enlightenment. In the story of Christ, his relationship with the Devil is similar to Buddha's relationship with Mara. The Devil tempted and threatened Jesus in a similar way when Jesus meditated in the desert. That the Devil appears here, at the beginning of the third section of the trumps, is in harmony with his role of gatekeeper to the higher realms. We have to deal with the Devil if we want to progress.

In Buddhist art, Mara is usually included in the background of a multifigured scene depicting the attacks of his demons and the temptations of his daughters. In the center sits a serene Gautama. Our card depicts three figures drawn in Buddhist style, but composed as they are on the Marseilles card. In the center is the large fanged and glaring Mara. He is blue and he wears the skins of a tiger and of a human. In the foreground on our left is one of his tempting daughters, and on our right is one of his fierce soldiers. Buddhist literature tells us that demons fall into two categories: those born of our hopes, and those born of our fears. This is the nature of the two attacks on Gautama. Mara's daughters are the demons of hope, and his army the demons of fear.

Divination

Mara represents the negative aspects of the ego. He is the consistent cravings and worries that fill one's consciousness daily and that stop one from achieving peace. Mara is bad. He is temptation, fear, and enslavement. He may represent a dead-end job or relationship, addiction, the threat of violence, or incarceration. If he is in the center of three cards, the cards to either side may be an illustration of our hopes and our fears.

XVI. The Flaming Disk - The Tower

I aspire to so great a treasure
That all pain for me is pleasure

St. Francis

The female seduction and the male assault, the two parts of Mara's attack on Gautama, had both failed. Mara realized that his only chance of defending his domain of delusion from Gautama was to take matters into his own hands. If he could not find any weakness in Gautama to exploit, he would simply destroy him. Mara prepared his ultimate weapon: a huge flaming disk that was capable of cleaving a mountain. Riding on a cloud, Mara flew to a spot in the sky above Gautama. With his right arm, Mara raised the disk over his head and heaved it with all of his strength directly at Gautama.

Because Gautama was sitting in the sacred center of the world, and because he had totally surrendered his ego, his aura was one with the unlimited creative potential of the cosmos. Nothing negative could enter this aura without being transformed. As the flaming disk entered Gautama's aura, it became a ring of flowers that hung in the air surrounding his head.

By now, the escalating ferocity of Mara's attacks had frightened away the gods who before this had gathered to witness Gautama's attainment of enlightenment. Seeing that Gautama was alone with no one to vouch for him, Mara decided to challenge Gautama's right to sit on the Diamond Throne. Mara commanded that Siddhartha leave the throne. After all, Mara was lord of the world, not Gautama. "Gautama, what right do you have to sit here?" Mara asked.

Gautama explained that during his last 547 lifetimes he had purified himself through rightful actions and had acquired the ten virtues. In this life, he had exhausted every extreme in his search for enlightenment, and now he had found the middle path and had earned the right to sit on the Diamond Throne.

Looking to the four directions and seeing that no one was there, Mara said, "I do not believe you. Who will bear witness to these deeds?"

Gautama did not say a word. Instead, he reached down with his right hand and touched the earth. Up from the earth rose the Earth Goddess. With a voice like thunder, the Earth Goddess replied:

> I have seen all of his previous lives. I have seen hundreds of thousands of lives in which he practiced the perfections. So I bear witness that on account of his practices of these perfections he is worthy to sit in the seat of the Buddhas of old.[9]

At this sight, Mara fled in fear.

Commentary

In the Tarot of Marseilles, the Tower card is called *La Maison Dieu*, "The House of God." It depicts a flamelike lightning bolt knocking the top off a tower. The crenellated top is depicted in a way that suggests a crown. One figure is falling from the top and another appears to be jumping out of the tower from the bottom. Like the other cards in this section of the trumps, this scene is most likely derived from the descriptions in Revelation of lightning and earthquakes that will cleanse the earth in preparation for the new millennium when the City of God will manifest on earth.

The Tower is missing from all the early hand-painted decks except the Gringonneur deck, which depicts a tower being struck by fire from above. The early printed cards are similar to the Tarot of Marseilles, except that the falling figures are not always included. In these, the fire from above is depicted as a flaming disk. In the Italian decks, it was usually called "Fire" or else "The House of the Devil" or other variations. In Mitelli's *Tarocco Bolognese* and the Belgian Tarot, it was sometimes called "Lightning" or "Thunderbolt," and a fiery lightning bolt would be shown striking a person or tree instead of the tower.

The fire from above is cleansing away negativity to prepare for a new spiritual awakening. In the Bolognese tradition, it strikes a man. On the Marseilles card, it topples the crown of pride or ego. It is like a reiteration of the falling figure on the Wheel of Fortune, who was crowned when sitting on top. The Tower shows the crown knocked from the summit and a man falling headfirst.

In the story of Buddha, this is the final defeat of Mara, who also represents the ego. Mara's fire dethrones its wielder and a new purified aura surrounds Gautama. The image of Buddha sitting in lotus position with his legs crossed and touching the ground with his right hand in what is known as the *Victory mudra* is one of the most prevalent icons in Buddhism. It is one of the four essential images of Buddha's life and maybe the most important. With this final victory over the ego, Gautama was becoming Buddha.

The fact that Mara, the evil one, is the ruler of the world may seem pessimistic. We might feel that Buddhist attitude is similar to the dualistic pessimism of the Gnostics. But this icon is essentially optimistic. By asking the earth for help and receiving it, Buddha is demonstrating that the state of enlightenment is part of the natural world and that the world welcomes it. To become enlightened is to become one with the world.

Divination

The Tower represents transformation, the shattering of illusion, and sudden change. This kind of transformation is abrupt and may be discomforting or unsettling. Also, it represents the overcoming of egotism and the ability to ask for help. The image of Buddha touching the earth is optimistic, and exhibits a trust that no matter what happens, the universe is on our side.

XVII. The Chakras - The Morning Star

Celestial bodies are not to be sought outside ourselves: the heavens, in fact, are within us, and we have within us the vigor of fire, the celestial origins.

from a letter by Marsilio Ficino

Mara had fled and now there was nothing to stop Gautama from reaching enlightenment. It was the end of the day and the sun had set. In Tantric Buddhism, it is believed that there is a latent psychic energy that resides at the base of the spine. This force is called the *kundalini* and it is symbolized as a coiled snake. In the process of enlightenment, the kundalini is awakened and it rises up the spine through a progression of psychic centers called *chakras*. We came across the word *chakra* earlier when we were discussing the chakravartin. It means "wheel." In

English we might call these locations on the spine *soul centers*. That would be the English equivalent of Plato's name for them. These are places where our physical body and our psyche interact. In the ancient literature, we find lists of three, four, five, six, seven, or more principal chakras. Today the most commonly accepted number in both the East and the West is seven, as can be seen in the illustration on this card. Each is pictured as a mandala or a wheel that turns when flowing with energy.

Although Tantric Buddhism teaches us that Gautama's kundalini would have activated his chakras on the night of his enlightenment, the chakras are not mentioned directly in the ancient texts. Instead, the chakras are depicted through symbolic aspects of the story. It is said that after the defeat of Mara, Gautama achieved full enlightenment during that night. In ancient India the night was divided into three sections called *watches,* and in each watch Gautama progressed through a higher state of consciousness. The last watch, in which he achieved the highest state of consciousness, was marked by the rise of the morning star. (We will discuss the three levels in more detail in the discussion of the next trump, the Moon.) These three divisions correspond to the three main divisions into which the seven chakras fall. The three lower ones are a group dealing with physical desire; the central heart chakra is the place of awakening to the higher consciousness and where the ego is overcome by love and selflessness; and the upper three deal with the wisdom that comes from above.

On the next morning, Gautama no longer existed. In his place there was a fully enlightened being, a Buddha. Buddha continued to sit in meditation for another seven days and remained close to that spot for seven weeks. By the seventh week (some say the sixth week), it was the season of the monsoon, a time when the sky pours a flood of water on the earth. King Mucalinda, the king of the serpent creatures called *nagas,* saw that Buddha would be helpless during the downpour. Mucalinda coiled around Buddha's body seven times and with his seven heads formed an umbrella over Buddha's head. After the rains had stopped, Mucalinda took the form of a beautiful youth, stood in front of Buddha, and bowed in salutation.

The rain was like a purification, or baptism, of this new being, the Buddha. Mucalinda, the snake king, rose around the body like the kundalini serpent rises through the spine. His seven heads are like the seven awakened soul centers and he used them to crown the fully awakened Buddha. The youth was a symbol of the rejuvenation brought about by the activation of the chakras.

Commentary

On some early Star cards we can find astronomers, and on others we find magi, following the star of Bethlehem. But the most popular image is a woman, or in one case, a man, holding a single star overhead. However, for this card, the Tarot of Marseilles contains the most evolved mystical image. On the Tarot of Marseilles card we find a female nude pouring water from two pitchers, one on the land and one on the sea (an alchemical symbol for the harmony of opposites). The nude is a Neoplatonic symbol of the soul. Above her are seven stars situated around a larger eighth one. The seven stars represent the Neoplatonic ladder of the planets. The eighth star represents the eighth sphere on which the fixed stars revolve, and is considered the gateway to heaven.

Neoplatonists believed that the World Soul entered physical creation by descending a ladder of seven planets that had been described by Plato. The word *planet* is derived from the Greek word *planetai*, which means "wanderer." To the Greeks, the wanderers were the seven celestial bodies, visible to the naked eye, which appeared to move independently from the constellations. They included the sun, the moon, Mercury, Venus, Mars, Jupiter, and Saturn. The ancients believed that Earth was in the center of the cosmos and that the seven planets circled it. Each orbit was thought of as a crystal sphere, one nesting inside the next with Earth in the center. Encasing the outermost crystal was the eighth sphere of the constellations, and beyond that was the home of the spirit. In Neoplatonic mystical visions, the soul ascended these seven planets like a ladder leading to heaven and the experience of enlightenment.

In Plato's *Timaeus* he describes the human body as a microcosm of the universe. He shows that the universe has a body and soul and describes the seven planets as seven soul centers:

> And when the whole structure of the soul had been finished to the liking of its framer, he proceeded to fashion the whole corporal world within it, fitting the two together center to center to the outmost heaven.[10]

These seven soul centers were believed to ascend the spine of each person in the same way that the planets ascend the axis mundi of the cosmos. In the following quotation from Iamblichus's fourth-century CE *The Life of Pythagoras,* we can see that Plato's ideas may have come from Pythagoras:

> He alone apparently hearing and grasping the universal harmony and consonance of the spheres, and the stars that are moved through them, producing a melody fuller and more intense than anything effected by mortal sounds . . .
>
> Divinely contriving mingling of certain diatonic, chromatic and enharmonic melodies, through which he easily switched and circulated the passions of the soul in a contrary direction, whenever they had accumulated recently, irrationally, or clandestinely—such as sorrow, rage, pity, over-emulation, fear, manifold desires, angers, appetites, pride, collapse or spasms. Each of these he corrected by the rule of virtue, attempering them through appropriate melodies, as through some salutary medicine.[11]

Pythagoras believed that each of the planets made a musical note as it circled on its sphere. Together they created "the music of the spheres."

Pythagoras could hear this music while in meditation, and he devised seven notes that captured these perfect sounds. These became the seven notes of our Western diatonic scale; the octave, or eighth note, is a return to the first note of the seven on a different frequency. Pythagoras created a seven-stringed lyre called a *cithara* to capture these notes and, when properly played, he found that each note brought the corresponding soul center in the human body into harmony and health.

In the mystery religions, these soul centers were the basis of seven degrees of initiation. All of these ancient ideas entered Christian culture and became the basis for the seven days of the week, the seven sacraments, the seven courses in the medieval scholastic curriculum, the seven virtues, the seven vices, and numerous other lists of seven. In the seventeenth century, the famous scientist Isaac Newton discovered that the spectrum of light contained seven colors. As the colors of the spectrum are a continuum with no breaks, one may wonder if Newton was predisposed to see seven divisions by his, now well-known, alchemical studies.

The Tantric system of chakras was introduced to the West in the early part of the twentieth century through books like *The Chakras* by the Theosophist C. W. Leadbeater and *The Serpent Power* by the Hindu writer Arthur Avalon. In Tantra, there are many systems of chakras with different numbers of centers. Although we do find that lists of seven are common, one of the most ancient texts from the Kaula school lists eight chakras. The Upanishads speak of the "five parts" of the body corresponding to the five cosmic elements—earth, water, fire, air, and aether—which relates them to the symbolism of the stupa. In Tibet we find a system that acknowledges four chakras (the navel, heart, throat, and head) and other systems that acknowledge five, seven, or ten chakras. However, the early Western writers chose a seven-chakra system to present to the West and this has been considered the norm ever since.

In the original Tantric conception, the chakras are psychic realities that are to be visualized along the spine—although the texts do not agree on their exact locations. The yogi creates them in his or her meditation. They are an aid to achieving higher consciousness. The Western writers, particularly in the Theosophic tradition, described them as a consistent part of our subtle anatomy—as having a physical as well as a psychic reality. They are described as a place where body and soul meet, an inner reality that can be perceived by a clairvoyant.

Since then, Western writers on the chakras have seized on their physical reality, even going as far as relating them to the seven endocrine glands. In our modern conception, the chakras are thought of as energy centers that may be blocked or flowing freely, and their proper functioning is believed to be necessary for psychic and physical health. In reality, we have used the Tantric system to help us rediscover our own Pythagorean system. In 1970 in his book *Nuclear Evolution*, spiritual writer Christopher Hills suggested for the first time that the colors of the spectrum correspond sequentially to the seven chakras. In the Indian texts, we find different color associations for each chakra. Almost all Western books on the chakras since Hills's have used his color association. Our modern system is truly a synthesis of Eastern and Western theories.

In the Buddhist texts, King Mucalinda is said to wrap himself around Buddha's body, but in the statues and paintings Buddha is usually shown sitting on the coils like a throne. These images are created primarily in southeast Asia—particularly Thailand—where they are used as amulets to protect their owner from attacks. A Thai amulet was used as a model for this card.

Here the chakras are depicted as seven internal stars. Each is given a color of the spectrum and the appropriate number of points to correspond to the number of petals on the lotuses that are usually depicted for each chakra. In the sky can be seen the morning star, which represents the third watch, the period of the night in which Buddha reached the highest level of meditation.

Divination

The Chakras card represents the ladder of ascent to a higher state of consciousness. It may represent the stages that are necessary in this ascent, and that it is necessary to go through stages. It may also be a reference to the chakras and to the balance and health that stems from free-flowing unblocked psychic energy. At the mundane level, it represents a breakthrough, an opportunity suddenly becoming available, a calm after a storm, or forgiveness after an argument. It is the calm in the center of our being.

XVIII. Wesak - The Full Moon

To see the world in a grain of sand,
And a Heaven in a wild flower,
Hold infinity in the palm of your hand,
And eternity in an hour.

William Blake

The night after Mara's defeat was Wesak, the night of the full moon in May. It was Gautama's thirty-fifth birthday. Without Mara, Gautama's path was now open. Gautama had begun planning for this moment from the time that he had broken his fast and embraced the middle path. In that moment, he had seen through the folly of excessive sensuality and asceticism, but he then had to decide how to proceed in a way that was not on either side, but embraced the middle.

Gautama remembered that when he was a child, his father had taken him to watch the annual festival of the plowing of the fields in the spring. On that day, he had found himself sitting alone under a rose-apple tree that protected him from the sun. As he sat there, he began to notice the dead insects, worms, and grass that had been turned up by the plow and felt sorrow for this destruction. In that moment, he escaped his ego and his sorrow was replaced by a feeling of bliss as he became one with the world. If he could fall into this state of bliss effortlessly as a child, then that was the path he was looking for. In his efforts before this, he was trying to achieve enlightenment for his own sake and, as long as his motivation was selfish, he could not escape his ego. Gautama realized that he had to add the love and compassion of bhakti yoga to his raja practice. Only through compassion could he escape selfishness. When he thought of others, he was no longer thinking of himself.

As Gautama sat there in meditation on that night, he repeated the practice that he had been developing in the days before. First, Gautama evoked the feeling of love and directed it toward the four corners of the world and to every creature in the world, whether a friend or a foe. He developed a sense of friendship with the entire world and he experienced the first Jina, or conqueror. When he had mastered this, he evoked compassion and again directed it to the four directions and to every living being. He empathized with the suffering of the world and this manifested the second Jina. Next, he projected sympathetic joy and again radiated it to the four directions. This created the third Jina. In the fourth stage, he immersed himself in contemplation beyond pleasure and pain and achieved a state of total equanimity in which the distinction between him and the world disappeared. This was the manifestation of the fourth Jina, and with this state, Gautama had reached the end of the first watch, or first third of the night.[12]

In the second watch, Gautama used his divine eye to see the vision of the Wheel of Life in its complete state. He understood the law of karma, and saw how all creatures were held to the endless beginnings and endings of incarnation after incarnation until they could free themselves from the wheel. He remembered all of his past lives and saw the process that led him to this moment. In the third watch, he remembered who he was before his first incarnation. At this moment he woke up. Gautama ceased to exist and in his place was the Buddha. His light radiated to the four corners of the world and the sun began to rise.

Commentary

All of the early Moon cards depict the moon in the upper portion of the card. On the bottom of the card we sometimes find astronomers making measurements or holding a clock, a reference to the moon as the gauge of time. In other decks, we find references to the moon goddess, such as a woman in a long dress holding the moon, or Diana with her hound. On an uncut sheet of sixteenth-century Italian printed cards in the Yale library, we can see one of the oldest examples of the design made popular by the Tarot of Marseilles in which a crayfish climbs out of a pool reaching for the moon. In the French versions, two dogs are added. The crayfish relates to the constellation Cancer, the native house of the moon, and the dogs are Diana's companions in mythology. The Marseilles Moon suggests the presence of Diana without showing her.

In the early hand-painted decks, the moon is depicted as a crescent, its most characteristic shape. In the early woodblock decks, a face is added to the crescent. This addition completes the circle and transforms the crescent into a full moon. This is the way that it is depicted in the Tarot of Marseilles.

It may seem odd that the Tarot of Marseilles depicts the seven planets, which includes the moon and the sun, on the Star card, and then depicts the moon and the sun on separate cards again. However, this is exactly how these symbols are used in alchemical texts. We find that although the moon and sun are part of the ladder of ascent, they also represent the feminine and masculine principles. The feminine force is passive and associated with the night. The masculine force is active and associated with the day. As rulers of the night and the day, the moon and the sun are the ultimate timekeepers. In alchemical texts they are singled out as symbols of the dual forces that must be harmonized for spiritual progress. Also, the brilliance of the full moon and the even greater light of the sun symbolize the growing radiance of the process of enlightenment. The moon represents the time of night and rest. This is when Buddha withdrew deep within himself and allowed the process of enlightenment to proceed. The sun represents the result made visible, its radiance being compared to the light of the sun.

The Buddha on this Moon card is in one of the most common poses in Buddhist art. He is sitting cross-legged with his hands in the mudra of meditation and his eyes closed. He has put his physical body to rest and is journeying within. The moon on this card is directly based on one of the oldest Italian-printed Moon cards.

Divination

The Moon represents unconditional love, compassion, forgiveness, night, a time of rest, and meditation. This is not a time to go forward; it is a time to rest and recuperate, to love ourselves as well as others. It is a time for reflection and to turn inward. To meditate is to relax and let go of our hopes and fears. When we let the clutter in our minds settle, we find our true mind. Inside we can also find tranquility and strength.

XIX. Buddha and Sakti - The Sun

Complextion is of complextion between two lights, male and female, and then they embrace themselves and couple together, and a perfect light is begotten between them, which there is no light like through all the world.

Rosarium Philosophorum, an alchemical text

As the sun came up on the morning of Wesak, Buddha was born. By completing the meditation of the third watch, Buddha had also manifested the fifth and most essential Jina ("conqueror"), the Jina of the sacred center called *Vairocana*.

Buddhahood is a totality. It is to be eternally one with the cosmos. Each Jina is a manifestation of that totality, but it also has a specific focus that gives a Jina individuality. Each Jina is part of Buddha, but he can also be thought of as a separate Buddha with an individual wisdom. There is a Jina for each of the four cardinal directions and there is a Jina for the center. Buddha is both masculine and feminine because he or she is beyond duality. However, the masculine and feminine aspects of Buddha can also manifest as separate Buddhas. The feminine Buddha is called a Sakti. Each Jina has a female half that is his Sakti. In the east, there is the Jina Aksobhya with his Sakti Locana; their color is blue and their element is air. To the south, there is Ratnasambhava and his Sakti Mamaki; their color is yellow and their element is earth. In the west, we find Amitabha and his Sakti Pandara; their color is red and their element is fire. In the north, there is Amoghasiddhi and Tara; their color is green and their element is water. In the center of all the Jinas in the center of the world, there is Vairocana and his Sakti Vajradharisvari; their color is pure white and their element is the celestial aether, the element of the stars.

To be a Buddha is to be in a state of eternal bliss. This bliss has two aspects: love and wisdom. Each Buddha is an expression of a particular love, and his Sakti is an expression of the complementary wisdom. In the bliss of Buddhahood, these two aspects are eternally locked together. As a symbol of this joined duality, and to express the blissfulness of their existence, each Jina is pictured existing in a sexual embrace with his Sakti. Tantric Buddhism teaches us that the seeds of this masculine and feminine spirit exist in each individual as a red and a white essence that is present in the body from birth. Through yogic practices, the essences are stirred, and yogis describe this experience in the following way:

> Bliss arises when the inner fire blazes throughout the body . . . [and] when the male and female essences unite in the heart . . . the whole body is suffused with undefiled rapture.[13]

As the sun rose, Vairocana was completely manifested and Gautama was indistinguishable from Vairocana. Vairocana's name means "the illuminator" and his symbol is the sun. Vairocana's skin is luminous and white and he is the sun of the spiritual universe, brighter than the physical sun and radiating the light of truth to all corners of the world. His Sakti, Vajradharisvari, is the space that embraces that light. Her name means "lady of the sphere of infinite space." Vairocana and Vajradharisvari are as inseparable as light and space. In the sacred Vedas of India, the name *Vairocana* is an epithet of the sun.

In the final addition to the Vedas, the Upanishads, we find a description of enlightenment that will help to explain another aspect of Buddhahood. The Chandogya Upanishad tells us that for the enlightened one, when the sun reaches the "zenith it will neither rise nor set any more. It will remain alone in the center."[14] The rising and setting of the sun represent time, and for the sun to stand still at the height of the day represents the sacred center of time. Buddha exists in the center of time as well as the center of space. For him, all time is one and all space is his body. This was his condition from the beginning before the wheel of time was set in motion.

Commentary

As a fitting counterpart to the Moon cards, the early Sun cards consistently display an image of the masculine celestial orb. On the lower half we may find an angelic child, called a *putto,* holding the sun or the sun god Apollo. The hand-painted deck made for the noble D'Este family depicts the Cynic philosopher Diogenes living in a barrel and asking Alexander the Great to move so as not to block the sunlight. In the Minchiate, as in some later decks, we find lovers on this card. In the hand-painted Gringonneur deck, as well as some early printed decks, there is a woman with a distaff, a stick used for winding wool, in her lap. This image seems to relate to the image of the goddess Necessity that we find in the myth of the soul's journey in the last chapter of Plato's *Republic.* In Plato's myth, the cosmos is described as a distaff or spindle in the lap of Necessity. The thread on her distaff suggests the role of her daughters, the three Fates, who would pull a thread to measure the life of each mortal and cut it when that life ended. As the measure of time, the moon and the sun are related to mortality and fate.

In the Tarot of Marseilles, we find a human-faced sun radiating above two youths wearing loincloths. Because of their youth and their clothing, their sex cannot be determined. However, on some of the earliest seventeenth-century versions of this image, and in a card from Sforza Castle dated circa 1700, they are clearly older male and female figures, with breasts depicted on the female. The youths may represent a male and female joined together in innocence in a new golden age. Some have suggested that they are the brothers Castor and Pollux, of the Gemini constellation, or the founders of Rome, Romulus and Remus. Although Castor and Pollux had the same mother (Leda), Castor's father was mortal, which made Castor mortal, and Pollux's father (Zeus) was immortal, which made Pollux immortal.

In the myth of the founders of Rome, we find the same polarity. In the myth of Romulus and Remus, they are born of a vestal virgin who was raped by the god Mars. Later they were exposed to the elements, but the twins were saved by a she-wolf. After the brothers founded Rome, Remus died, but his brother never did. After forty years of rule, Romulus vanished and became the god Quirinus.

So whether the pair is masculine or feminine or mortal and immortal, they represent the joining of opposites. They are personifications of the sun and moon being joined. This is what the alchemists call the *greater conjunction*. An alchemical description of the greater conjunction is provided in the quotation above. This quotation demonstrates the masculine and feminine sexual symbolism that the alchemists used to describe the state of unity that precedes the final mystical state.

In Buddhist art, we find this same sexual symbolism for the highest mystical state of unity and bliss. On this Sun card, Vairocana and his Sakti Vajradharisvari are sitting in a yogic posture of sexual embrace that is called *yab-yum,* which means "father-mother." The sun above is based on the sun in the same Italian deck that provided the model for the Moon card.

Divination

This card represents completeness, love, harmony, and peace. It can depict a state of self-satisfaction, especially when derived from bringing two polarities together in harmony, such as a peace treaty, a partnership, or an ideal marriage. Buddha and his Sakti are like a marriage of the conscious and the unconscious, or soul mates. To be bathed in sunlight is to be one with the world, to be loved. It also allows us to see clearly, as if the lights were turned on. Sunrise is the time to wake up and let go of illusions.

XX. The First Sermon - Judgement

The soul, then, as being immortal, and having been born again many times, and having seen all things that are, whether in this world or in the world below, has knowledge of them all . . . all inquiry and all learning is but recollection.

Socrates, in Plato's Meno

After his enlightenment, Buddha stayed near the Diamond Throne meditating, bathing, and purifying himself for seven weeks. At the end of this time, a choice was presented to him. Once again, Mara visited Buddha for one last try to stop Buddha's teachings from reaching the world.[15]

"Buddha, this exalted state that you have achieved is unique throughout the world," Mara said. "Even I have to admit that it is a marvelous accomplishment. You have achieved a state that is so far above ordinary consciousness that I doubt any other humans, with their vision clouded with the dust of ignorance, as you know, would be able to comprehend it. I doubt that anyone would even be able to appreciate it. If you were to teach, I am afraid that your words would fall on deaf ears. It would be better for you to sit here in silence, and when your body is gone, there will only be Nirvana, the absolute. This would be a just reward for all of your efforts."

Buddha saw that there was some truth in Mara's words. He doubted if people would be able to understand a truth so sublime and abstract. As he sat there, he pondered. "Would it be worth it to teach?" he asked himself. "Is the nature of truth too much for people to comprehend?"

However, as Buddha sat there, a great light appeared in front of him. From this light, the god Brahma, Lord of a Thousand Worlds, appeared. Then Brahma began to speak. "Buddha, you must preach the truth that you have discovered. Some are ready to listen," he pleaded.

While Brahma spoke to him, Buddha had a vision. He saw a pond with many lotuses. Some held their flowers up above the surface of the water where they could blossom in the sunlight. Others were too short or tangled in the muck at the bottom of the pond—their buds would never reach the sunlight. But another third of the plants were between these two extremes. Some were just below the surface and beginning to blossom. Buddha realized that the sun was like the truth. There were some who already knew the truth, and some who were prisoners to the mud of ignorance. Then there were those who were nearing the truth and needed his help.

Buddha left the center of the world and looked for his first students. He realized that of the people he knew, his two former teachers were closest to the truth, but with his inner eye he saw that they had already died. Next he thought of his five former disciples. He saw that they were staying in Deer Park, so he made his way there.

On the way to Deer Park, Buddha came across an old acquaintance, a Jain ascetic named Upaka. Upaka noticed the radiance and serenity in Buddha's face and inquired, "Who is your master now, Gautama, and what teaching are you following?"

Buddha replied that he had no teacher. "I have followed my own path . . . and reached enlightenment," he added.

Upaka could not believe what he had heard. "Are you saying that you are a Buddha?" he asked incredulously. Upaka walked away shaking his head. Buddha continued on his journey undisturbed.

As Buddha approached Deer Park, his former disciples saw him coming. At first they were not happy to see him. When Buddha had broken his fast, they believed that he had abandoned his search and they felt betrayed. But as he came closer, they could see the serenity and glowing acceptance in his face. They felt waves of peace emanating from his aura. They were won over by his presence and each decided to listen to what he had to say.

Buddha sat down and delivered his first sermon. It was the full moon of Ashadha, which is our July. For the first watch of the night, Buddha sat in silence. In the second watch, he explained that excessive asceticism would not lead to enlightenment. In the third watch, Buddha listed for the first time the Four Noble Truths.

"All life is dukkha. It is off-center, it is like an illness. The cause of dukkha is *tanha,* or selfish desire. The cure to life's illness, or *dukkha,* is to let go of tanha. The method for overcoming tanha is called the *Eightfold Path.* The eight essentials are the development of right knowledge, healthy desire, truthfulness, virtuous behavior, right livelihood, perseverance, self-awareness, and the practice of meditation. When these eight essential elements are developed in one's life, one will proceed to enlightenment."

Then Buddha fully explained each part of the Eightfold Path. These eight elements are like the eight spokes of a wheel, and this wheel came to be called the *Dharmachakra,* the "Wheel of the Law."

With this sermon, Buddha set the Wheel of the Law into motion. This gave humanity a replacement for the wheel of fate, a path out of death and toward eternal life. His five disciples saw that Buddha spoke the truth and they became the first members of the Buddhist *sangha,* or community.

Commentary

In the hand-painted Italian decks, we find on this card two angels with trumpets hovering over open graves with three to seven men and women waking from their death. This card in the Visconti-Sforza deck and one card that was a copy from that deck are the only ones to add God the Father to the scene. In the printed decks, the image becomes more uniform. There is one trumpeting angel above and two to four emerging from the graves. The Tarot of Marseilles contains the same image, with the number of figures rising fixed at three: two men and a woman. This is clearly a depiction of the Christian Last Judgment, when the dead are called from their graves to eternal life and their final reward or punishment. It is a Christian icon representing victory over death. In alchemical symbolism and to the more esoteric mind, it can also symbolize rebirth or rejuvenation.

In the Florentine Minchiate, this card is Fame, an allegory that is also commonly depicted as an angel with a trumpet. Fame represents one's personal reputation and accomplishment as a victory over death, but in Petrarch's *I Trionphi,* discussed in chapter 2, we see that he was not satisfied with this shallow victory. His allegory presses on to eternal life in the presence of God.

To mystics, life seems like a state of sleep or death. In Plato's works, for example, we find a description of life as a tomb. Also in the *Apology,* he has Socrates describe himself as a gadfly sent by God to wake up the Athenians with his annoyance. All great mystical teachers are like the angels of Judgment. They call out to us in an attempt to wake us from our sleep of delusion and from the grave of ignorance. Buddha is one of these angels and in Deer Park he resurrected his first five disciples.

On our card, Buddha sits between the polarities of the sun and moon as a third and greater illuminator. His hands are in the mudra of teaching. This is the mudra associated with Vairocana. This image is one the four essential icons of the life of Buddha. Below are his five disciples being called up to the truth. In the center is the golden Wheel of the Law—another symbol of Vairocana. As in many Buddhist icons of this symbol, the wheel is flanked by a pair of deer facing into it, although they often look more like antelopes. These are a reference to Deer Park, where the sermon took place. However, a pair of animals facing a central object or point is the most ancient form for depicting the archetypal sacred center. The Wheel of the Law has four elaborated points, which are the Four Noble Truths. It has eight spokes, which represent the Eightfold Path. In the center there are three jewels, colored red, yellow, and blue. These represent the Three Jewels of Buddhism: the Buddha, the Dharma (teaching), and the Sangha (community). Buddha presented these three jewels as a refuge for one on a Buddhist path and as a cure for the three poisons found in the center of the Wheel of Life.

Divination

This card is a call to wisdom and to a higher state of being. It is a wake-up call. On a worldly level, this card signifies calling up the past, making decisions based on our experience, or simply reminiscing. It can also refer to revitalizing parts of ourselves that we have blocked or denied. It is the universal medicine. It can represent teaching and a path that is made available to us. It is sound judgment. It is an offer of help.

XXI. WHITE TARA - THE WORLD

The Nature of God is a Circle of which the center is everywhere and the circumference is nowhere.

Pythagorean philosopher Empedocles

Over the next forty-five years, Buddha's disciples grew in number until they were a large monastic community that included both men and women from all classes of society. Buddha's parents, his wife, his son, his half-brother, and even his cousin became his disciples. Everywhere Buddha went he made converts, and his teachings spread throughout the world. Buddha worked tirelessly because he knew that many would be lost without his teaching. Buddha taught through his words and his actions. He even taught through silence. During one sermon, Buddha simply held a flower in his hand and did not speak.

The Sakti Tara is green, the color of vegetation and the world. Originally she was considered a goddess of fortune. Through Buddha's teachings, a new Tara emerged—a white Tara, the color of the sacred center, of purity, and of the transcendent truth. White Tara moved to the top of Mount Meru where her radiance could reach all areas of the world. She opened her seven eyes and faced east. At her feet, a blue light of wisdom radiated to the east. At her right, a yellow light of beauty radiated to the south. Behind her, the red light of love radiated west. And to her left, the green light of rightful action radiated north. The spiritual mandala and the world were one.

Commentary

The Marseilles World card is a more evolved symbol than the earlier cards. It is a Neoplatonic mandala called a *quincunx*. It represents the individual soul joined with the World Soul deified in the sacred center. The card depicts a beautiful nude standing on one foot, like a Dakini, in the center of an oval wreath. In her right hand she holds a rounded object with a knob on top that looks like a bell. In her left hand she holds a short wand or scepter. These objects are similar to the bell and *vajra* (*rdorje* in Tibetan) scepters that Tibetan monks hold during meditation. They represent the feminine and masculine forces of wisdom and love, the polarities that must be joined to reach enlightenment. The implements on the World card are most likely derived from the orb and scepter that are the symbols of royalty in the West. These symbols have a similar feminine and masculine association. Around her are the symbols of the Four Evangelists from the Christ in Majesty icon. They symbolize the four Gospels of the New Testament, but through their association with the fixed signs of the zodiac, they also symbolize the four directions and the four elements, as can be seen in Chart 5.

White Tara is similar to the figure of the World Soul. In her original green form she was an earth mother or a goddess of fortune and the Sakti of Amoghasiddhi, the Jina of the north. Now she has moved to

Chart 5

Evangelist	Symbol	Zodiac Sign	Element	Direction	Virtue
Matthew	Human	Aquarius	Air	West	Prudence
Mark	Lion	Leo	Fire	East	Strength
Luke	Bull	Taurus	Earth	North	Temperance
John	Eagle	Scorpio	Water	South	Justice

the center and is purified and white. She is the world made beautiful by the truth of Buddha's vision. Her seven eyes—three on her face and one on the palm of each hand and the sole of each foot—are the seven chakras that have opened and that allow clear vision. She can see into every aspect of reality. She has knowledge of all past, present, and future Buddhas, and can see the past and the future of all humanity. She is a symbol of purity and transcendent knowledge. In her left hand she holds a white lotus, a symbol of purity and tranquility. She stands in the center of the sacred mandala of the world.

The colors that radiate out from Tara to the four cardinal directions are the colors that represent the four Jinas of the cardinal directions. These Buddhas are depicted as the top royal card in each minor suit, and each minor suit is dedicated to them and to their symbols. The borders of these suits are colored with the color from the World card that corresponds to the Buddha of each suit. White Tara can be used as a central key to organize the entire deck into a mandala of the archetypal Buddha. This will be explained in more detail in the final chapter.

Divination

At the highest level, the World represents an attainment of oneness with the universe. This is called *enlightenment*. At its simplest level, she represents what is good or desirable, a more enlightened way of behaving, or the culmination of our goals. Tara is the world made beautiful.

She represents having order and harmony in our lives and maintaining balance. This card can be called the Good. She nurtures all people and satisfies all needs. She is a cure for the sick and shelter for the poor. She asks us to become her agent in this process.

XXII. Parinirvana

It was on his birthday that he departed life, when he had fulfilled eighty-one years and not a day less. For this reason the Magi who were then in Athens made sacrifice to Plato.

Marsilio Ficino, writing about the death of Plato

In his eightieth year, Buddha's body grew weak and he knew that he was reaching the end of his human existence. Although he had gathered many dedicated followers and spread truth in the world, the kingdoms of India were still mired in egotistical struggles and the Ganges valley was in a constant state of war. Even within Buddha's sangha (his religious community), there had been egotistical struggles for power. The great orator Devadatta, who was Buddha's brother-in-law and who had become a disciple, had grown resentful of Buddha's control of the sangha. Devadatta wanted to become the leader of the sangha instead of Buddha. But Buddha did not think of himself as a leader, only as a teacher. Buddha did not feel that monks needed a leader. He urged each of them to follow their own guidance and to not take anything that he had said on faith, but to find out for themselves if it led to truth. He denounced Devadatta for his egotism and Devadatta left the sangha.

Devadatta now tried to take over by force. He made an alliance with an ambitious young prince and acquired the aid of royal assassins, whom he sent to kill Buddha. But every assassin that he sent was won over by the aura of love that surrounded the Buddha and became a member of the sangha instead. Devadatta gave up his murderous plot, but managed to convince a faction of the sangha to leave and follow his leadership.

Now in his eightieth year, Buddha, whom devils and assassins could not kill, was dying of old age. Knowing that he would not be there for his disciples much longer, he worked diligently to clarify his teaching and to stress that this dharma, or teaching, was the true teacher, not Buddha the man. He visited all of the communities that he had founded and prepared them for his end.

In May, Buddha arrived in Papa and was invited to dinner at the house of Cunda, the blacksmith. For dinner, Cunda served Buddha a "pork treat." Some say it was the meat of a pig, others say that it was a dish of mushrooms that were dug up by pigs. The treat pushed Buddha over the edge into fatal illness. Buddha made a last painful trip from Papa to Kusinagara. When he arrived, he had his faithful servant Ananda prepare a bed for him in a grove by the river.

Buddha lay on his right side with his head to the north. The flowering trees began to blossom and the full moon rose. It was Wesak, Buddha's eightieth birthday. He instructed his disciples throughout the night. During the third watch, he ended his sermon with the words: "All compounds grow old. Work out your own salvation with diligence."[16] After this speech, the life of the historic Buddha came to an end, but the true body of the Buddha—the Dharma Body—was eternally present.

After his death, the Buddha's teachings were handed down by word of mouth from one Buddhist to another. The practice of yoga had given the monks highly developed memories and they had diligently memorized the Buddha's discourses. Sometimes they set them to verse or sang them as an aid to memory. When three generations had passed, the monks began to write down these discourses, and this became the basis of the Buddhist sutras.

By the third century BCE, the endless warfare of the Indian kings led to one victor who established an empire over all of India—like the legendary chakravartin. His name was Asoka. Asoka was so sickened by the violence that he had caused in creating his empire, that he embraced the teaching of the Buddha as his cure for the angst in his soul. He became a devout Buddhist and initiated a legendary golden age of peace and devotion. All over India he set up columns commemorating the dharma. Asoka founded monasteries and sent missionaries to spread Buddha's words to the other countries of the known world. He spread the dharma through Asia and as far as Europe and Africa.

Commentary

There is no twenty-third card in the fifth suit of the traditional Tarot, although there are forty-nine cards in this suit in the Minchiate and there may have been other quantities in the earliest decks. After I made *The Alchemical Tarot* with my coauthor Rosemary Ellen Guiley, Rosemary had a vision. In the middle of the night, Hermes Trismegistus came and stood at the foot of her bed holding a large Tarot card with a mystical pyramid on it labeled "Truth." Hermes told her that it was the twenty-third card of the fifth suit. I made a painting of that image as it was described to me by Rosemary, and since then I have been considering adding an additional trump to my decks.

In one of the early known orders for the trumps, the Judgement card comes after the World card. The Parinirvana card can be thought of as another version of the Judgement card. Nirvana is the ultimate state of enlightenment, and the Parinirvana represents the historic Buddha's physical death and his attainment of the total state of oneness. *Nirvana* means "to extinguish," like the flame of a candle, but what is extinguished is separateness and illusion. The Parinirvana is one of the four essential icons of the life of Buddha, which is why I did not want to leave it out of this story. Any statues or paintings of the Buddha lying on his side are a representation of the Parinirvana.

Divination

The Parinirvana is the ultimate reward. It is the trust that when something comes to an end there is a new beginning, a rebirth, and that when all rebirths come to an end there is eternal life. Its most basic meaning is a move up or the receipt of a reward. It tells us that we are more than our limits, to relax and be our better self. On the card Buddha appears to be dreaming, but he is really becoming totally awake.

Chapter 6

THE WORLD OF THE FOUR BUDDHAS

Each of the minor suits in *The Buddha Tarot* is assigned to one of the four Buddhas of the cardinal directions called *Jinas*. The royal cards contain the Buddha as the King, his Sakti as his Queen, his Guardian Animal as the Knight, and his Dakini as the Page. In Buddhist iconography, each of the Jinas is assigned a magical implement as his symbol. He is also assigned a color, a cardinal direction, and an element. The four implements make a natural substitution for the traditional suit symbols in the Tarot. They have been equated to the traditional Tarot symbols through the elemental association that they both share: vajras for swords, jewels for coins, lotuses for staffs, and double vajras for cups. Surprisingly, the Buddhist symbols are a good match for the traditional suit symbols. The borders of each suit display the color that is associated with each Jina and make the suits easily identifiable. For a more detailed discussion of these relationships, read chapter 4.

The pip cards in the Tarot originally displayed only a repetition of the suit symbol appropriate to the number on each card, from one to ten. Since the Waite-Smith deck was published in 1910, pip cards in modern Tarots have typically contained a scene that illustrates the divinatory meaning. *The Buddha Tarot* combines these two traditions. All of the pips in *The Buddha Tarot* contain a repetition of suit symbols, and from Two to Ten they have an additional illustration that pertains to the meaning. The meaning of each pip is determined by numerical symbolism combined with associations derived from the suit symbol and its elemental and psychological connection. The meanings associated with the pips are Western. However, Buddhist symbols and concepts are used to illustrate the meaning of each card. The symbols used include all of the Eight Lucky Symbols that were given to Siddhartha at his birth and on other occasions by the gods; the five mudras, or hand gestures, of the Five Jinas; and the three poisons from the Wheel of Life.

ACE OF VAJRAS

The vajra (*rdorje* in Tibetan) is the symbol of Aksobhya, the blue Buddha of the east and the element air. In some Buddhist icons, Aksobhya's color is white. When that is the case, blue is assigned to the sacred center. The vajra, as we see in the card, is a short scepter with a pronged point at each end. This is a three-pronged vajra, but they may have from one to nine prongs. *Vajra* means "thunderbolt." In Hindu tradition, it was the weapon of the god Indra, and similar weapons have been found on ancient Mesopotamian carvings. In Buddhism, it is the weapon of Aksobhya, who is the Buddha of wisdom. His vajra represents the power of knowledge over ignorance. It is a weapon against evil thoughts and desires.

It is fitting that this weapon should be connected with the sword of the Tarot. Both weapons are associated with air. Aces represent a new beginning. In this case, it may be a new idea or a positive direction. This card represents positive thinking and constructive ideas. Words are connected to thoughts, and this card also represents affirmations. This suit is associated with the thinking function of Jungian psychology and with jnana yoga.

Two of Vajras

On the Two of Vajras we find the Dharmachakra mudra. This is the hand gesture of teaching or debate. It is associated with Buddha setting the Wheel of the Law into motion in Deer Park, and with the white Jina of the center, Vairocana. The index finger and thumb touching symbolize a point being made. Usually in icons the other hand would display an open palm or the index finger pointing up to reinforce the point. Here there are two points being made. This card represents a debate. This is a debate of words; a calm attempt to find truth, not a power struggle engendered by negative emotions. Each opinion must be respected, and everyone involved must be free to accept or reject what is said based on his or her own experience. This is how Buddha expected his teachings to be received. Do not take what is said on faith.

Three of Vajras

In the Waite-Smith Tarot we find three swords piercing a heart on this card. Smith derived this image from a Renaissance Three of Swords card found in the Sola Busca deck. The Sola Busca is a fifteenth-century engraved deck that contains images on the pips but a different allegory on the trumps. In keeping with the theme of pain in the heart, this card contains an image based on an illustration from the Tibetan healing tantras. It is called *The Blue Beryl,* and it depicts an arrow-wound to the heart. This card represents pain and suffering. The wound to the heart suggests emotional suffering. Buddha taught that suffering is unavoidable in life. Through suffering, one learns to empathize with the suffering of others. In this light, suffering is love. It is better not to deny suffering. Let it run its course; you will heal.

FOUR OF VAJRAS

Four is the number of physical manifestation, and this is the suit of air and of thought. The material world generates from the immaterial world. Everything that we create stems from our thoughts, and our thoughts rise from unseen depths from within our unconscious. This is the process we observe when we meditate. Through meditation, we bring concentration and freedom to this creative process and re-create our lives. This is a card of meditation.

The hands on this card are in Dhyana mudra, the hand gesture symbolizing meditation. This is the mudra associated with Amitabha, the red Jina of the west. The thumbs joining form a triangle in relation to the hands. This is a symbol of the mystic fire of Amitabha. From this fire, like an emerging thought, the white lotus rises. This is one of the Eight Glorious Emblems of Buddha. It symbolizes peace, tranquility, and spontaneous generation.

Five of Vajras

This is another scene from the Tibetan *The Blue Beryl*. A healer takes a man's pulse to determine how to proceed to cure him. Pulse diagnosis is practiced in China and Tibet. Its origins are from before the time that Buddhism entered both of these countries. The doctor has attuned himself to the subtle energies in his patient's body, and from their rhythms he can gather detailed information about the patient's health.

This card represents someone or something that needs healing or fixing. It also represents the ability to heal or fix.

SIX OF VAJRAS

The Precious Umbrella is one of the Eight Glorious Emblems that were given to Siddhartha by the gods. The Precious Umbrella was one that was given at the time of his birth. In ancient India it was a symbol of royalty. Servants would hold the umbrella over Siddhartha to protect him from sun and rain, and one of his titles was "Lord of the White Umbrella." Some icons of Siddhartha's life include the umbrella being held over him. For several hundred years after Buddha's death he was not depicted in art. Instead, objects like the umbrella were depicted as symbols of his presence.

This card denotes protection from harm, illness, and obstacles. This protection comes from a higher power. We should go with the flow. The Precious Umbrella of Buddha was said to protect him from all evil and to offer shade from the heat of evil desires.

Seven of Vajras

In the scene on this card we see a warehouse with cushions and jewels stored inside. A thief is leaving with a bag of jewels. His suspicious glance gives him away. This card represents dishonesty.

The Five Precepts tell to avoid dishonesty of various kinds. We are told not to steal, not to lie, and not to cheat on our spouse. These rules are not for the sake of others, but for our own sake. These negative actions stem from the false belief that we can prosper from the misfortunes of others. This ignorant behavior separates us from others and does violence to our ability to become one with the world. However, it is not enough to refrain from negative behavior; we must cultivate positive behavior instead. Instead of not stealing, we must develop generosity; instead of not lying, we must develop truthfulness; and instead of not cheating, we must develop contentment.

If a dishonest action is not engendered by negative selfish interest, then it does not fall into the same category. For example, if we stole a weapon from a would-be killer to stop him from killing, this is not a negative action. If the reading is referring to this kind of action, it is describing a heroic act. Look for what is being stolen and why.

Eight of Vajras

On this card we find a Tibetan dog tethered to a stake. The dog is a Tibetan spaniel, a small dog with a loud bark that has been bred in Buddhist monasteries since before the sixth century. Supposedly they were watchdogs. Because the dog's freedom is curtailed, she strains at the end of her leash. One might imagine that if her leash were untied, she would turn around and eat the food in the dish instead of running away. She is not straining because she wants to go somewhere else, but because she cannot accept the restriction of her leash.

Our psychic energy is like this when we restrain it by trying to hold on to past expectations and patterns instead of living in the present. Every situation requires a unique approach. If we were in a relationship and it ended badly, it does not mean that all relationships will end badly. If we had an uncomfortable relationship with our parents, it does not mean that all our relationships with figures of authority will be uncomfortable. This card represents restraint. It may refer to a psychic block. This block may also refer to ideas that we think are positive, but that we are still attached to. The Buddha said:

> To be attached to a certain view and to look down upon other views as inferior—this the wise call a fetter.[1]

Nine of Vajras

A dragon swallows the sun and the moon. A dream or vision of this nature is believed to foretell a serious threat or illness. This card represents fear of the future. In the Lotus Sutra, Buddha told the story of a man who, when he became drunk at his friend's house, fell into a deep sleep. While he was asleep, his friend sewed a precious jewel into his clothes as a present to him. The next morning the man continued on his travels. Eventually he reached a foreign land where, because of the fear of hunger and cold, he worked as a slave. During the time that he slaved and worked at difficult tasks, he did not realize that he owned a precious jewel that could buy him any comfort. We are all like this man. We fear more than we need to, and therefore make ourselves more uncomfortable than we need to. Work should be constructive, not fearful.

Ten of Vajras

A ten-headed demon curses a man. Demons of this nature bring illness and misfortune. In Tibetan medicine, diseases are commonly attributed to demons that arise from the environment. As some of these environmental demons are associated with certain occupations and the workplace, and others are unseen forces of nature, we might think of them as pollutants and allergens. However, the Tibetan doctor is able to cure their effects through ritual. This card represents misfortune that has come to us apparently through no fault of our own.

Buddha's teaching is the ultimate cure. When we have attained wisdom and clarity of mind, all demons depart because all demons are born of our hopes and fears. Everything in the world is intimately connected to our minds.

Vajradakini - The Dakini of Vajras

In Tantric Buddhism, Dakinis are dancing goddesses. Their name is derived from the Sanskrit word for space. Their name in Tibetan, *Khandroma,* means "sky-walker." The space that the Dakini dances in with such freedom and abandon is the mind. Each Dakini is a representation of an aspect of a Buddha manifesting in the world through our minds. They are like the Anima Mundi of Western alchemy.

Vajradakini is the manifestation of Aksobhya. She holds his vajra in her right hand. Because Aksobhya favors wrathful manifestations, she is sometimes shown holding a skull cup or standing on a corpse. She is the manifestation of wisdom in one's psyche. She is a good idea or clear, unobstructed thinking.

THE ELEPHANT - THE ANIMAL OF VAJRAS

The elephant is a symbol of strength and wisdom. In ancient India, elephants were used for heavy labor and as moving fortresses in battle. They were royal symbols of power, strength, and universal sovereignty. In Hinduism, they were associated with the royal god Indra. In the West, also, the elephant is credited with great wisdom. It is said that an elephant never forgets. In a mystic sense, to not forget is to awaken from our sleep of forgetfulness and remember who we are. The elephant's massive presence represents the unmovable power and presence of wisdom. This card represents power, memory, and wisdom.

Locana - The Sakti of Vajras

Locana is the blue Sakti of the east and the consort of Aksobhya. She shares his throne. Her name means "the clear-visioned one" or "the one with the eye." She is the embodiment of pure awareness of the truth. It is because her pure awareness is inseparable from Aksobhya that his wisdom is unshakable. All Saktis are an embodiment of wisdom and this is the suit of wisdom. Locana's wisdom is absolute awareness, absolute knowledge. She is the bedrock of wisdom.

Locana holds a lotus—the symbol of purity—in her left hand, and with her right she expresses a mudra that is a combination of teaching and giving. Her lessons are her gift. Locana helps us to live up to the first precept: to refrain from harming any living creature, and to develop kindness. She teaches us to accomplish this by meditating on the deliberate, mindful development of compassion and to visualize sending this compassion out to all living beings. This is the antidote for the poison of anger. It is through positive direction that we gain mastery, not through fighting with our negative thoughts.

Aksobhya - The Buddha of Vajras

Aksobhya is the blue Jina of the east, the land of the rising sun. The growing radiance of the rising sun is one of his symbols. His name means "immovable." His name is Ashuku Nyorai in Japanese, Achu in Chinese, and Mibskyodpa in Tibetan. What is immovable and unshakable about him is his trust and confidence. His trust stems from wisdom, from direct knowledge of the One, not from theory. All Buddhas represent love, but Aksobhya represents the love of wisdom, which is what it means to be a philosopher. To demonstrate his immovable trust and wisdom, he is performing the Victory mudra that Gautama used when he conquered Mara, and his throne is supported by the strongest and wisest of animals: the elephant. His emblem is the vajra, the ancient thunder weapon of the gods, and he is the head of the Vajra family of Bodhisattvas and Buddhas. His family contains more wrathful Buddhas, called *Herukas,* than any other Jina. This card represents wisdom, confidence, and mastery of the thinking function, which is related to the element air.

Ace of Jewels

In Sanskrit this is called *cintamani,* which is the "wish-granting jewel." It is the symbol of Ratnasambhava, the yellow Buddha of the south and the element earth. The jewel is a ball of precious stone with a point on top. It is often shown sitting on a lotus, and may have flames emanating from it—a symbol of its power. Its origins can be found in the legend of the chakravartin where it was one of his seven jewels. The seven jewels are likely to be a reference to the seven metals of alchemy, but the cintamani has more in common with the alchemical Philosopher's Stone. Like the alchemical stone, this jewel has the power to grant any wish. In Buddhist symbolism, it is the tool of Ratnasambhava, the Buddha of beauty. His gem can satisfy any desire, but its ultimate power is the ability to bring freedom from desire through understanding and tranquility. Sometimes the jewel is represented as a group of three jewels. This is a reference to the Three Jewels that Buddha presented as a cure for the three poisons: the Buddha, the Dharma, and the Sangha.

Here, the jewel is equated to the coin of the Tarot, another symbol of value that is associated with earth. The equivalent French suit symbol in modern playing cards is the diamond, another gem. This Ace represents a beginning that has to do with physical aspects of our life. It can represent money, a job, a physical relationship with a sexual partner, or a cure for an ailment. It can represent having our desires satiated, but its highest meaning is the overcoming of desire. This suit is associated with the sensation function of Jungian psychology and with karma yoga.

Two of Jewels

Two hands reach up. The moon is in the left hand and the sun is in the right. This card represents polarity and a situation that is fixed, stagnant, or in a dormant stage. The sun represents the masculine, yang force, and the moon the feminine, yin force. When these two forces mingle, we have a flow of energy that brings health. In Chinese medicine this is called *chi*. In all things in nature, the forces of yin and yang are mingled in numerous and subtle ways—they become indistinguishable. Here the forces are clearly identified and they are in their own place. This is stagnation and polarization. The Chinese oracle *I Ching* tells us that when we have stagnation, creativity ceases, but it also comforts us with the truth that the way of nature is to work against stagnation. This state cannot last. It contains great potential for creativity and this cannot remain stuck for long.

Three of Jewels

Three is the number of creativity. On this card an artist draws a Buddha with pen and ink. He is working on an icon that is part of an established tradition. This card represents creative work, art, and concentrated study or focus. It also represents having both spiritual and material support in this work.

In Buddhism, art is the gateway to the inner truth, and the artist both heals and instructs with his or her work. Through carefully constructed mandalas, the artist manifests the true spiritual world and provides a map of the psyche that can be used as a guide in meditation. By learning to create precisely proportioned Buddhas, the artist manifests the spiritual essence of each Buddha and each pose. This is a magical act.

Four of Jewels

Four is a number of physical manifestation and this is the suit of jewels, which relate to the element earth and are therefore also physical. This card is too heavily grounded. The man in the picture is hoarding his jewels. We must determine if he is wisely saving his wealth for its creative potential, or if he is a miser who has lost the true understanding of his possession. Most often he is stingy. Buddhist literature warns that this type of wealth may not profit one at all.

> But by charity, goodness, restraint, and self-control man and woman alike can store up a well-hidden treasure—a treasure which cannot be given to others and which robbers cannot steal—that is the treasure which will not leave one.[2]

Five of Jewels

The man in the picture is sick and begging for help. This card represents illness and poverty. This condition is a manifestation of an inner imbalance. The man in the picture is engulfed in blue-green flames. In Tibetan medicine this does not represent a fever and heat, but the cool flame of a wind imbalance. In the Ayurvedic healing of India and Tibet, the ancient elements are seen as dynamic systems in the body, called the three *doshas: vata* for air, *pitta* for fire, and *kapha* for water. In Tibet they are called *loong* ("wind"), *tripa* ("bile"), and *beygen* ("phlegm"). Disease occurs when these humors are imbalanced through improper diet, improper behavior, deficiencies, or external influences.

The symptoms of disease are a communication from the unconscious. When these symptoms are worked on in yogic practice, they are aids on the path to enlightenment. As in alchemy, a poison is turned into a healing elixir.

Six of Jewels

A woman is about to share food with a beggar. This card represents generosity. In Buddhism, generosity is the positive dharma that corresponds to the second precept: to refrain from taking what is not ours. When one gives to those in need, one gains spiritual benefits. The Tibetan master Shantideva tells us that:

> Whatever joy there is in the world comes from desiring the happiness of others. Whatever suffering there is comes from desiring happiness for oneself . . . The childish work for their own benefit; the Buddhas work for the benefit of others. Just look at the difference between them![3]

We find similar wisdom in the Christian Bible:

Inasmuch as ye have done it unto one of the least of these my brethren, ye have done it unto me.[4]

Seven of Jewels

In the center of this card we see a stupa with a statue of a Buddha inside. The stupa is a symbol of the axis mundi. The different sections of this tower represent the five elements, and their order demonstrates the descent of spirit into matter. At the top there is a teardrop form that represents Buddha nature descending into the aether. The sun and moon symbolize the aether. Below this, Buddha nature continues its descent into a half-dome representing air, a stack of cones that represents fire, a large dome that represents water, and at the base a rectangular box that represents earth. In meditation, this creative descent can be reversed. Starting from the material state, the yogi contemplates the progressively more subtle states of matter and rises up toward Buddha nature. This is a journey through the chakras as well.

This card represents a progression. We have to go through stages to advance toward our goal. The gifts that are coming to us have to descend through stages as well. This may also be a reference to the chakras.

Eight of Jewels

A blacksmith hammers a red-hot strip of metal. This card represents labor and livelihood. It is repetitive work that earns a living. The Tibetan medical tantras warn us that certain occupations can be harmful to our health. The fumes that a blacksmith breathes can endanger his well-being. Likewise, Buddha warned that certain occupations can be harmful to our spiritual health. The fifth part of the Eightfold Path tells that development of right livelihood is necessary for spiritual progress. By its nature, work is repetitive and time-consuming. By this repetition, whatever is worked on is reinforced in our psyche. It is impossible to progress spiritually if we undermine our practice by spending our working time in activities that are poisonous to our consciousness. Yet, work that is of benefit to others and that is done without attachment becomes a form of yoga. This is the way an artist or craftsperson works when the goal of his or her work is beauty.

NINE OF JEWELS

Nine is a number of perfection, and in the center of this card the Treasure Vase is depicted. This is one of the Eight Glorious Emblems of Buddha, representing gifts that were given to him by the gods. The Treasure Vase is an inexhaustible source of wealth, and represents all of the benefits that one can have in life, longevity, prosperity, and abundance. It also symbolizes rain, which is a key to its deeper meaning. Real wealth is to be in harmony with nature. When our internal systems are in balance and we are in harmony with the seasons of nature, our work prospers and nature continues to provide for our needs. This is endless abundance. In ancient symbolism, the king was the guardian of this vase and therefore of rain. He was responsible for the continued fertility and prosperity of the kingdom. In Buddhist symbolism, the treasure in the vase is the spiritual jewel that takes us beyond desire.

Ten of Jewels

Here we find the rooster that we saw in the center of the Wheel of Life. It represents greed, one of the three poisons that drives the wheel. This card represents going beyond the prosperity of the Nine of Jewels by losing balance. Greed is the belief that one can benefit at the expense of others. This is a delusion. When we imbalance the world through our self-centered desires, everyone suffers. When one individual hoards money by improper activity or unfair deals, money does not circulate properly and real prosperity suffers.

In Ayurvedic medicine, the three poisons of the Wheel of Life are associated with imbalances of the three doshas. Greed creates an imbalance of the air dosha, vata. Conversely, people who are predominately vata are more prone to fall into this poisonous behavior. It may also manifest as worry and sleeplessness. When vata types are in balance, this poison is replaced by singing and laughter.

Ratnadakini - The Dakini of Jewels

Dakinis are goddesses joyously dancing in infinite space. Their name is derived from the Sanskrit word for space, and the space that they dance in is the mind. In the unconscious, our minds are unlimited, and this is where we find the Dakinis, rising up from the endless depths of the unconscious. Each Dakini is a representation of an aspect of a Buddha manifesting in the world through our minds. They are like the Anima Mundi of Western alchemy.

Ratnadakini is the manifestation of Ratnasambhava. She holds his jewel in her right hand. As Ratnasambhava has the power to grant any wish, Ratnadakini is how that power is delivered to us. She is an inspiration that is a divine gift. Act on this inspiration. Do not waste it.

The Horse - The Animal of Jewels

Having a horse for a guardian relates Ratnasambhava to Siddhartha's departure from his palace on the back of his horse, Kantaka. As the gods lifted Kantaka's hooves, he rode through the air. Likewise, Ratnasambhava's horse, called the "Wind-Horse," gallops through the air. It seems that Ratnasambhava's horse is influenced in its symbolism by the mythic horse-dragon or "Long-Horse" of China, who carried the Book of the Law on its back. The Wind-Horse carries the wish-granting jewel on his back, or the three jewels from the center of the Wheel of the Law.

All horses are symbols of speed and energy, but the Wind-Horse symbolizes the psychic energy called *prana*. In Hinduism and Buddhism, this mystical energy is associated with the breath, and breathing exercises are prescribed for the increase of one's prana. Like Siddhartha's steed, prana can carry us to higher states of awareness. This card represents energy, speed, and prana.

Mamaki - The Sakti of Jewels

Mamaki is the yellow Sakti of the south and the consort of Ratnasambhava, whose throne she shares. Her name means "mine-maker." Just as Ratnasambhava is continually giving, Mamaki is continually taking in the sense that she makes everything part of her. However, this is not selfish. It is because she breaks down all distinction between the giver and the recipient that Ratnasambhava can be continually generous. Mamaki's wisdom is that to help others is actually to help ourselves. In Buddha mind, there is no separation between self-interest and empathy.

Mamaki holds two peacock feathers, symbols of beauty. It is believed that the peacock is able to create this beauty by transforming poisons in its body. She makes the world beautiful. Mamaki teaches us to refrain from lying and to develop truthfulness. She also helps us to overcome conceit. To remedy this, she recommends the meditation on the five elements of the body that is described in detail in the last chapter. This card represents sincerity and empathy.

Ratnasambhava - The Buddha of Jewels

Ratnasambhava is the yellow Jina of the south. His name means "the jewel-born one." His name is Hosho Nyorai in Japanese, Baosheng Fo in Chinese, and Rinchenhbyung in Tibetan. Naturally, his emblem is the jewel. His mudra is Varada mudra, the gesture of giving. Sometimes there is one jewel or three jewels in this hand. Ratnasambhava represents beauty and prosperity.

We may think that to be prosperous, we need to hold on to our wealth and to stop it from going out away from us, but Ratnasambhava teaches us the opposite. He is continually giving and he is the embodiment of wealth. If we are truly wealthy, then it is ours to give and we are not the slaves of wealth. Prosperity happens when wealth is allowed to flow to where it is needed. Ratnasambhava is also the master of the flow of prana, the mystical life energy that is associated with breath. His horse, which is called the Wind-Horse, is a symbol of psychic energy called *prana*. Ratnasambhava is the head of the Jewel family of Bodhisattvas and Buddhas. His family includes the god of wealth and the earth goddess. This card represents mastery of the sensation function, which is related to the earth element and which is the key to material creation, comfort, and beauty.

ACE OF LOTUSES

The lotus is the symbol of Amitabha, the red Buddha of the west and the element fire. This flower is one of the most familiar symbols of Buddhism, and may be equated with the Christian rose. The lotus is a symbol of tranquility, purity, and spontaneous generation—hence it also symbolizes divine birth. All Buddhas and Bodhisattvas are depicted sitting or standing on a lotus to signify their divine status and the attainment of tranquility. In Buddha's vision before his first sermon, the stages in the development of the lotus plant symbolized the stages of progress of individuals toward enlightenment. It is said that everyone has a lotus bud in his or her heart, waiting dormant in the mud. The light of truth draws this lotus out of the mud and brings it to full bloom. Amitabha is the Buddha of love.

Lotuses are a good match for the staffs of the Tarot. Staffs are made of wood, the product of a plant, and like the lotus, they are associated with fire. In this suit in the Waite-Smith deck, the staffs or wands bear leaves, which shows that the fire they symbolize is the force of life that drives the leaf to form and the flower to bloom. Aces are a beginning and lotuses can represent a newfound passion or direction. It means that energy will be directed toward a new endeavor or a new love. This suit is associated with the feeling function of Jungian psychology and with bhakti yoga, the yoga of love.

Two of Lotuses

Two women work together as one pouring milk into a large cauldron. This card represents love and harmony between two people, teamwork, and common interest. In Tibet, milk—particularly the milk of the *dri,* the female yak—is considered an ambrosia. Milk is poured into large cauldrons like the one on this card and boiled with equal parts water to enhance its healing power. The milk of cows, goats, sheep, dris, horses, and donkeys is used and turned into yogurt, whey, and butter. These products and the different milks each have specific healing properties. But their healing power is more than physical. Milk is the physical embodiment of love. Clarified butter is used to fuel the altar lamps, and sculptures of butter are made as offerings to the Bodhisattvas and Buddhas.

Three of Lotuses

The man on this card is performing a Tibetan magic ritual designed to renew his life force and heal his body. He has obtained a fish that was captured with the intention of being cooked and eaten and he is returning it to the waters. Birds, cows, sheep, dogs or cats in the animal pound, or any other animal that is imprisoned and is in danger of imminent death can be set free in this way. The effectiveness of this cure stems from the truth that compassion and generosity are more powerful than any herb or medicine. The greatest cure—the true medicine—is inside of us and available at all times. It is our love and compassion. Through love and compassion we are continually renewed. This card represents renewed energy and freedom.

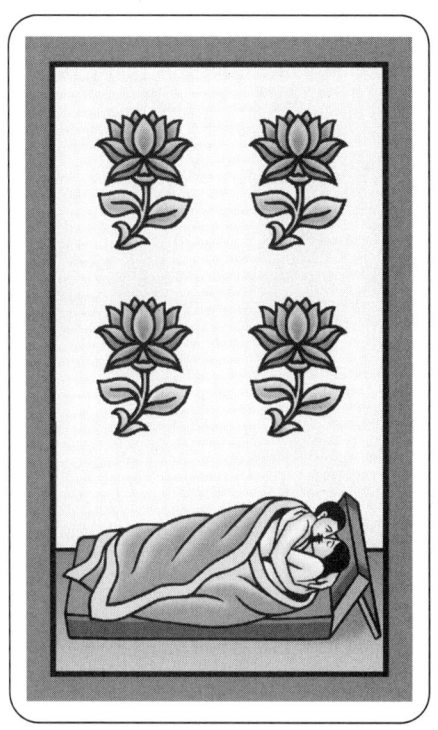

Four of Lotuses

A husband and wife embrace in their bed. Four is the number of physical manifestation and this is the suit of fire and feeling. This card represents commitment to love, faithful partnerships, and other relationships. The fourth of Buddha's Five Precepts warns us not to commit sexual misconduct. This means being true to the commitments one has made. For a monk that could mean celibacy, but for a householder or a married monk it means being true to one's marriage vows. In Tibet, marriages may be between one man and one woman, or a man may have more than one wife or a woman more than one husband. These are all acceptable forms of marriage, and if one is true to the commitments one has made, one is true to the fourth precept. The positive form of this precept is to develop contentment. Without contentment, we cannot really enjoy any relationship. The discontented person is always wishing for something else and not appreciating what he or she has. Without contentment, one does not really have anything.

FIVE OF LOTUSES

This card depicts the Abhaya mudra, the hand gesture that represents protection, benevolence, and peace. This mudra dispels fear. The hand is held at shoulder height and the fingers are together and pointing up. It is a gesture that allows the energy of Buddha mind to flow through the fingers. It demonstrates that the one making the gesture is without fear, and this absence of fear dispels fear in others. This mudra is associated with Amoghasiddhi, the green Jina of the north, and was used by the historic Buddha to calm an attacking elephant. We can find this same hand gesture in most cultures. It is a universal gesture of trust and friendship. It demonstrates that one is unarmed and that one's heart is open. This card represents trust, the unimpeded flow of creative energy, and openness.

Six of Lotuses

On this card we see the Victory Banner. This is one of the Eight Glorious Emblems of Buddha, which were given to him as gifts from the gods. This is a circular banner with a central pole that was erected on the peak of the roof of a palace to declare victory. This card represents being praised for our accomplishments, receiving recognition, and achieving success. In Buddhist symbolism, the banner represents victory on the path to enlightenment, victory over the negative forces in one's ego that would stop progress, and victory over desire and suffering. It also stands for the victory of the Buddha's teachings over forces that would stop it. It is said that the Victory Banner flies from the summit of the palace of salvation.

SEVEN OF LOTUSES

A man attacks a serpent with a large knife. The serpent is anger, one of the three poisons from the center of the Wheel of Life. This card represents anger. By responding to anger with anger, one falls into its poisonous trap. If one lets go of anger by offering it to one's higher self, this energy will become a positive force. By not echoing the anger of others, we may find that their anger will be dispersed. However, it is not enough to let go of anger to be free of it, one must develop the complementary positive quality: kindness. In the martial arts, it is said that the best defense is to develop friendships.

In Ayurvedic medicine, the three poisons of the Wheel of Life are associated with imbalances of the three doshas. Anger creates an imbalance of the fire dosha, pitta, and people who are predominately pitta are more prone to fall into anger. A pitta imbalance may also manifest as an insatiable hunger or thirst. When pitta types are in balance, the poison of anger is replaced by energy and intelligence.

Eight of Lotuses

A man is pruning a shrub. He is cutting it back, but he is also harvesting. This card represents cutting back on our activities or emotions and making use of what we already have. It is not a time to push ahead; it is a time to harvest. In Tibet, every plant is believed to have medicinal value, and a healer must learn the proper time to gather herbs to assure their maximum potency. Leaves such as these are gathered in the summer, fruit in the fall, barks and stems in the spring, and roots are dug up in the winter. The proper attitude is also important. As the harvesting is completed, the proper mantra must be sung to increase the power of the herb. We sometimes think of cutting back on activity as something negative, but when we cut back, we are editing our lives, focusing our energy, and increasing the power of what we accomplish.

Nine of Lotuses

A man with a knife is preparing to sacrifice a bull. This card represents sacrifice. In most ancient cultures, animal sacrifice was the primary form of ritual worship, and examining the entrails of the sacrificed animal was a primary form of divination. In the Axial Age, religious leaders like Buddha and Pythagoras rejected this form of sacrifice and preached that the highest form of sacrifice was to sacrifice one's unvirtuous behavior and one's ignorance. Along with this change of worship, new forms of divination were formed that made use of combinations of numbers. To ask for a sacrifice from another may be easier, but it's not as meaningful and effective as making a personal sacrifice.

> If anyone with a pure heart undertakes a commitment to virtue—to refrain from taking life, from taking what is not

given, from sexual immorality, from lying speech, and from taking strong drink and sloth-producing drugs—that constitutes a sacrifice better than giving alms, better than giving shelter, and better than going for refuge.[5]

Ten of Lotuses

On this card we see the Golden Wheel. This is one of the Eight Glorious Emblems of Buddha, which were given to him as gifts from the gods. The Golden Wheel was originally the emblem of the ancient warrior king called the *chakravartin*. It is a symbol of the sun and of the wheel of the year similar to solar symbols that we can find in Celtic culture. In Hinduism it is related to the disk of the god Vishnu. As a symbol of the year, it can be related to the Wheel of Life. This is the same wheel that we find in the Tarot as the Wheel of Fortune, a symbol of fate and of the impermanence of life. Buddha transformed it into the Wheel of the Law, which conquers fate and death with its teaching. This card represents rebirth and renewal. It is related to the Western symbol of the phoenix rising from flames.

PADMADAKINI - THE DAKINI OF LOTUSES

Dakinis are goddesses dancing in the vast empty space that is consciousness. They are sky-walkers. Their home is the unobstructed space of the mind that is unbounded and connected to all life in its depths. They are thought or inspiration that comes directly from the Jinas. They are powerful energies that rise into consciousness and bring freedom and joy and teach us that we are not isolated egos living in a world of doubt. They connect us with the divine.

Padmadakini is a manifestation of Amitabha, the Buddha of fire and love. She holds his lotus in her right hand. Padmadakini is a feeling of love deep in one's psyche. She is a feeling that can comfort one in a time of need and bring joy when this feeling is allowed to bloom. Cherish this feeling.

The Peacock - The Animal of Lotuses

Because of its beauty, the peacock is a bird found in the heaven of the gods. In Buddhism, it is believed that the peacock creates such beautiful plumage by living on a diet of poisonous plants and snakes. It takes what is poisonous and transforms it into beauty. Therefore, the peacock is a symbol of the Tantric path, which transforms destructive desires into spiritual energy and heightened awareness. There are three poisons depicted in the center of the Wheel of Life, but each of the Five Precepts describes a poison as well. These poisons can form blocks in our chakras. However, if we free this energy and send it up through the chakras unimpeded, it will feed our higher self. Like the peacock, we will transform poison into beauty. This card represents transformative power. When a poisonous thought comes into consciousness, let go of it and watch it ascend out the top of your head.

Pandara - The Sakti of Lotuses

Pandara is the red Sakti of the west. Her consort is Amitabha and she shares his throne. Her name means "the white-robed one." She is the embodiment of purity and she is holding two lotuses, symbols of purity. Pandara is clothed in purity. She is the atmosphere that surrounds Amitabha as he meditates. Her protective enclosure allows him to withdraw from material reality in safety. She is like a protective white light. She is the wisdom of love.

Pandara instructs us not to commit sexual misdeeds and promotes contentment. Without contentment, we are continually desiring what we don't have and we cannot enjoy what we do have. As a cure for distraction and discontentment, she recommends meditating on the breath and bringing the mind to one pointed concentration. This is the wisdom of love.

Amitabha - The Buddha of Lotuses

Amitabha is the red Jina of the west, the land of the setting sun. His name means "he whose splendor is immeasurable" or "infinite light." His name is Amida in Japanese, which means "immortal," and in China he is invoked with the phrase "Nanwu Omituo Fo." His mudra is Dhyana mudra, the mudra of meditation, and he sits with his eyes closed in meditation. It may seem strange that he is associated with the setting sun and growing darkness and he is also called infinite light. But the setting sun is a fitting symbol for the process of withdrawing into oneself that is meditation, and the infinite light of his name refers to the internal light that one perceives in meditation. All Jinas are associated with love, but Amitabha represents the love aspect of Buddhahood. He is the love of love and he is one of the most popular Jinas.

In Japan, many people venerate Amida to the exclusion of all other Buddhas. His followers pray to him, hoping that they will be reborn in their next life in his paradise in the west. There in their next life, they will find ideal circumstances for reaching enlightenment. Amitabha is the head of the Lotus family of Bodhisattvas and Buddhas. The most famous member of his family is Avalokitesvara, the Bodhisattva of compassion. In China, Avalokitesvara takes the form of the famous female Bodhisattva called Kuan Yin. His animal is the peacock, which is said to have the power to transform poison into a healing sustenance.

    This card represents mastery of the feeling function and is related to the element fire. This mastery gives one the ability to choose not to act from emotion, but instead to make decisions based on deeply held values. Feelings tell us what is right and what is wrong.

Ace of Double Vajras

The double vajra is the symbol of Amoghasiddhi, the green Buddha of the north and the element water. The double vajra is like two single vajras connected at their center to form a cross. *Vajra* means "thunderbolt," and the double vajra represents thunderbolts radiating to the four cardinal directions of the four Jinas and the four winds. This is associated with the power of storms, rain, and water. The double vajra is sometimes equated to the Wheel of the Law that proclaims the truth to the four directions with a voice like thunder and illumination like lightning. The great Buddhist emperor Asoka set up columns in India with four lions on the top joined together at the rear and facing the four directions. The lions, with their thunderlike roar, were a symbol of Buddha's law radiating to the four directions. Amoghasiddhi, the Buddha of action, uses his tool to conquer passion and promote fearlessness. The double vajra is also a symbol of the joining of opposites. It has a vertical masculine pole and horizontal feminine pole joined at the center.

A double vajra is not a vessel like the cup of the Tarot, but the two are connected through their common association with water and therefore with the unconscious. The double vajra represents action radiating out from a center that is hidden in the center of our soul. It is like the lotus in our heart when it blossoms. If we look deep into our unconscious—into our soul—we will find that our deepest desires are not our own creations. They are like seeds of love and compassion that are planted there before we were born. They need to be nurtured and they need to grow. This card represents the beginning of that growth. This suit is associated with the intuitive function of Jungian psychology and with raja yoga.

Two of Double Vajras

Here we find the Golden Fish, which is one of the Eight Glorious Emblems of Buddha. The two fish swim in effortless freedom and take endless joy in each other's company. This card represents love and attraction. In universal symbolism, the fish is a messenger from the depths of the sea of the unconscious. That the two fish swim on the surface of the sea symbolizes the unconscious waking to consciousness.

We find fish being used as symbols of waking up from ignorance in many myths and religions. For example, Jesus called his disciple Peter to become a fisher of men. Similarly, when we fall in love, it is as if we woke up. We see the world with new eyes and it is beautiful. In Buddhist symbolism, the two fish are said to be the two eyes of Buddha. When we can see with Buddha's eyes, we are saved from the ocean of suffering and delusion and can swim freely through life.

Three of Double Vajras

A teacher passes on a written text to a student. This card represents support and guidance. In yogic practice there is a close relationship between the teacher, or guru, and the student. The teacher passes on more than knowledge of what is written, more than instruction in the practice of yoga, and more than words can convey. The best teacher is one who is an example of the goal—who is enlightened. Enlightenment is contagious. To be in the presence of unconditional love is to resonate unconditional love.

To list what not to do, to complain, and draw attention to what is done wrong helps to promote frustration and negativity. When we explain what is desired and praise the student for achieving it, the student begins to understand the goal. This is teaching. When the teacher is one with the goal, teaching becomes effortless.

Four of Double Vajras

Here we find the boar from the center of the Wheel of Life. This pig represents the poison that is both sloth and ignorance in Buddhist thought. Sloth and ignorance may not seem as negative as the other poisons on the Wheel of Life (anger and greed), but much suffering is caused in the world by ignorant activity and by simply not stopping evil from happening. Socrates said that he believed that all evil in the world was perpetrated by those who ignorantly believed that they were accomplishing good. The opposite of this poison is intelligence and energy. These are two of the virtues that Buddha found essential for progress on the path to enlightenment.

In Ayurvedic medicine, the three poisons of the Wheel of Life are associated with imbalances of the three doshas. Sloth creates an imbalance of the water dosha, *kapha,* and people who are predominantly kapha are more prone to fall into laziness. A kapha imbalance may also manifest as obesity and sleepiness. When kapha types are in balance, the poison of sloth and ignorance is replaced by faithfulness and contentment.

FIVE OF DOUBLE VAJRAS

A pot topples, spilling milk. Milk is considered a precious ambrosia in Tibet. To spill milk is a tragedy and a symbol of carelessness. To spill milk is compared to being careless with the cherished Buddhist teachings. However, at times, the preciousness and veneration of a teaching robs it of its meaning.

The Zen Buddhist monk Sato-Kaiseki was disturbed when he heard of Copernicus's heliocentric cosmology. If the sun was in the center of the cosmos, he reasoned, the Buddhist cosmology with Mount Meru in the center is false. Also, other aspects of the cosmology that were taught, such as the triple world and the twenty-five forms of existence, will be proven nonsense. Perhaps this would prove that Buddhism is nonsense. He wrote a book defending the Buddhist cosmology and presented it to his teacher, Master Ekido. Master Ekido leafed through the book and handed it back to Sato. Then he said, "How stupid! Don't you realize that the basic aim of Buddhism is to shatter the triple world and the twenty-five forms of existence?"[6] The Zen approach to Buddhism is to spill milk.

Six of Double Vajras

A mother sits under a tree, like a Buddha. She nurses her child. Six is a number of love, and here the love is between a mother and child. This card represents nurturing, the type of love that provides what is needed—no more, no less. To love in this way actually involves detachment. If we are too involved, we are motivated by selfish interest and we may feed too much or too little. To do what is right, we must observe and listen without self-interest. The child will tell us what he or she needs, and we feed the child for the sake of the child, not for our own gain.

> Here a Bodhisattva gives a gift, and he does not apprehend a self, nor a recipient, nor a gift; also no reward of his giving. He surrenders that gift to all beings, but he apprehends

neither being nor self. He dedicates that gift to supreme enlightenment, but he does not apprehend any enlightenment. This is called the supramundane perfection of giving.[7]

Seven of Double Vajras

This card depicts the Varada mudra, the hand gesture that represents compassion, charity, and giving. The hand is held down with the fingers together and the palm facing out. Hence, it is extending down from the top of the card. This mudra is associated with Ratnasambhava, the yellow Jina of the south. It is also associated with the Bodhisattva Avalokitesvara, who used this gesture to allow the water of life to flow from his hand and soothe the tormented souls in one of the Buddhist hells. At the bottom of the card we find three pots containing the gifts of Ratnasambhava. There is a pot of jewels, representing wealth; a pot of herbs, representing health; and a pot of fruit, representing sustenance and strength. These gifts are designed to soothe our pains in this world. However, we are asked to make a choice. What gift is needed?

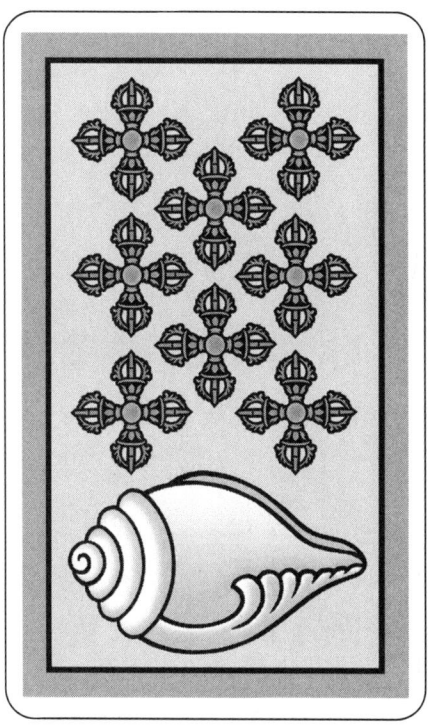

EIGHT OF DOUBLE VAJRAS

Here we see a depiction of the Joyous Conch Shell Trumpet, which is one of the Eight Glorious Emblems of Buddha. It is also called the Trumpet of Victory. This card represents joyous sound, music, and creative expression. The conch was used as a trumpet in ancient India during religious rituals and by armies during war. It is one of the royal emblems of Siddhartha. In Hinduism, it is one of the four emblems of the god Vishnu. In Buddhism, the coiling of the white conch and its far-reaching sound symbolizes the Dharma, the teaching of Buddha. The teaching is compared to the beautiful, voluminous sound of the Conch Shell Trumpet that reaches in all directions and wakens all who hear it from the sleep of their delusions. In readings, we may think of this card as a wake-up call that breaks a monotonous routine and calls us to a more creative endeavor.

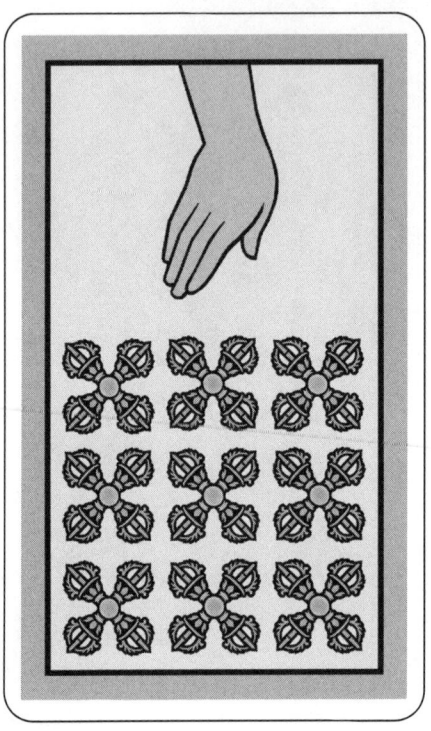

NINE OF DOUBLE VAJRAS

This card depicts the Bhumisparsa mudra, the hand gesture that represents faith, resolution, and confidence. This mudra is associated with Aksobhya, the blue Jina of the east. This is the mudra that Gautama used during his victory over Mara. It is also called the Victory mudra. When Mara challenged Gautama's right to attain enlightenment, Gautama responded by touching the ground with his fingertips and the earth bore him witness. This is one of the most important images in Buddhism. It is the supreme act of optimism and trust. To be where we are in life, we have all accomplished many things. These accomplishments are ours, and we can stand on them with confidence and look to the future with optimism. Sometimes we may forget our accomplishments and doubt our worth, but the earth never forgets. We only need to trust the world and know that she supports us.

Ten of Double Vajras

On this card we see the Lucky Knot. This is one of the Eight Glorious Emblems of Buddha, which were given to him as gifts from the gods. This design is also the symbol of the tenth Jina of the Jain religion, and may be related to designs depicting the intestines of animals used as an offering. In design, it is close to the endless knots of medieval Celtic art and its meaning is similar. It represents interconnectedness. We may think of this interconnectedness as the invisible bonds that connect people to their family, friends, neighbors, and to all people, or we may think of it as the life force that connects all living creatures. To the Buddha it symbolizes that all is one and the continual interlocking of the wisdom of the Sakti with the love of the Buddha. They are as inseparable as form and space. In a reading, think of this as representing a group or network that one is connected to by invisible bonds.

VISVADAKINI - THE DAKINI OF DOUBLE VAJRAS

Dakinis are female forms of a Buddha. They are like goddesses that are dancing with freedom and abandon in our psyches. Their name in Tibetan means "sky-walker." The sky that they dance in is the unlimited space of consciousness. At its deepest level, our consciousness is open-ended. The Dakinis come to us from the Buddhas.

Visvadakini is a manifestation of Amoghasiddhi. She holds his double vajra aloft in the air with the joyous sound of her music. Amoghasiddhi is the Jina of fearlessness, and his Dakini is deep inside of everyone. This means that there is a part of one's psyche that is beyond fear. In times of stress and turmoil, we can call on Visvadakini and find our inner confidence and fearlessness. This fearlessness comes from the realization that we are not isolated beings in an uncaring world. We are one with the world and this has always been so. Death and suffering stem from the illusion of separateness. Visvadakini's music dispels this illusion.

THE GARUDA - THE ANIMAL OF DOUBLE VAJRAS

Garudas are mythical animals that are part bird and part man or woman. They usually have bird's wings, legs, and beaks. Sometimes they are shown in armor or playing a flute. They are said to live inside Mount Meru. In Hindu mythology, the garuda is the celestial mount of the god Vishnu. In Buddhism, the garuda is the sworn enemy of the serpent creatures called nagas. We spoke of nagas in the previous chapter when we were discussing Mucalinda, the king of the nagas who protected Buddha during the rains. Mucalinda is a beneficial naga. However, most nagas are believed to be the cause of disease. Only if a naga has converted to Buddhism or performed a deed of merit like Mucalinda is it safe from the wrath of the garudas. Because of this, garudas are considered great healers. The four books of the tantra of Tibetan healing *The Blue Beryl* are compared to a garuda. This card represents a healer and protector.

Tara - The Sakti of Double Vajras

Tara is the green Sakti of the north and the consort of Amoghasiddhi. She shares his throne. Her name means "the one who ferries across" or "savioress." Tara is "the one who ferries" in that she can carry us across the river of birth and death and deliver us to the shore of Nirvana. It is her compassionate embrace that allows Amoghasiddhi to be unobstructed and fearless. She has seven eyes: three on her face, one on each palm, and one on the sole of each foot. They are like seven psychic centers, or chakras, that are open and allowing her energy to flow freely. Green Tara is popular and she has sister aspects in other colors, the most important being white Tara, whom we can see on the World card. Tara is like the night after Amoghasiddhi, the setting sun, has retired. In contrast, white Tara is the brightness of noon. There are also blue, red, and yellow Taras.

Tara is the wisdom of action. She instructs us to refrain from taking what is not offered to us and to develop generosity. As a cure to this self-centered activity, she recommends that we meditate on the impermanence of life.

Amoghasiddhi - The Buddha of Double Vajras

Amoghasiddhi is the green Jina of the north and his paradise is located in the north where the stars never set. His name means "infallible success" or "unobstructed accomplishment." His name is Fukujoju Nyorai in Japanese and Don-grub in Tibetan. His mudra is Abhaya mudra, the mudra of fearlessness. Fearlessness and wisdom are his virtues, which is fitting of the Buddha of action. Amoghasiddhi is fearless and unobstructed because he is one with the depth of the sea of the unconscious. He perceives where things are going and knows where they have been and acts accordingly. He is the head of the Karma or Action family of Bodhisattvas and Buddhas. The most famous member of his family is his Sakti Tara. His animal is the garuda, the man-bird that is a wise healer. This card represents mastery of the intuitive function, which brings unconscious wisdom into the light and allows one to act fearlessly. Intuition is related to the element water.

Chapter 7

DIVINATION

Many people think of the Tarot primarily as a tool for divination. Often the word *divination* is equated to *fortunetelling,* which means to predict what Fortuna has in store for us in the future. When people go to fortunetellers, they are hoping that they will receive good news about their future. Then, they don't have to do anything but sit back and wait for it to happen. With this hope comes the fear that the news will be bad. To relinquish the responsibility for one's future in this way is fatalistic. The downside of leaving things to fate is that if the future is bad, there is nothing that can be done but wait and dread the event.

The word *divination* actually means "to get in touch with the divine." It is derived from the Latin *divinus,* which meant "soothsayer," which in turn was derived from *deus,* meaning "God." We often think of the ancient soothsayers or oracles as making predictions. However, we have written records, inscribed on lead tablets, of questions that were put to the oracle of Zeus at Dodona, and the answers that were given. They show that the majority of statements of the oracles were not predictions, but advice on how to make improvements and keep the favor of the divine. Advice was given on the proper forms of cult practice, the proper sacrifices to the gods, the wisdom of beginning a journey or a marriage, or how to heal an illness.

Rather than being fatalistic, these responses were designed to improve the future.[1]

In the ancient world, it was generally believed that the gods desired to communicate with people, and divination was how that communication happened. Besides oracles, techniques for divination included dream interpretation, the interpretation of the flight of birds and other omens, the examination of the entrails of sacrificial animals (particularly the liver), astrology, and throwing dice or lots. All important decisions at a personal or state level involved divination. As there was no central authority to decide religious issues, often the questions that were asked were concerned with the will of the gods.

Buddhist culture is similar to that of ancient Greeks and Romans in its reliance on divination as a religious practice. In traditional Tibetan culture, for example, we find numerous forms. Every monastery contained at least one learned astrologer who advised the people. In their practice of astrology, the Tibetans are influenced by their neighbors. From the Chinese, they have borrowed the animals of the zodiac that are assigned to consecutive years. From India, Persia, and Greece they have borrowed other elements, such as the seven days of the week named after the seven ancient planets, and the division of the day into auspicious and inauspicious hours. In addition to these elaborate horoscopes, every lama and layperson made use of rosary beads, sheep bones, dice, or even cards for divination.

In most Tibetan homes, one can still find a manual for divination called *Mo* or *Mo-pe*. This book contains lists of interpretations, which pertain to the throws of dice. Two six-sided dice are used. On each side of the dice is inscribed one syllable from the chant, "AH RA PA TSA NA DHI." Because the order in which the syllables appear is important—for example, AH RA is considered a different throw than RA AH—there are thirty-six possible throws. This is unlike the Western system, which uses numbered dice and does not attach significance to which emerges first and therefore only has twenty-one possible combinations. For each of the thirty-six throws in the Mo system, the manual lists eleven interpretations that fit all possible types of questions. Also, there are directions for the proper prayers and sacrifices to maintain or improve one's fortune.

The Tibetan cards used for divination are small strips of cardboard painted with either favorable or sinister symbols and a string attached to each. When consulting the cards, first the Bodhisattva Tara or another deity is asked to help. Then the cards are held at face level in the left hand, and with the eyes closed, a thread is grasped. By this means, a card is pulled from the stack. When three cards are drawn in this way, the results are compared and interpreted.[2]

Like the ancient Greeks, the Tibetans maintain state oracles. For hundreds of years, during the New Year's festival the Dalai Lama and government officials have consulted a state oracle called *Nechung*. Although the Tibetan government is now in exile, the present Dalai Lama continues this practice. When the Dalai Lama has been criticized by "progressive" thinkers for maintaining this "outdated" practice, his defense was that Nechung's advice has always been truthful.

Buddha taught that the greatest good is to help others, and that one should use any means available toward this end. Buddhists see divination as one means of practicing this teaching. Divination gives one insight into the present. It allows one to see the situation clearly and make informed decisions. At the highest level, it helps one move along the path to enlightenment.

The highest teaching of the Buddha is called *pratiya samutpada*. This teaching explains that all things are interdependent. It is the realization of ultimate reality, in which we come to see that the entire world is one and we cease to be conscious of ourselves as separate entities. All causation arises from the void (which is at the base of consciousness), and what we now think of as cause-and-effect relationships vanish. When we practice divination, we are participating in reality at a higher level beyond normal cause-and-effect observations. Although there is no direct connection between cards or dice and the events that we question them about, the seemingly random patterns that they form are connected to our affairs at a deeper level. The practice of divination prods us toward the realization that all is one.

In Jungian terms, this realization is called *individuation*. Jung found that the part of ourselves that we usually identify with is only a small part of our total self. He labeled this conscious aspect the *ego* and the entire personality the *Self*. The ego is like a small point of light in comparison to the endless immensity of the Self. Therefore, the largest portion of the psyche is unconscious. To progress toward individuation, we must begin to communicate with the unconscious, and bring its wisdom into consciousness. Divination is a tool to assist in this process.

The Tarot consists of a series of symbolic pictures, similar to the images in dreams. Symbolism is the voice of the unconscious. It is a language that can take us beyond the confines of words. The creators of the Tarot in the Renaissance were involved with the same interaction, although they would not have used modern psychological terminology to explain it.

In the Renaissance, artists and philosophers were deliberately trying to capture powerful symbols in images and organize them into a meaningful philosophic structure, and one manifestation of this was the Tarot. Therefore, the Tarot consists of a series of symbols—of hieroglyphs—that our unconscious can use to write to us. Beyond the individual symbols, the entire deck contains a mystical structure that can keep the communication on a high philosophical level. The trumps outline the story of the hero's journey, and the entire deck contains the archetypal, mystical, symbolic structure that Jung referred to as a mandala. Jung said that the mandala is an archetypal symbol for the Self, the totality of consciousness. If we are aware of this when we use the cards and use it as a tool for corresponding with the unconscious instead of predicting the future, the readings help us to create a better future and can nudge us along to higher consciousness.

In our unconscious—in our higher Self—we have a vast resource of knowledge and wisdom that is ours when we open up a dialogue and bring it into consciousness. All readings are about the present. However, in the present, through the higher Self, we can see what others are thinking and feeling, we can see the aspects of the past that we and others are carrying with us, and we can see where we are headed in the future and decide if we want to change direction.

THE THREE-CARD MESSAGE

As I said above, the Tarot cards are hieroglyphs. Therefore, they can be used by our higher self to create sentences and communicate with the conscious mind. The simplest and most powerful way that we can combine them and allow this communication to take place is the three-card reading. Once we have learned this technique, it can be used to build many different types of spreads to address different issues.

Three is considered a sacred number in most ancient cultures. In Christianity, it is related to the mystery of the Trinity. To the ancient Greeks, it defined the three points necessary to make the first geometric form and begin creation. To the Buddhists, there are three desires that drive the Wheel of Life forward, and Three Jewels offered by Buddha as a substitute for these desires. Every complete sentence needs a subject and a predicate, but to go beyond the most rudimentary form, it will also need an object. Every story or situation has a beginning, middle, and an end. The Tarot trumps themselves are a three-part story. The three-card reading allows communication to happen.

I recommend using the cards right-side up in your reading. Right-side up cards allow the pictures to communicate more clearly and are less likely to throw unnecessary negativity into a reading. Some people feel that it is necessary to use upside-down cards to increase the vocabulary of the cards by allowing for more possibilities, but this only doubles the possibilities. When we use three cards, we find that we have 456,456 possible combinations. If we use three cards for each position in a more complex reading, we have 456,456 possible combinations for the first place, 405,150 for the second, and 357,840 for the third place. With one card for each place with upside-down possibilities, we have 156 possibilities for the first place, 154 for the second, and 152 for the third. It is not necessary to use upside-down images. If you prefer to use upside-down images, then it will change the direction of the images and you will have to determine what being upside-down in relation to the other images means in each spread.

Next, the querent must decide the purpose of the reading. The purpose can be a clarification of a past or present situation, to attain wisdom or advice, to investigate the possible outcome of a course of action, or to gain perspective.

Let the querent cut the cards once with his or her left hand (symbolizing the unconscious) while stating the purpose of the reading—it should be specific. Then take the cards and shuffle them loosely, stopping only when you feel the intuition to cease; or, let the querent shuffle until the process comes to a natural state of completion. Let the querent cut the cards—again with the left hand—by removing a block of cards from the top of the deck and setting it aside. Lay the first three cards from the remaining portion of the cut deck out in a line from left to right.

Now look at the cards as one picture. Look at the flow of energy in the picture, and interpret it as you would a dream or a story in a picture book. It is essential to notice in what direction the characters are facing. There are six basic patterns that can come up, although each has subdivisions, and at times, two patterns can merge. The center card is most important to the action. The characters on each card can be facing left, right, center, or upward. At times the body is in one direction, but a head or gesture points to the other, or the figure may be pointing to either side. It is usually possible to state the action as one sentence or expand it into a more detailed story. The six patterns are:

1. **Linear:** The cards could show a story that begins on the left and ends on the right, or the action could start on the right and proceed to the left. The figures will tend to be facing in the same direction, left or right. Sometimes the end card, instead of facing forward, may be facing the opposite way to meet the action.

2. **Choice:** The central figure may have his or her back toward the back of the figure on one of the flanking cards. When two figures are back-to-back in this way, it indicates that the central figure is moving away from one side and all that that symbolizes and toward the other—choosing one direction and rejecting the other.

3. **The Central Origin:** Perhaps the central figure is looking directly at you or up to a higher plane. This may indicate that the action starts in the center and moves out to both sides, or to one side and not the other. Look at the direction of the figures on the flanking cards. If they are moving away from the center, this is the central origin pattern.

4. **The Central Destination:** When the central figure is looking at you or looking up, and the end figures are facing the center, the action may start on both sides and converge in the middle. Thus, the middle has become the destination for the action.

5. **The Central Problem:** At times, there may be no flow of energy. The central card may be blocking the action or dispersing the energy. For example, if placed in the center, the Eight of Vajras may represent a block. It wants to move to the right, but it cannot.

6. **The Central Teacher:** The central figure may be instructional and comment on or point to two possibilities illustrated by the cards that flank it. The center card may illustrate that two choices are available, or recommend one choice over the other. For example, the Two of Vajras in the center would represent a debate between the two choices represented by the cards flanking it.

Sometimes the layout may be interpreted as fitting more than one pattern. Use your intuition to determine which one feels right. If a card confuses you, you may expand it for clarification. This involves shuffling and obtaining another three cards, which are an expanded message related to the card in question. It is best to place these three above the card that they refer to. To find out the causes of a situation, we may also place three cards below any card we need to know more about.

It is possible to use the three-card message for each position in many different spreads. You can also make up spreads of your own. Below are some that I have found useful.

The Relationship Spread

The Relationship Spread is a useful short reading that can be used to focus on almost any question. It can be applied to relationships between two persons, or between a person and a job, home, culture, city, or other environment. It can be a health reading showing the relationship between the querent's mind and body. It can give a detailed analysis of the situation and be used creatively to solve problems.

The cards are laid out left to right in three groups of three. Start by letting the querent shuffle and cut as before. On the left, lay out the first line of three cards. These represent the querent. Skip a space, and on the right lay out the second line of three cards. These represent the other party in the relationship—person, place, job, and so on. If you feel that the three cards representing the other party belong to the left of the querent instead of the right, then follow your intuition. On top, bridging the gap between the two sides, place a third line of three cards. The first will be over the last card of the group on the left, the second will be over the gap, and the third will be over the first card on the right, as illustrated in Figure 16. This will represent the relationship itself, and reveals the dynamics at work. Use the story approach to read each line of three as one picture. Then look at all three lines to see the bigger picture. It is helpful to notice how the cards in each group change as they approach each other from the outside into the center. Always end with three additional cards of advice.

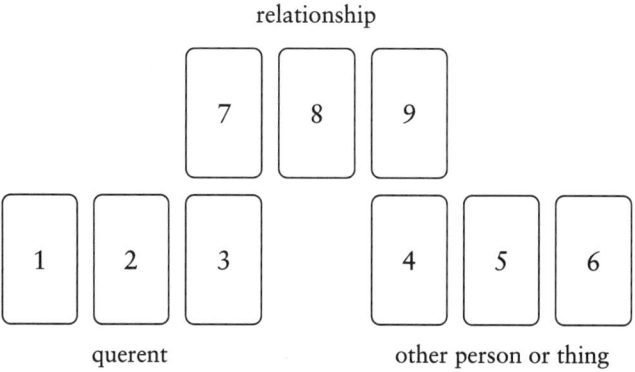

Figure 16—The Relationship Spread

THE CHAKRA READING

We have discussed the chakras in chapter 4 and under the Chakras card in chapter 5. In our modern conception, the chakras are thought of as seven energy or soul centers located in ascending order on the spine and cranium. They may be blocked or flow freely, and their proper functioning is believed to be necessary for psychic and physical health. This reading gives us a picture of what is happening in the querent's chakras. This is also an important reading to do for oneself. Just seeing the energy patterns in these centers is healing, and the reading can go a step further and suggest changes in behavior that will begin to dissolve blocks. It can also be combined with other forms of chakra therapy. I recommend reading more books or taking classes on the chakras if one is interested in this type of therapy.

Start as before and have the querent shuffle and cut with the left hand. After a block of cards is removed, draw from the top of the remaining block and lay out seven cards in a column from the bottom up as indicated by the numbers on the cards in Figure 17. As you lay down the cards, describe each chakra for the querent. Just describe each chakra and what energies are associated with it without attempting to analyze what is happening there. Analysis will come later when we lay down the cards that flank this central column. The following is a list of each chakra with its name in Sanskrit, a translation in English, an equivalent English name, and a list of associations:

1. **Muladhara/"Root"/Sacrum:** This center is located at the base of the spine, which is called the sacrum. It is interesting to note that the word *sacrum* is Latin for "sacred." This is the group mind, the first part of the psyche that is developed in an infant. This center deals with issues of survival and self-preservation and is important for physical health and prosperity. Here we may find patterns that tell us about the childhood of the querent. At first we are dependent on our parents, our family, and our culture and try to conform, and those conservative patterns or patterns that stem from the rejection of conservative values are found here. The more conservative and the less individuated the querent is, the more influence this area has on the other chakras.

2. **Svadhisthana/"Sweetness"/Genitals:** This center is located on the spine at the level of the genitals. This is the area of desire—not just sexual desire, but all desires: comfort, wealth, respect, and so on. It is desire that pulls one out of the group mind and helps one to become an individual, and this is where we begin to define our individuality. It contains patterns that show how one goes about satisfying desire. Often these patterns were formed in adolescence. This area is important for our emotional well-being and for developing the ability to find pleasure.

3. **Manipura/"Precious Jewel"/Solar Plexus:** This center is located on the spine at the level of the upper abdomen. This is where we digest our food and begin to create our body, and this is where we create our self-identity. It is the center of one's ego. It is fully developed in young adulthood. The patterns here describe the querent's will, self-esteem, and power. We will find patterns that indicate if the querent is weak and shy, dominating and aggressive, or self-

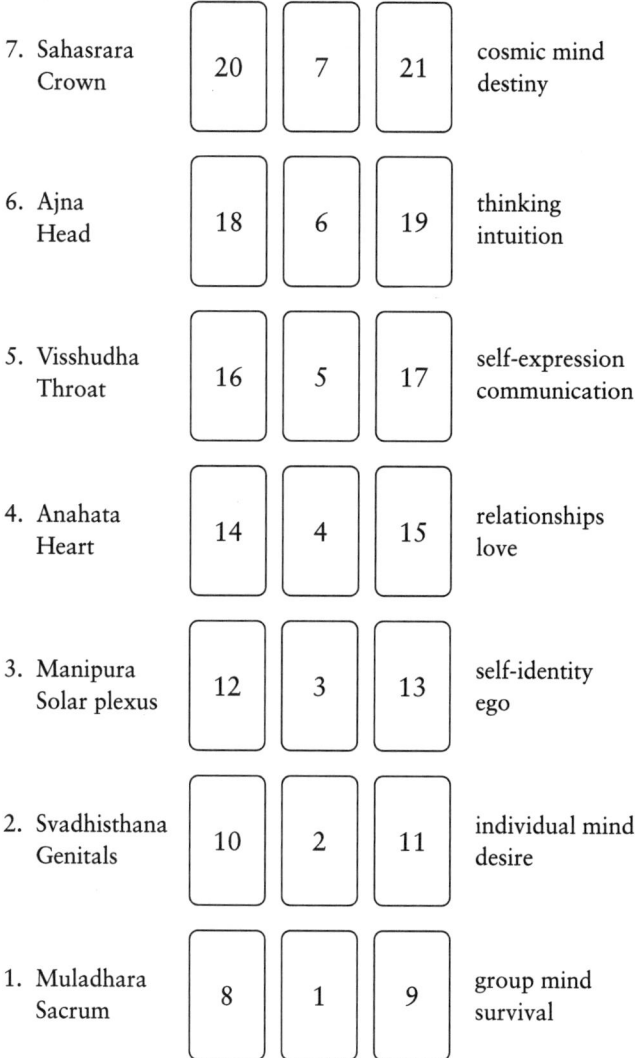

Figure 17—The Chakra Spread

confident with a good self-image and a sense of humor. A healthy ego is a necessary stage of development and allows one to progress to higher states of consciousness. Blocking the development of the ego is not the same thing as overcoming egotism. Although enlightenment is described as letting go of the ego, one must first have an ego to let go of.

4. **Anahata/"Unstruck"/Heart:** This center is located at the level of the heart. This is the area of true maturity, where we go beyond thinking only about ourselves and develop compassion. The heart is where we interact with the world and others. It is the center of feeling, which is not emotion, but a deep decision-making function where our values are created. The heart is of central importance to the whole system of the chakras. It allows the energy from the sacrum to rise to the crown, the energy from the crown to descend to the sacrum, and it allows energy to interact with others. Until Buddha fully embraced compassion, he could not proceed to enlightenment. The heart is the door. We may find patterns here that depict jealousy, shyness, love, grief, empathy, or courage.

5. **Visshudha/"Purification"/Throat:** This center is located in the cervical vertebrae of the neck. This is the center of self-expression and communication. It has to do with one's occupation, creativity, and ability to speak. The chakras above the heart tend to relate to their parallel center below the heart. The throat relates to the solar plexus. A healthy ego supports eloquence and creative expression. A negative self-image will lead to the inability to speak or to express emotions, or may lead one into a stifling job. What we do for a living and how we express ourselves will also affect our self-image. We may find patterns here of shyness or excessive talking, an energy block, or artistic ability and free expression.

6. **Ajna/"To Perceive"/Head:** This center is often thought of as the third eye and located in the center of the brow, but in Western

Platonic thought, it is the head and the brain. This is the center of thinking and intuition. This is where we develop our perception and philosophy and make decisions. I have found that thinking is a product of the energy rising up from the lower chakras. It parallels the desires of the genitals and seeks ways of fulfilling these desires, or it can go beyond thinking about hopes and fears and allow this energy to ascend to the crown, its ultimate goal. Intuition stems from the energy that comes down from the crown. It is a message from the higher self and can help to clarify our thoughts. This energy wants to descend to the sacrum and manifest in physical reality. In this area we may find patterns of obsession, delusion, or denial, or clear-sightedness, intelligence, imagination, and intuition.

7. **Sahasrara/"Thousandfold"/Crown:** The crown is located at the top of the cranium. This center is actually the place where the system opens to the psychic energy of the cosmos and transforms this energy into the individual personality. It parallels the tribal group of the sacrum center with the universal collective of the unconscious. This is where we are in contact with the higher self. Just as the patterns that are found in the sacrum have to do with the past, the patterns found in the crown have to do with the future. This is advice from the higher self about where we should head. We may call it destiny. We do not have to listen to the advice or head in that direction, but life will be easier if we do.

Once these cards are laid on the table, a map of the querent's soul has begun to emerge. There is a connection between this map and the actual energies in the querent's chakras. At this point, pass your left palm over the cards, keeping it about two inches above the surface. Repeat this process as many times as necessary to allow yourself to become sensitized to the energy in the cards. With practice, this will become easier. When you are sensitized, you will notice a flow of energy in the cards. Over certain cards you may feel a large mass of energy or a hot spot. This area may feel spongy or slow up your hand. In other places you may feel a depression or a cold spot, and still other areas may seem slippery or free-flowing.

Once you have done this, you may invite the querent to do the same and share his or her impressions. I have found that every time I have done this, the querent was able to feel something and it almost always was the same as what I felt.

This information has already begun to give you information about the condition of the querent's chakras. Ideally, the energy in the chakras should be free-flowing and unobstructed. The energy from the base wants to liberate itself in the crown, and the energy in the crown wants to manifest in the base. At the heart there should be a free flow with the hearts of others. When this is the case, we have good health, confidence, and creativity. However, this is almost never totally the way we will find the energies in the reading. When we hold on to certain patterns of thought and behavior, we create blocks in our psyche, and this creates thick or hot spots where the energy is being hoarded and thin or cool spots in the areas that are being starved of energy. Our job as a healer is to help dissolve these blocks and to promote the flow of energy.

Now we are ready to complete the layout. Have the querent shuffle the cards again and cut. Taking from the top of the remaining portion of the deck, lay out cards to the left and the right of the card at the base of the column, as indicated in Figure 17. Replace the block of cards that was removed from the top of the deck back on top of the remaining block of cards and ask the querent to cut again. Now lay cards to the left and the right of the second card of the column. Repeat this process until the entire layout is complete.

Each section of the column can be read as a three-card message that will give information about the energy patterns and behavior that is held in each chakra. Pay special attention to the thick or hot spots that you discovered earlier. The reading will tell you what preconceptions or false expectations are causing these blocks. They may be the result of positive expectations as well as negative. Also give special attention to the advice from the higher self in the crown.

After all of the chakras have been discussed and the querent has absorbed the information, it is time to work creatively with the energy blocks. Have the querent shuffle the remaining cards while asking the higher self how he or she may heal this area in question. After the querent cuts, place three cards directly over the three cards representing the blocked chakra, so that the original cards are covered by the new cards and are now out of sight. Again, read this new section as a three-card message. Repeat this with any problem areas. I have found that often problems in the sacrum create other problems in the chakras above. Therefore, it is a good idea to work on the sacrum no matter where problems show up. As in all readings, it is also a good idea to finish with three cards of advice.

The Mandala Meditation

Historian of religion Mircea Eliade tells us that the construction of a mandala "is equivalent to the magical recreation of the world."[3] The mandala is the true pattern of the world—the inner, mythical pattern—and to recreate it is to share in the creative magical force that created the world in the beginning. Shamans the world over use sacred patterns to gain personal knowledge of the origins of things in the world and to therefore gain magical power over these things. By completing this meditation, one will gain a deeper magical understanding of this deck and the archetypal forces that it represents. This process will help to make this deck an expression of the higher self.

Find an area of floor that is large enough to lay out the entire deck according to Figure 18. You will need approximately six feet by six feet and room outside of this for a place to sit. Take White Tara (the World card) and place her in the center of the area with her feet facing east. She is the key to the layout. Now, sitting on the west side of Tara, lay out the blue suit of vajras radiating out from her feet to the east with the bottom of the cards facing you, as illustrated in Figure 18. Start by putting the Ace on the first level; the Two and the Three left to right on the second level away from Tara; the Four, Five, and Six on the third level; the Seven, Eight, Nine, and Ten on the fourth level; and, still left to right, the Dakini, the Buddha, the Sakti, and the Animal on the fifth level.

Move to the north side of Tara and lay out the yellow suit of jewels on the south side of Tara so that, again, the cards are facing you. Proceed to the east side of the layout and place the red suit of lotuses on the west side in the same way. Then complete the cross by moving to the south and laying out the green suit of double vajras in the same way on the north side.

The progression of the pips—with one on the first level, two on the second, three on the third, and four on the fourth—is an ancient Pythagorean symbol of emanation called the *tetractys*. This symbolizes the transcendent truth that is Tara in the sacred center, which is the One, radiating out to the physical world, which is symbolized by the number four. This fourfold emanation is then repeated in the four aspects of the four Jinas—the Dakini, the Buddha, the Sakti, and the Animal—which are repeated four times, one for each of the four directions of the manifest world. Mandalas of the Jinas usually take the form of a cross to demonstrate that they are the wisdom of Buddha manifest in the world. For an example, see Figure 12.

Around this cross we will make a circle of the Fool and the remaining trumps. Go to the east side of the mandala and place the Fool on the bottom, just left of the center of the blue arm of the cross. Then proceed to lay down trump numbers one to twenty and then number twenty-two clockwise in a circle as shown in Figure 18. This represents the life of Buddha in the physical world. It starts with his descent from the center and ends with his realization that he is the whole mandala. In the process he becomes one with Vairocana, the Jina of the center. As in the assertion in the quotation from Empedocles on page 223, the circle is an extension of the center, the center is everywhere, and there is no circumference.

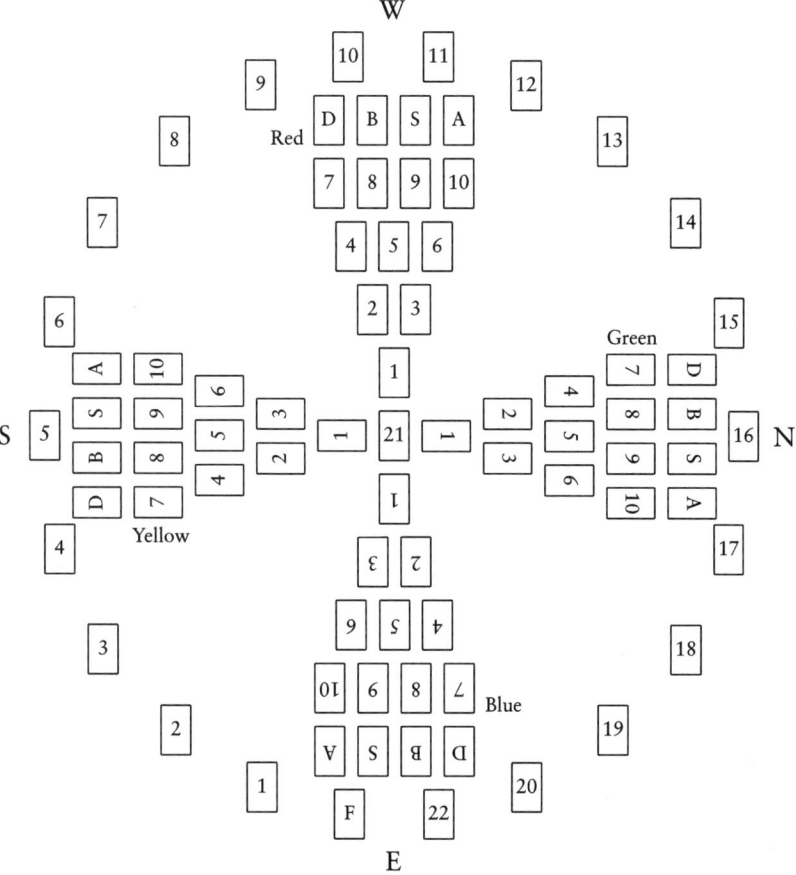

Figure 18—A Mandala of Cards

Make a comfortable seat for yourself on the east side of the mandala. You can use a cushion and sit on the floor or use a short stool or even a chair. You have to be comfortable to be able to relax your body. Sit and contemplate the mandala and observe your inhalations and exhalations. After a few minutes, your breathing will become deeper and you will begin to relax. As you relax, let your eyes follow the story of the Buddha from the descent from Tusita Heaven to the Parinirvana.

Then bring your eyes to the yellow arm of the cross. This is the earth element. Contemplate the nature of the earth element within yourself. Notice what is hard and solid in your body, and what parts of yourself are sustained by cravings. Contemplate your body, your head, your hair, nails, teeth, skin, muscles, and tendons. Proceed through the organs of the body—kidneys, heart, liver, and so on—and on to the bones, and then the marrow. Notice that this internal earth element is essentially no different than the earth element in any part of external reality such as rocks or wood. This is not your true self. Think of these things the way you think of rocks and fallen branches as something that you can observe with detachment.

Now, move your eyes to the green section of the cross, which represents the element water. Contemplate all the aspects of your body that are liquid. Think of your blood, sweat, tears, bile, phlegm, the oils of the body, urine, or anything else that is watery in the body. Take your time; don't leave anything out. Notice that this internal water is essentially no different from the external element of water. Think of salt water and of fresh water, of oil in the ground, of puddles, and sap. Water is not your true self. Think of the watery elements of your body with detachment—the way that you think of a stream or a puddle.

Now, move your eyes to the red arm of the cross directly across from you. This represents the fire element. Think of the parts of your self that are fiery. Pay attention to any part of the body that is warm, that takes part in the process of consuming your food and turning it into heat. Think of chewing or drinking, and digestion in the stomach and in the intestines. Think of the energy that is produced and what you can do with that energy: lift a heavy object, run or walk, or any other thing. Then picture a flame, perhaps in a campfire or on a stove, and realize that the fire in you is essentially the same as that external fire. This is not your true self. Think of the fire within with the same detachment as you think of the fire on the stove.

Now, move your eyes to the blue arm of the cross, directly at your feet. This represents the element air. Contemplate the wind inside your body. Think of your breath and any other winds in the body. See how the air moves from the outside of your body, comes into your nose and mouth, and fills your lungs. Exhale, and see how the body contracts as the air inside the body becomes the air outside of the body. The wind is not your true self. Think of this internal wind with detachment as you think of wind in the trees.

Now, contemplate the space between the arms of the cross and the space between the cards themselves. With your inner eye, look inside your body and contemplate the spaces within. Look at your chest and measure the space in your lungs, heart, and other organs. Ask yourself, *How much space is there between my sternum and my spine, and from my collarbone to the base of my pelvis?* There are air passages and space for food to go in. Now, think of your head. Ask yourself, *How much space is there between my nose and the back of my head?* There are sinuses and space for the brain to function. Contemplate the other parts of the body in the same way. Think of the space in bones and in nerves. Think of the space in molecules and atoms. The particles in each atom in the body are so small that the vast majority of the atom is all space. How is this space any different than external space? Space is not your true self. Think of this space with detachment.

Now, move your eyes to the center of the mandala—to Tara. If you are not the earth of your body, not the water of your body, not the fire, not the air, and not the space of your body, what are you? There is only consciousness. Contemplate your consciousness. As you contemplate Tara, look at each thought and examine it. If a thought comes up that is a desire related to the needs and pleasures of the body, let go of it. Feel it moving up and out of the top of your head. This thought stems from what is not you. If a negative thought comes up such as fear or anger, do not dwell on it. Let go of this thought also. These thoughts are not you. Close your eyes. Watch as these thoughts come into you, and watch as they leave. When these thoughts cease, look beyond these thoughts to what is still there. If a light appears that is not a thought, contemplate that light as long as you desire.

The pure mind, the source of everything, shines forever and on all with the brilliance of its own perfection. But the people of the world do not awake to it, regarding only that which sees, hears, feels, and knows as mind. Blinded by their own sight, hearing, feeling, and knowing, they do not perceive the spiritual brilliance of the source-substance. If they would only eliminate all conceptual thought in a flash, that source-substance would manifest itself like a sun ascending through the void and illuminating the whole universe without hindrance or bounds.[4]

Acknowledgments

I wish to thank my wife for her encouragement while I was working on this book, and Robert Kohls and Lisa Bach for their encouragement when I was first developing this idea. I want to thank historians Robert O'Neill and Ron Decker for answering my inquiries about Tarot history, and Robert O'Neill again for his foreword to this book; Barbara Moore, Tarot acquisitions editor at Llewellyn, for her enthusiasm about this project; Lynne Menturweck, the art director at Llewellyn, for her skill and consideration in handling the art; and my editor, Joanna Willis, for making a hard job look easy.

Notes

Introduction

1. John Snelling, *The Buddhist Handbook: A Complete Guide to Buddhist Schools, Teaching, Practice, and History* (Rochester, VT: Inner Traditions, 1991), 119.
2. *Encyclopaedia Britannica,* 2001 Standard Edition CD, s.v. "Hinduism."
3. Carl Kerenyi, *Eleusis: Archetypal Image of Mother and Daughter* (Princeton, NJ: Princeton University Press, 1991), 100.
4. *Encyclopaedia Britannica,* 2001 Standard Edition CD, s.v. "Polo, Marco."
5. David Fideler, ed., *The Pythagorean Sourcebook and Library,* trans. Kenneth Sylvan Guthrie (Grand Rapids, MI: Phanes Press, 1988), 74.
6. Ibid., 14.

Chapter 1

1. Stuart R. Kaplan, *The Encyclopedia of the Tarot* (New York: U.S. Games Systems, Inc., 1978), 1:24.
2. Michael Dummett, *The Visconti-Sforza Tarot Cards* (New York: George Braziller, Inc., 1986), 6.
3. Ronald Decker and Michael Dummett, *A History of the Occult Tarot 1870–1970* (London: Duckworth, 2002), ix.
4. Dummett, *The Visconti-Sforza Tarot Cards,* 9.

Chapter 2

1. Ted Honderich, ed., *The Oxford Companion to Philosophy* (Oxford, UK: Oxford University Press, 1995), 686.

2. Walter Scott, ed. and trans., *Hermetica* (Boston: Shambhala, 1985), 1:123.
3. Ibid., 123.
4. Ibid., 127.
5. Alain de Botton, ed., *The Essential Plato,* trans. Benjamin Jowett (New York: Quality Paperback Book Club, 1999), 741.
6. Ibid., 743.
7. Ibid., 745.
8. Fideler, *The Pythagorean Sourcebook and Library,* 274.
9. Ibid., 174.
10. Ibid., 70.
11. Laleh Bakhtiar, *Sufi: Expressions of the Mystic Quest* (New York: Thames and Hudson, 1997), 7.
12. Omer Englebert, *St. Francis of Assisi: A Biography* (Ann Arbor, MI: Servant Books, 1979), 72.
13. Ibid., 251.
14. Ramon Lull, *Blanquerna,* trans. E. A. Peers (London: Dedalus/Hippocrene Books, n.d.), 455.
15. Sarel Eimerl, *The World of Giotto: c. 1267–1337* (New York: Time Incorporated, 1967), 163.
16. Jacob Burckhardt, *The Civilization of the Renaissance in Italy* (New York: Harper & Row, 1958), 2:467.
17. Ibid., 2:411.
18. Kaplan, *The Encyclopedia of the Tarot,* 2:142.
19. Ibid., 2:144.
20. Ibid.
21. Ibid.
22. Ibid., 2:146.
23. Ibid., 2:147.
24. Burckhardt, *Civilization,* 2:479, footnote 4.
25. Marsilio Ficino, *Meditations on the Soul: Selected Letters of Marsilio Ficino,* trans. Language Department of the School of Economic Science, London (Rochester, VT: Inner Traditions International, 1996), xii.
26. Erwin Panofsky, *Studies in Iconology: Humanistic Themes in the Art of the Renaissance* (New York: Harper & Row, 1972), 121.
27. Ibid., 77.

28. Ficino, *Meditations on the Soul*, 53.
29. Peter Kingsley, *Ancient Philosophy, Mystery, and Magic: Empedocles and Pythagorean Tradition* (Oxford, UK: Clarendon Press, 1995), 13.

Chapter 3

1. Karen Armstrong, *Buddha* (New York: Penguin Putnam Inc., 2001), xi–xxix.
2. Huston Smith, *The Illustrated World's Religions: A Guide to Our Wisdom Traditions* (San Francisco: HarperCollins Publishers, 1994), 63.
3. Sangharakshita, *A Guide to the Buddhist Path* (Birmingham, UK: Windhorse Publications, 1997), 130–31.
4. Ibid., 130.
5. Snelling, *The Buddhist Handbook*, 26.
6. Smith, *The Illustrated World's Religions*, 75.

Chapter 4

1. Mircea Eliade, *Images and Symbols: Studies in Religious Symbolism* (Princeton, NJ: Princeton University Press, 1991), 27–56.
2. Esther M. Harding, *Woman's Mysteries: Ancient and Modern* (New York: Harper & Row Publishers, 1971), 90.
3. Although the archetypal hero is being referred to as male in this paragraph, the same description is applicable to female heroes.
4. L. Austine Waddell, *Tibetan Buddhism: With Its Mystic Cults, Symbolism, and Mythology* (New York: Dover Publications, 1972), 78–86.
5. Ibid., 417.
6. The information in this list is based on C. G. Jung, *Psychological Types*, Bollingen Series 20 (Princeton, NJ: Princeton University Press, 1990), 330–408.
7. The information in this list is based on Smith, *The Illustrated World's Religions*, 26–38.

Chapter 5

1. John Opsopaus, *Guide to the Pythagorean Tarot* (St. Paul, MN: Llewellyn Publications, 2001), 21–22.

2. Kaplan, *The Encyclopedia of the Tarot,* 1:28, 345.
3. Fideler, *The Pythagorean Sourcebook and Library,* 158.
4. Armstrong, *Buddha,* 30.
5. *The Oxford Classical Dictionary,* 3rd ed., ed. Simon Hornblower and Antony Spawforth (Oxford, UK: Oxford University Press, 1996), s.v. "Asceticism."
6. Ian J. Baker, *The Tibetan Art of Healing* (San Francisco: Chronicle Books, 1997), 16.
7. Ibid., 89.
8. Armstrong, *Buddha,* 89.
9. Sangharakshita, *A Guide to the Buddhist Path,* 41.
10. Plato, *Timaeus and Critias,* trans. Desmond Lee (London: Penguin Books, 1977), 50.
11. Fideler, *The Pythagorean Sourcebook and Library,* 72.
12. Armstrong, *Buddha,* 77.
13. Baker, *The Tibetan Art of Healing,* 183.
14. Eliade, *Images and Symbols,* 75.
15. This dialogue has been created by the author to dramatize the event.
16. Smith, *The Illustrated World's Religions,* 63.

Chapter 6

1. Jack Kornfield, ed., *Teachings of the Buddha* (New York: Barnes & Noble Books, 1996), 101.
2. Ibid., 107.
3. Baker, *The Tibetan Art of Healing,* 165.
4. Matthew 25:40
5. Kornfield, *Teachings of the Buddha,* 108.
6. Lucien Stryk and Takashi Ikemoto, eds., *Zen: Poems, Prayers, Sermons, Anecdotes, Interviews* (Garden City, NY: Doubleday Anchor, 1965), 113.
7. Kornfield, *Teachings of the Buddha,* 186–87.

Chapter 7

1. *The Oxford Classical Dictionary,* ed. Hornblower and Spawforth, s.v. "Oracles."

2. Waddell, *Tibetan Buddhism*, 465.
3. Mircea Eliade, *Myth and Reality* (New York: Harper & Row Publishers, 1963), 25.
4. Kornfield, *Teachings of the Buddha*, 195.

Glossary

Note: The oldest Buddhist texts are written in Pali, which is close to the language of northern India used during Buddha's lifetime. Early Buddhists chose Pali, a common language, rather than Sanskrit, the learned language, to relate Buddha's teachings because they wanted them to be accessible to common people. However, later texts were written in Sanskrit and it is the Sanskrit versions of the Buddhist terms that are best known in America today. The Sanskrit terms and names are used in this book because they are the ones that are now more accessible to the public. In transliterating them from the Sanskrit alphabet to the Roman alphabet, the letter or combination of letters that are the best equivalent to the original sound were chosen.

Adi Buddha: The archetypal Buddha that is one with everything, the totality. He exists in the highest heaven above Mount Meru from where he can permeate all reality.

Aksobhya: (Also spelled *Akshobhya* because the *s* is pronounced like the *sh* in *she*.) The name of one of the five great Buddhas called *Jinas*. Aksobhya is the blue Jina of the east. His emblem is the vajra, his element is air, and his Sakti is Locana. His name means "immovable" or "unshakable."

Amitabha: The name of one of the five great Buddhas called *Jinas*. Amitabha is the red Jina of the west. His emblem is the lotus, his element is fire, and his Sakti is Pandara. His name means "he whose splendor is immeasurable" or "infinite light."

Amoghasiddhi: The name of one of the five great Buddhas called *Jinas*. Amoghasiddhi is the green Jina of the north. His emblem is the double vajra, his element is water, and his Sakti is Tara. His name means "infallible success" or "unobstructed accomplishment."

anamnesis: Greek word meaning to "cease to forget." Plato believed that all knowledge was within us from before we were born, but at birth we fell into forgetfulness. When we come into knowledge, we are really remembering it. Therefore, he used this term for "knowledge." This is similar to the title *Buddha,* which means "to wake up."

Ananda: Literally, "bliss." This is the name of Buddha's most loyal disciple and companion. He was born on Wesak, the same day as Buddha.

Anima Mundi: Latin for "the soul of the world." In Neoplatonic philosophy, the Anima Mundi is the second emanation down from the One or the Godhead. The first emanation is Nous, which is a masculine word meaning "mind" or "intelligence." The *Anima—Psyche* in Greek—is a feminine word meaning "soul." She is the love or compassion that permeates the physical world. It is interesting that the masculine and feminine attributes of wisdom and compassion are the opposite in Buddhism. The alchemists associated the Anima Mundi with the quinta essentia.

ascetic: Self-denial, particularly the denial of food and sex, as a spiritual discipline. It is derived from the ancient Greek word *askesis,* which referred to the labor or exercise necessary to become an athlete. Ancient athletes were also known for their self-denial. They placed strict limits on their diets and on their sexual activity. This was also called *askesis*. As this discipline led to self-mastery, the term came to be used for spiritual discipline as well. In the ancient world, *askesis* was used to distinguish the spiritual practices of philosophers, which included fasting and silent meditation, from the ritual practices of the priests. In the Greek view, Buddha would obviously be regarded as a philosopher.

Asita: A respected and learned Brahman who lived in a retreat in the Himalayan mountains. When Siddhartha was born, he heard news of the child and came to see him. After examining Siddhartha's body, he found on him the thirty-two marks and eighty signs that proved that he was a great man. Afterward, Asita began to weep because he realized that he would not live to hear this future Buddha's teachings.

Asura: A race of giants that live at the base of Mount Meru. At one time they were gods, but because of their pridefulness they were expelled to this lowly realm. Because of their pride, they live in a constant state of war and die in futile battles against the gods. An Asura can be seen near the center of the Wheel of Life representing pride pulling a human down.

Ayurveda: (The *ay* is pronounced like a long *i*.) It means "the science of life." Ayurveda is an ancient Indian healing system in which health is attained by balancing three bodily humors called *doshas*. The doshas are related to the elements. *Vata* is related to air, *pitta* is related to fire, and *kapha* is related to water. Ayurveda is comparable to Western alchemy and to medicine as practiced in the Renaissance (except that in Renaissance medicine there are four humors because there is also one related to earth).

bhakti yoga: The yoga of love and the fire of devotion. This is the simplest and most popular form of religious devotion. It involves transferring the love that one normally feels for a mate or another loved one to a god or goddess. At its root is the power of compassion. It is related to the feeling function in Jungian depth psychology.

Bodhi Tree: (Also called the *Bo Tree*—both pronounced with a long *o*.) *Bodhi* or *bo* means "enlightenment." The Bodhi Tree is a pipal tree—a type of fig tree (*Ficus religiosa*)—that Buddha sat under when he attained enlightenment. It is believed to be in the center of the world and to have sprouted on the day that Buddha was born.

Bodhisattva: Means "pure-minded one." It refers to a person who is in the process of becoming a Buddha. Technically everyone is a Bodhisattva, but it is primarily used to describe individuals who are on the verge of becoming a Buddha but hold off the final attainment of Nirvana so that they can help others to progress toward enlightenment. In Mahayana Buddhism, Bodhisattvas are comparable to saints in Christianity.

Brahma: The creator god in Hinduism. Part of the trinity Brahma, Vishnu, and Shiva. *Brahma* also means "the ultimate ground of being," the ultimate experience of the true nature of reality.

Brahman: The highest caste in Indian society, traditionally fulfilling the role of priests in Hinduism.

Buddha: Literally, "one who is awake." A Buddha is a title like "Christ." It refers to one who has attained enlightenment. In Mahayana Buddhism, the most prevalent form, there are numerous Buddhas besides Siddhartha Gautama, the historic Buddha.

cardinal virtues: The four virtues that were deemed essential for spiritual progress in the works of Plato and other philosophers: temperance, strength, justice, and prudence. St. Ambrose, the fourth-century "Doctor of the Church," labeled them "cardinal." The word *cardinal* is derived from the Latin word *cardo,* which means "axis." *Cardinal* refers to something that turns a wheel on its axis. By using this word, St. Ambrose was saying that the practice of virtue is like a wheel of our making that can replace the irrational wheel of fate.

castes: The four hereditary social classes of Hindu society that are formed into a hierarchical structure with Brahmans on the top. Each caste is restricted in what occupations and social roles the members can participate.

chakra: (Pronounced *"sha-kra,"* the first *a* like in *father,* the second like the last *a* in *banana.*) This is the Sanskrit word for "wheel." It is used as the name of the psychic energy centers located in the body, especially ascending the spine. There are different numbers of chakras in various Hindu and Buddhist theories, but the system with seven is the one most commonly known in the West. The Western equivalent would be the soul centers mentioned by Plato.

chakravartin: Literally, "wheel-turner." The title of the great man or emperor in Indian mythology. The chakravartin, by purifying his karma through good deeds in past lives, has earned the right and ability to subjugate lesser kings and conquer an empire. His rule is characterized by harmony and justice like King Arthur in British myth.

Chandaka: Siddhartha's squire, to whom he gave his horse when he left home. Chandaka was born on Wesak, the same day as Siddhartha.

cintamani: The wish-granting jewel of Buddhist mythology.

Cunda: The blacksmith from Papa who served Buddha a dinner with a "pork treat." The dish started Buddha on the road to death.

Dakini: A dancing goddess, the Buddhist equivalent to an angel. The name is derived from the Sanskrit word for space. Her name in Tibetan is *Khandroma,* which means "sky-walker." The space that the Dakini dances in with freedom and abandon is the mind. Each Dakini is a representation of an aspect of a Buddha manifesting in the world through our minds. They can be threatening or sexually alluring. They inspire, teach, and admonish.

Dharmachakra: Usually translated as "the wheel of the law." *Chakra* means "wheel" and *dharma* means "the fundamental law of existence," "the truth," or "true understanding of reality." Therefore, *Dharmachakra* could also be translated as "the wheel of truth." Buddha is said to have set the Dharmachakra in motion when he delivered his first sermon in Deer Park. The Dharmachakra represents the salvation offered by Buddha's teaching. It symbolically replaces the Wheel of Life, the Buddhist equivalent of the Wheel of Fortuna.

dosha: *See* Ayurveda.

dukkha: Usually translated as "suffering," but more accurately meaning "off center" or "not right." It was used to describe a wheel with a bent axial. In the first noble truth, Buddha identified dukkha as the problem that permeates life.

emanation: A theory of creation in which the One or First Cause is continually creating reality by manifesting into progressively lesser beings. The resulting hierarchical structure becomes a ladder of ascent that a mystic can visualize and use as a means of progressing toward the experience of oneness.

enlightenment: The direct understanding of the true nature of reality. Enlightenment is achieved through a combination of wisdom and compassion that allows one to let go of the ego and the illusion of separateness and achieve oneness. To become enlightened is to become a Buddha. *Gnosis* is a similar term in Greek.

garuda: A mythical animal that is part bird and part man or woman. They usually have bird's wings, legs, and beaks. Sometimes they are shown in armor or playing a flute. They are said to live inside Mount Meru. In Hindu mythology, the garuda is the celestial mount of the god Vishnu. In Buddhism, the garuda is the sworn enemy of the serpent creatures called *nagas*. Nagas are snakelike creatures that are said to be evil and cause disease. Because they destroy nagas, garudas are great healers and are used as a symbol of healing.

Gautama: *See* Siddhartha.

gnosis: (The *g* is silent.) *Gnosis* is a Greek word for knowledge that is gained through a spiritual experience—similar to the word *enlightenment*. The *Hermetica* says that with the attainment of gnosis, one becomes a god. *Gnostic* is a modern term used to refer to ancient mystics who sought gnosis. It is now mostly used as a name of heretical Christian groups, but it can also refer to Hermetic and Jewish mystics.

guru: (Pronounced *"gu-ru."* The *u*'s are like the double *o* in the word *too*.) *Guru* is the Sanskrit word for "teacher," but it literally means "heavy" or "grave," which shows the respect a guru is given. The Tibetan equivalent is *lama,* which means "unexcelled."

Hellenistic: This word is derived from the Greek name for their homeland. *Hellenistic* refers to the historic cultural period initiated by Alexander the Great in the fourth century BCE. Alexander made an effort to spread Greek language, art, and culture throughout his empire. This common language, artistic style, and education helped to create a prosperous cosmopolitan atmosphere in the area from Greece and Egypt east to India that lasted even after his death and the political disunity that followed. The center of Hellenistic culture was Alexandria in Egypt where a synthesis of Greek, Egyptian, and Jewish culture flourished. Although the Hellenistic kingdoms were conquered by Rome and absorbed into the empire, Rome also was influenced by Hellenistic culture.

Hermetica: The religious philosophical texts written by a group of mystical philosophers in Alexandria from the second to the fourth centuries CE. Although they are written by numerous authors, all of the texts are ascribed to Hermes Trismegistus. Hermes Trismegistus is a synthesis of the Greek god Hermes with the Egyptian god Thoth. In the texts he is presented as a sage who lived long before the birth of Christ. The *Hermetica* explains how Hermes attained gnosis and became a god.

Heruka: Literally, "blood-drinker." The name of the wrathful aspect of a Buddha or a Jina conceived as a separate being. Each Heruka has a Heruka Sakti.

Indra: The Hindu god of the sky and of storms, rain, and fertility. He is comparable to the Greek god Zeus. His weapon is the vajra, which symbolizes his lightning and thunder and his power. His importance was eclipsed by the Hindu trinity: Brahma, Vishnu, and Shiva.

Jains: Members of a religious group in India founded in the sixth century BCE. The founder is called the Jina, the "conqueror," or Mahavira, the "great man." Like Buddhists, Jains seek to free themselves from the wheel of reincarnation. Many Jains were known for their severe ascetic practices.

Jina: Literally, "conqueror." The title of the enlightened master in Jainism. In Buddhism it became an alternative title for a Buddha, particularly used for the five archetypal Buddhas of the five directions.

jnana yoga: The yoga of knowledge. Although this is an intellectual path and involves reading and study, the ultimate goal of oneness is beyond reason. Therefore, yogis have developed a system for using the intellect to explore its limits and to expose the inability of logic to express ultimate reality. Jnana yoga is related to the thinking function in Jungian depth psychology.

jongleurs: (Pronounced *"zho-'gler"*; the *o* is long.) Professional musicians who traveled from one castle to another in France, Spain, and Italy in the late Middle Ages singing for their keep. They performed songs composed by troubadours and occasionally fulfilled both roles. Jongleurs could also perform as jugglers, acrobats, and fools. *Jongleur* is related to the English words *juggler* and *jester*.

Kabbalah: (Also spelled *Qabala, Qabalah, Qabbalah, Cabala, Cabbala, Cabbalah,* or *Kabbala.*) Literally, "tradition." The Kabbalah is Jewish Neoplatonism, said to be derived from an ancient, mystical, oral tradition. Kabbalists believe that God creates through a ladder of emanation. The ladder contains ten emanations, called *sefirot* (also spelled *sephiroth*), usually depicted as circles connected by pathways in a diagram called the *Tree of Life.*

Kantaka: Siddhartha's horse, which he rode when he left home to become an ascetic. Once away from home, he gave Kantaka to his squire Chandaka. Kantaka was born on Wesak, the same day as Siddhartha.

Kapilavastu: A small kingdom in what is now northern India and southern Nepal. This is where Siddhartha lived and where his father ruled.

karma: The Buddhist and Hindu equivalent of divine justice. *Karma* means that one's past actions will determine the conditions of each incarnation. If one falls into ignorant, unskillful actions dominated by greed, hatred, and confusion, the karma one has earned will lead to a life of hardship. If one overcomes ignorance and begins to act skillfully, motivated by generosity, love, and awareness, this will earn the karma that brings rebirth in a life of ease.

karma yoga: The yoga of work practiced in the workplace. To practice, one must be involved in commerce, but not lose one's way in the self-centered desires that the workplace can engender. To accomplish this, one can detach oneself from the outcome of one's work by working for the sake of the activity with no thought of reward, or by offering the rewards to a deity. It is related to the sensation function in Jungian depth psychology.

Ksatriya: (Pronounced *"ksha-tree-a"*; the *i* is like a long *e.*) The third highest caste in Indian society. Ksatriyas are the warriors and the protectors of the people. In the West we would call them the landed gentry. This is the caste into which Siddhartha was born.

Kundalini: A goddess who takes the form of a coiled serpent that resides at the base of the spine in all humans. When the chakras are fully activated, she awakes and stretches up the spine. She represents vital energy that is activated. Her name is the feminine form of the word for "ring" or "coil."

Locana: The Sakti of Aksobhya. She is blue and lives in the east. Her name means "the clear-visioned one."

Mahaprajapati: Maya's younger sister, who acted as a mother to Siddhartha after Maya's death.

Mamaki: The Sakti of Ratnasambhava. She is yellow and lives in the south. Her name means "mine-maker."

mandala: Sanskrit for "circle." A mandala is a sacred map of the world that captures the inner psychic reality. Mandalas are geometric patterns that often make use of circles and fourfold divisions. They illustrate the sacred center of the world and often place a deity or sacred being in the center. Leonardo da Vinci's drawing *Vitruvian Man,* which depicts a man simultaneously fitting into a circle and into a square, and the Christ in Majesty icon are Western examples of mandalas.

Mara: One of the gods, but also the king of the demons called *maras*. He is the Buddhist equivalent of the Christian Devil. His name means "delusion." When Siddhartha approached enlightenment, Mara interceded to try and stop him. Mara is said to be the ruler of this world. He is symbolic of the ego.

Maya: (The *ay* is pronounced like a long *i*.) Siddhartha's mother. Although she was married to Suddhodhana, the king of Kapilavastu, she was a virgin when she conceived Siddhartha. She was traveling when Siddhartha was born. She stopped in Lumbini Park and, while holding on to a Sala Tree, Siddhartha came out of her side. Seven days later she died of joy and was reincarnated in Tusita Heaven.

meditation: *See* raja yoga.

Mucalinda: King of the serpent creatures called *nagas*. After Buddha attained enlightenment, Buddha sat under the Bodhi Tree for seven weeks. It became monsoon season, and Mucalinda protected Buddha from the rain by coiling around Buddha's body with his own seven times and sheltering Buddha's head with his seven heads fanned out like an umbrella. Although nagas are evil, Mucalinda proved that he was not by aiding the Buddha. Mucalinda may be considered a symbol of the kundalini.

mudra: A Buddhist hand gesture that has symbolic meaning, such as the gestures of instruction, dispelling fear, meditation, and so on. Each Jina has a characteristic mudra. The hand sign for benediction in Christianity is a Western equivalent.

mystic: Derived from the Greek word *mystes,* which referred to an initiate in one of the ancient mystery cults. Mystics strive for knowledge and to experience the oneness of reality. In Christianity, this is described as a beatific vision of God, a face-to-face relationship with God and God's love. In Buddhism, this is described as Nirvana, in which separateness is extinguished.

nagas: *See* Garuda; Mucalinda.

Necessity: *Ananke* in Greek. The name of the goddess who ruled over the workings of the cosmos and the fate of individual souls. She is the mother of the three Fates, and even Zeus is said to be subject to her. Plato places the cosmos in her lap. Her Latin equivalent is the goddess Fortuna.

Nemesis: The Greek goddess of divine punishment. She is one aspect of Fate.

Neoplatonists: The modern name for Platonic philosophers who think of Plato as a mystic and combine his philosophy with various mystical systems. Historians usually credit Plotinus (205–270 CE) as being the first Neoplatonist.

Nirvana: This means "to extinguish," like the flame of a candle, but what is extinguished is ego and separateness. Nirvana is the supreme state of bliss that comes when enlightenment is attained. Some Buddhists believe that it can be attained while still in the body; others believe it can only be attained after death.

Nous: *See* Anima Mundi.

The One: In Platonic philosophy, the divine unity that is the source of all creation. It is also called the Good and the Beautiful. To experience the One is the goal of the mystic.

ouroboros: A Greek word meaning "tail-devourer." It is the name of an image of a serpent that forms a circle by biting its tail. The ouroboros is a symbol for the cyclical nature of time and for the limits of time and space. It is related to the circle of the zodiac, which was believed to be the edge of the cosmos and the measure of the yearly cycle of time. It is also related to the wheel of Fortuna.

Pali: The language that the oldest Buddhist scriptures are written in. It is close to the common language used in Kapilavastu and the Ganges valley in Buddha's lifetime. Because Buddhist terms are more commonly known in Sanskrit in the West today, the Pali forms may seem strange to the Western reader. For example, *Nirvana* in Pali is *Nibbana*.

Pandara: The Sakti of Amitabha. She is red and lives in the west. Her name means "the white-robed one."

Parinirvana: The death of a Buddha. Parinirvana is the transition that happens at death when the physical life of a Buddha comes to an end but the state of Nirvana remains. All icons and statues depicting Buddha lying on his right side are images of the Parinirvana.

quincunx: A design containing five objects in which four of them are placed one to each corner and the fifth is in the center, like the five on a die. It is a type of mandala used to illustrate the sacred center or the fifth element in sacred art. The World card in the Tarot of Marseilles is a quincunx.

quinta essentia: Literally, the "essential fifth," an alchemical term for the fifth element, the unseen spirit that holds the four mundane elements together and permeates all matter. It is the spirit in matter that the alchemist works to uncover. When found, it is the immaterial substance that comprises the Philosopher's Stone. The word *quintessence* is derived from it.

Rahula: The name of Siddhartha's son. His mother is Yasodhara.

raja yoga: *Raja* means "royal" and this path is called royal because it is the principal path to enlightenment. It makes use of meditation. Meditation involves progressively taking attention away from the body, the ego, and the unconscious until the mind is like still water. In this stillness, the Ground of Being can be experienced. Raja yoga is related to the intuitive function in Jungian depth psychology.

Ratnasambhava: One of the five great Buddhas called *Jinas*. He is the yellow Jina of the south. His emblem is the jewel, his element is earth, and his Sakti is Mamaki. His name means "the jewel-born one."

sadhu: A Hindu mendicant. He is a wandering holy man who lives by begging for food, similar to the first Franciscans.

Sakti: (Also spelled *Shakti*. Pronounced *"shak-tee."* The *a* is pronounced like the *a* in *father* and the *i* is pronounced like the *e* in *beat*. Because this Sanskrit *s* is pronounced like an *sh*, it is sometimes written that way.) A female Buddha or goddess who personifies the dynamic energy of a male Buddha or a Hindu god. The name comes from the Sanskrit words meaning "power." In Buddhism, the Sakti personifies the wisdom and the Buddha personifies the compassion of the same entity. The Buddha and the Sakti are often depicted in a sexual embrace called *yab-yum* ("father-mother") to symbolize the blissful state of enlightenment.

Sakyamuni: *See* Siddhartha.

Siddhartha: The name of the historic Buddha born in 563 BCE. At birth, he was given the name Siddhartha, and his family name was Gautama. During his ascetic period, he is usually referred to by his family name. Technically, *Buddha* is a title, not a name. It means "one who is awake." To the Buddhists, a Buddha is no longer a man, he is something superior to the gods. Siddhartha is only called Buddha after he is transformed through the experience of enlightenment. He is also called *Sakyamuni*, which means "the sage (*-muni*) of the Sakya clan."

Stoicism: A Greek philosophical school stemming from the teaching of Zeno in about 300 BCE. The name is derived from *stoa*, the Greek word for "porch" or "portico," because Zeno lectured at the Painted

Portico in Athens. Stoics believe that the wise can achieve a state of calm beyond hope and fear, and place a strong emphasis on the role of the Anima Mundi.

stupa: A Buddhist monument derived from Indian tumuli. It is a symbol of the axis mundi. The earliest ones housed the relics of Buddha. The different sections of this tower represent the five elements. Their order demonstrates the descent of spirit into matter, a concept similar to the ladder of emanations found in Neoplatonism. The floor plan of a stupa is related to the mandala.

Suddhodhana: Siddhartha's father, the king or ruler of Kapilavastu.

Sudra: (Pronounced *"shu-dra."* The *u* is pronounced as the *u* in *rule*.) The lowest caste in traditional Indian society. Sudra are farmers and tradesmen of low standing. The lowest members of this group were called *Untouchables*. These were laborers, and their duty was to serve.

Sufis: Members of an Islamic mystical sect that incorporates Neoplatonism into Islam. The word *Sufi* is derived from the root *suf,* which means "wool" and referred to wool-wearing ascetics from the time of Mohammed. In the late Middle Ages and up to the present, Sufis are characterized as optimistic mystics that create love poetry and songs that make use of erotic imagery to symbolize their quest for Allah or God.

Sujata: A beautiful young woman from a village who offered Gautama rice and milk in a golden bowl when he broke his fast.

sutras: Buddhist sacred texts, which are named after the string used to tie the ancient loose-leaf books together.

tanha: Selfish desire or selfishness. The root of the three poisons: greed, aggression, and ignorance. In the second noble truth, Buddha identifies tanha as the cause of dukkha (*see* dukkha).

Tantra: An esoteric teaching found in Hinduism, Jainism, and Buddhism, particularly in Tibet. Tantra focuses on yogic practices instead of philosophy and theory.

Tara: The Sakti of Amoghasiddhi. She is green and lives in the north. Her name means "the one who ferries over." There is also a white Tara associated with wisdom and the center, and other colored Taras including yellow, blue, and red, each ruling a different aspect.

Tarocchi: The Italian name for Tarot.

Themis: The ancient Greek goddess of divine justice. Themis was the second wife of Zeus. She continued to be his companion after he married Hera.

troubadours: Mostly nobles living in southern France in the late Middle Ages who composed love poems in the vernacular that were performed by professional musicians called *jongleurs*. The subject of their songs was always love and beauty, which they saw as a force of spiritual transformation. Their work was strongly influenced by Sufi poetry.

Tusita Heaven: A paradise in the sky above Mount Meru in the sacred center of the world. Tusita is the fourth heaven in the first section above the mountain. The beings who live there are gods and Bodhisattvas, and they live in a constant state of joy. In Buddhist theology, the gods and Bodhisattvas enjoy exceptionally long lives, but they are not immortal. Siddhartha lived there before his last incarnation in the world of humans.

Upanishads: The last addition to the Vedas, the Hindu sacred texts. The Upanishads give a mystical interpretation to the Vedas that is the basis of Hindu thought.

Vairocana: The name of one of the five great Buddhas called *Jinas*. The white Jina of the center of the world. His emblem is the wheel, and his element is aether, the immaterial substance of the center. His Sakti is Vajradharisvari. His name means "illuminator" or "shining one."

Vaisya: (Pronounced *"vish-ya."* The *ai* is like a long *i*.) The second highest caste in traditional Indian society. Vaisya was made up of commoners, which included merchants and bankers. They tended to avoid manual labor and sometimes were managers of farms.

vajra: A Sanskrit word that is not translatable. It combines the meanings "diamond," "lightning," and "ultimate power." It is the weapon of the Hindu god Indra. In Buddhist art it is the name of a scepter that represents the ultimate power. Buddhists conceive of this power as compassion. In one Buddhist meditation, the vajra is held in one hand and the bell, representing wisdom, is held in the other. The two hands interact in dancelike movements. It is the emblem of the Jina Aksobhya.

Vajradharisvari: The Sakti of Vairocana. She is white and lives in the center of the world. Her name means "the sovereign lady of the sphere of infinite space."

Vedas: The collection of inspired sacred texts that form the basis of Hinduism. The Vedas are interpreted and recited by Brahmans, the priest caste.

Wesak: (Also spelled *Vesak* or *Vaisaka*.) In the ancient Indian lunar calendar, each month is named after the full moon. The full moon is the magical center of the month when, as it is mostly done today, the new moon is considered the first day of the month. However, in ancient India, it was only reckoned this way in the south. In the north where Siddhartha was born, the full moon was the first day of the month. Siddhartha was born on the full moon of Wesak, which is equivalent to our month of May or sometimes June. It was on Wesak (of different years) that he also left home to become an ascetic, achieved enlightenment, and died and passed into Nirvana. On the day of his birth, his wife Yasodhara was born, his horse Kantaka was born, his squire Chandaka was born, his closest disciple Ananda was born, and the Bodhi Tree sprouted.

In Buddhism, Wesak is the most sacred day of the year. However, it is mostly observed in southern Asia. In the northern countries, particularly China, the Western calendar has been adopted and Buddha's birth is celebrated consistently on April 8, his enlightenment on December 8, and his Parinirvana on February 15.

yab-yum: Literally, "father-mother." This refers to the artistic convention of depicting the Buddha and Sakti together in a sexual embrace to symbolize the bliss of the state of Nirvana. Although the Buddha and Sakti are depicted as two individuals, they actually represent one being, and yab-yum helps to illustrate that concept.

yantras: Sacred geometric diagrams used in meditation and related to mandalas.

Yasodhara: Siddhartha's wife, a beautiful princess who bore him their son Rahula.

Yggdrasill: (The *ygg* is pronounced *"ig"* with a short *i* like in the word *pit*.) In Norse mythology, the tree in the center of the world that connects our world, Middle Earth, with the world of the gods above and the underworld below.

yoga: Primarily mental exercise or meditations, but also used to denote physical exercises that are used in connection with meditation. The purpose of yoga is to build spiritual ability and strength, and to help one to progress toward enlightenment. Some forms of yoga are ascetic.

Bibliography and Recommended Reading

Armstrong, Karen. *Buddha*. New York: Penguin Putnam Inc., 2001.

Baker, Ian J. *The Tibetan Art of Healing*. San Francisco: Chronicle Books, 1997.

Bakhtiar, Laleh. *Sufi: Expressions of the Mystic Quest*. New York: Thames and Hudson, 1997.

Boisselier, Jean. *The Wisdom of the Buddha*. New York: Harry N. Abrams, Inc., 1993.

Burke, Peter. *The Italian Renaissance: Culture and Society in Italy*. Princeton, NJ: Princeton University Press, 1986.

Burckhardt, Jacob. *The Civilization of the Renaissance in Italy*. 2 vols. New York: Harper & Row, 1958.

Carus, Paul. *The Gospel of Buddha*. Chicago: The Open Court Publishing Co., 1995.

The Concise Oxford Dictionary of Current English. 9th ed. Edited by Della Thompson. Oxford, UK: Clarendon Press, 1995.

de Botton, Alain. *The Essential Plato*. Translated by Benjamin Jowett. New York: Quality Paperback Book Club, 1999.

Decker, Ronald, Thierry Depaulis, and Michael Dummett. *A Wicked Pack of Cards: The Origins of the Occult Tarot*. New York: St. Martins Press, 1996.

Decker, Ronald, and Michael Dummett. *A History of the Occult Tarot 1870–1970*. London: Duckworth, 2002.

de Gebelin, Court. *Monde Primitif*. Vol. 8. Paris: de Gebelin, 1781.

Dummett, Michael. *The Visconti-Sforza Tarot Cards*. New York: George Braziller Inc., 1986.

Dunn-Mascetti, Manuela. *Saints: The Chosen Few*. New York: Ballantine Books, 1994.

Eimerl, Sarel. *The World of Giotto: c. 1267–1337*. New York: Time Incorporated, 1967.

Eliade, Mircea. *Images and Symbols: Studies in Religious Symbolism*. Princeton, NJ: Princeton University Press, 1991.

———. *Myth and Reality*. New York: Harper & Row Publishers, 1963.

———. *The Sacred and the Profane: The Nature of Religion*. Translated by Willard R. Trask. New York: Harper & Row Publishers, 1961.

Englebert, Omer. *St. Francis of Assisi: A Biography*. Ann Arbor, MI: Servant Books, 1979.

Ferguson, George. *Signs and Symbols in Christian Art*. New York: Oxford University Press, 1961.

Ficino, Marsilio. *Meditations on the Soul: Selected Letters of Marsilio Ficino*. Translated by the Language Department of the School of Economic Science, London. Rochester, VT: Inner Traditions International, 1996.

Fideler, David. *Jesus Christ Sun of God: Ancient Cosmology and Early Christian Symbolism*. Wheaton, IL: Quest Books, 1993.

———, ed. *The Pythagorean Sourcebook and Library.* Translated by Kenneth Sylvan Guthrie. Grand Rapids, MI: Phanes Press, 1988.

Frawley, David. *Ayurvedic Healing: A Comprehensive Guide.* Salt Lake City, UT: Morson Publishing, 1989.

Frederic, Louis. *Buddhism.* Flammarion Iconographic Guides. Paris: Flammarion, 1995.

Graves, Robert. *The Greek Myths.* 2 vols. Harmondsworth, UK: Penguin Books, Ltd., 1968–1971.

Guiley, Rosemary Ellen, and Robert M. Place. *The Alchemical Tarot.* London: Thorsons, 1995.

Guirand, Felix, ed. *Larousse Encyclopedia of Mythology.* Translated by Richard Aldington and Delano Ames. London: Paul Hamlyn, 1959.

Hall, James. *A History of Ideas and Images in Italian Art.* New York: Harper & Row Publishers, 1983.

Harding, Esther M. *Woman's Mysteries: Ancient and Modern.* New York: Harper & Row Publishers, 1971.

Hind, Arthur M. *An Introduction to a History of Woodcut.* Vol. 1. New York: Dover Publications, 1963.

Honderich, Ted, ed. *The Oxford Companion to Philosophy.* Oxford, UK: Oxford University Press, 1995.

Judith, Anodea. *The Sevenfold Journey: Reclaiming Mind, Body & Spirit Through the Chakras.* Freedom, CA: The Crossing Press, 1993.

Jung, C. G. *Psychological Types.* Bollingen Series 20. Princeton, NJ: Princeton University Press, 1971.

Kaplan, Stuart R. *The Encyclopedia of the Tarot.* 2 vols. New York: U.S. Games Systems, Inc., 1978–1986.

Kerenyi, Carl. *Eleusis: Archetypal Image of Mother and Daughter.* Princeton, NJ: Princeton University Press, 1991.

Kingsley, Peter. *Ancient Philosophy, Mystery, and Magic: Empedocles and Pythagorean Tradition.* Oxford, UK: Clarendon Paperbacks, 1995.

Knight, Gareth. *Magic and the Western Mind.* St. Paul, MN: Llewellyn Publications, 1991.

Kornfield, Jack, ed. *Teachings of the Buddha.* New York: Barnes & Noble Books, 1996.

Leonard, George. "The Teachings of Iamblichus: Between Eros and Anteros." *Lapis* 13 (2001): 61–66.

Lull, Ramon. *Blanquerna.* Translated by E. A. Peers. London: Dedalus/Hippocrene Books, n.d.

Moakley, Gertrude. *The Tarot Cards Painted by Bonifacio Bembo.* New York: The New York Public Library, 1966.

O'Neill, Robert. *Tarot Symbolism.* Lima, OH: Fairway Press, 1986.

Opsopaus, John. *Guide to the Pythagorean Tarot.* St. Paul, MN: Llewellyn Publications, 2001.

The Oxford Classical Dictionary. 3rd ed. Edited by Simon Hornblower and Antony Spawforth. Oxford, UK: Oxford University Press, 1996.

Panati, Charles. *Sacred Origins of Profound Things.* New York: Penguin, 1996.

Panofsky, Erwin. *Studies in Iconology: Humanistic Themes in the Art of the Renaissance.* New York: Harper & Row, 1972.

Patry Leidy, Denise, and Robert A. F. Thurman. *Mandala: The Architecture of Enlightenment.* Boston: Shambhala Publications, 1998.

Pennick, Nigel. *Games of the Gods: The Origin of Board Games in Magic and Divination.* York Beach, ME: Samuel Weiser, Inc., 1989.

Place, Robert M. *A Gnostic Book of Saints.* St. Paul, MN: Llewellyn Publications, 2001.

Plamintr, Phra Sunthorn, Ph.D. *Basic Buddhism Course.* Carmel, NY: The Buddhist Association of the United States, 2001.

Plato. *Timaeus and Critias.* Translated by Desmond Lee. London: Penguin Books, 1977.

Rawson, Philip. *The Art of Tantra.* London: Thames and Hudson, 1973.

———. *Tantra: The Indian Cult of Ecstasy.* London: Thames and Hudson, 1987.

Sangharakshita. *A Guide to the Buddhist Path.* Birmingham, UK: Windhorse Publications, 1997.

Santina, Peter D. *Fundamentals of Buddhism.* Carmel, NY: The Institute for Advanced Studies of World Religions, n.d.

Schiller, David. *The Little Zen Companion.* New York: Workman Publishing, 1994.

Scott, Walter, ed. and trans. *Hermetica: The Ancient Greek and Latin Writings Which Contain Religious or Philosophic Teachings Ascribed to Hermes Trismegistus.* Vol. 1. Boston: Shambhala Publications, 1985.

Sharp, Daryl. *Personality Types: Jung's Model of Typology.* Toronto: Inner City Books, 1987.

Shearer, Alastair. *Buddha: The Enlightened Heart.* London: Thames and Hudson, 1992.

Smith, Huston. *The Illustrated World's Religions: A Guide to Our Wisdom Traditions.* San Francisco: HarperCollins Publishers, 1994.

Snelling, John. *The Buddhist Handbook: A Complete Guide to Buddhist Schools, Teaching, Practice, and History.* Rochester, VT: Inner Traditions, 1991.

Spiegelman, J. Marvin, Ph.D., and Mokusen Miyuki, Ph.D. *Buddhism and Jungian Psychology.* Temple, AZ: New Falcon Publications, 1994.

Stryk, Lucien, and Takashi Ikemoto, eds. *Zen: Poems, Prayers, Sermons, Anecdotes, Interviews.* Garden City, NY: Doubleday Anchor, 1965.

Sumrdho, Ajahn. *The Four Noble Truths.* Hertfordshire, UK: Amaravati Publications, 1992.

Taylor, Thomas, and Floyer Sydenham, trans. *The Works of Plato.* Vol. 1. Somerset, UK: The Promethius Trust, 1995.

van den Brock, Roelof, and Wouter J. Hanegraaff, eds. *Gnosis and Hermeticism: From Antiquity to Modern Times.* Albany, NY: State University of New York Press, 1998.

Waddell, L. Austine. *Tibetan Buddhism: With Its Mystic Cults, Symbolism, and Mythology.* New York: Dover Publications, 1972.

Webster's Word Histories. Springfield, MA: Merriam-Webster Publishers, Inc., 1989.

Wu Shang Shih, Ching Hai. *The Key of Immediate Enlightenment.* Taiwan: Infinite Light Publishing, 1993.

Yates, Frances A. *The Art of Memory.* London: Pimlico, 1966.

Index

aether, 53, 107, 121, 206, 214, 260
Aksobhya, 117, 121, 214, 233, 246, 248, 250, 302
alchemy, xiv, 6–8, 12, 42–47, 55, 59, 67–68, 73, 80, 101–102, 104, 111–113, 115, 144–145, 150, 177–178, 192, 204, 206, 211–213, 216, 221, 229, 246, 252, 257, 265
Alexandria, 10–11, 33, 35, 42
Ambrose, Saint, 79, 87, 176
Amitabha, 117, 121, 214, 237, 271, 285, 287–289
Amoghasiddhi, 117, 121, 214, 224, 277, 290, 304, 306, 308
Ananda, 144, 228
anamnesis, 5, 27
Anima Mundi, 31, 44, 67, 80, 111–113, 115, 125, 246, 265
Aristotle, 6, 26, 33–34, 42, 59, 176
asceticism, xiii, 41, 44–45, 51, 81, 83, 85, 97, 99, 166, 181–182, 184–185, 188, 191, 195, 209, 219–220
Asoka, 10, 229, 290
Asita, 83, 138–139, 142
astrology, 34, 55, 76, 141, 310
Asura, 105, 178
Avalokitesvara, 289, 300
Avalon, Arthur, 206

Axial Age, 4, 282
axis mundi, 102–103, 106, 205, 260
Ayurveda, 257, 264, 279, 294

Bateleur, 76–77
bhakti yoga. *See under* yoga
Bible, 65–66, 73, 103, 109, 111, 258
Blanquerna, 12, 56–58, 78, 135, 155, 158, 165, 169
Blue Beryl, The, 236, 238, 305
boar, 294
Boccaccio, 59–60
Bodhisattva, 2, 8, 82, 101, 107, 134–136, 182, 270–271, 273, 289, 298, 300, 308, 311
Bodhi Tree, 7, 85, 92, 97, 128, 144, 173, 192
Bologna, 19, 79, 185
Book of the Lover and the Beloved, The, 57, 133
Botticelli, 13, 71
Brahma, 144, 219
Brahman, 2, 11, 45, 81, 83–84, 94, 138–139

Campbell, Joseph, 3, 99
"Canticle to Brother Sun, The," 52, 80
Carnival, 61, 95
Cary-Yale Visconti deck, 20, 67

caste, 9, 82–83, 93–94
Cathars, 12, 156, 175
Celts, 46, 109, 173, 284, 303
chakras, 5, 11, 30, 34, 99, 146, 202–204, 206–208, 225, 260–261, 286, 306, 317–323
chakravartin, 83, 138, 173–174, 180, 202, 229, 252, 284
Chandaka, 144, 159, 165, 179
Chariot, the, 20, 22, 62, 65, 78, 162–164, 177
Charlemagne, 19, 149
chi, 254
chivalry, 47, 49, 51, 55
China, 1–2, 11–12, 15–16, 81–82, 100, 106, 115, 131, 164, 167, 177, 238, 250, 254, 266, 269, 288–289, 310
Christ, 6, 11, 32, 42–44, 46, 50–51, 53–56, 59, 66, 68, 70, 73–76, 109, 111–113, 115–116, 128, 131, 196
Christ in Majesty, 73–75, 109–110, 114–115, 131, 224
Christianity, 2–3, 6, 11–12, 20, 23–24, 27, 32, 34, 39–43, 45–47, 50, 53–55, 58–61, 64, 67–71, 73, 79, 95–96, 102, 104, 109, 111, 115–116, 128, 131, 146, 156, 175–176, 194–196, 206, 221, 258, 271, 313
cintamani, 252
Claudianus, 39
Clement of Alexandria, 2, 39
cock, 120, 178
coins, 9, 16–17, 78, 95, 121, 139, 231
conch, 122, 301
Cunda, 228
Cupid, 62–63, 65, 72, 78, 98, 146, 154, 159, 163

cups, 17, 47, 78, 95, 121, 139, 188, 231

Dakini, 120–121, 224, 231, 246, 265, 285, 304, 324
Dalai Lama, 311
Dante, xi, 59–61, 63, 65, 103
de Fiore, Joachim, 54
Death, 20–21, 23, 62–63, 65, 79, 98, 187–189
Decker, Ronald, 19
Deer Park, 87, 131, 219–222, 235
della Mirandola, Pico, 58, 70
Devil, the, 20, 23, 65, 80, 98, 194–196
Dharmachakra, 87, 115, 174, 220, 235
diatonic scale, 205–206
dice, 76–77, 139–142, 310–311
Diotima, 38–39
divination, 17, 76–77, 124, 129, 132, 136, 138, 140–142, 147, 151, 154, 157, 161, 164, 168, 171, 178, 182, 186, 189, 193, 197, 201, 208, 212, 217, 222, 225, 230, 282, 309–313, 315, 317, 321, 323, 325, 327
Divine Comedy, The, 60, 103
Dominic, Saint, 55
dosha, 193, 257, 264, 279, 294
Dream of Poliphilo, The, 145
dukkha, 88, 186, 220
Dummett, Michael, 19

Egypt, 1, 4, 6, 9–10, 12–13, 15–16, 27, 32–33, 35, 43, 103, 124
Eightfold Path, 89, 92, 128, 220, 222, 262
Eight Glorious Emblems, 122–123, 232, 237, 239, 263, 278, 284, 292, 301, 303

Eight Lucky Symbols. *See* Eight Glorious Emblems
elements, 28–29, 36, 52–53, 77–78, 105, 107, 109, 111–112, 115–116, 120–121, 124–126, 129, 193, 206, 214, 216, 224–225, 231, 233, 251–252, 256–257, 260, 268, 270–271, 289–290, 308
Eleusis, 2, 11
Eliade, Mircea, 102, 323
emanation, 28–29, 31, 33–35, 42, 52, 107–109, 324
Empedocles, 77, 223, 324
Emperor, the, xiii, 77–78, 96, 98, 145–146, 150, 152–154
Empress, the, 22, 77–78, 96, 98, 145–146, 148–151, 153–154
enlightenment, xi–xiv, 4–5, 9, 15, 28, 37, 43, 59, 81, 84–86, 89, 91, 94, 96–97, 99, 118, 123, 126, 128, 136, 177, 180, 191, 193, 196, 199, 201–203, 205, 210, 212, 215, 218, 220, 224–225, 230, 257, 271, 278, 289, 293–294, 299, 302, 311, 320
Enneads, The, 33

Fante, 76, 141
Fates, 31, 215
Ferrara, 13, 18–19, 70
Ficino, Marsilio, 13, 25, 70–74, 148, 152, 172, 178, 194, 202, 227
fish, 122, 274, 292
Five Dharmas, 90, 116, 120
Five Poisons, 116, 120
Five Precepts, 90, 116, 120, 240, 275, 286
Five Wisdoms, 90, 116, 120
flag, 122–123
Florence, 19, 62, 70, 72, 175

Fool, the, xi, 20–22, 24, 51, 57–58, 76, 79, 95–96, 133–137, 142, 155, 158, 169, 177, 194, 324
Fortuna, 31, 47, 76, 141, 156, 160, 176–177, 185, 309
Four Evangelists, 62, 73, 109, 111, 224
four functions, 28, 124–125, 129, 174
Four Noble Truths, 4, 87, 220, 222
France, 12–13, 20–22, 46, 49, 72, 76, 109, 111, 113, 132, 140, 159, 175, 185, 192, 196, 211, 253
Francis, Saint, 49–55, 58, 80, 96, 127–128, 135, 183, 187, 190, 198

Gandhara, 1, 10
garuda, 121–122, 305, 308
Gautama, xi, 9, 41, 81, 115, 180–181, 184–185, 188, 190–193, 195–196, 198–200, 202–203, 209–211, 214, 220, 250, 302
Germany, 13, 19, 25, 47, 103, 149–150
Giotto, 59–60
gnosis, 27, 29, 35, 37, 150
Gnosticism, 40, 45, 175, 196, 201
Godwin, Joscelyn, 6
Goldschmidt cards, 47–48
Grail, the, 46–48, 53, 96
Greece, 1–4, 9–11, 27–29, 31–32, 35, 70, 78–79, 97, 103–104, 109, 111, 124, 150, 160, 163, 167, 175, 181, 204, 310–311, 313
Gringonneur deck, 200, 215
Guglielmites, 145
Guiley, Rosemary Ellen, 229
guru, 180–181, 184, 293

Hanged Man, the, 23, 79, 98, 177, 184–185
Hellenist, 1, 10, 31–32, 35, 45
Hercules, 3, 99, 153, 181
Hermes, 35, 37, 42–43, 45, 68–70, 141–142, 147, 192, 229
Hermes Trismegistus, 35, 70, 229
Hermeticism, 27, 34–35, 40, 42–43, 45, 142, 144, 147
Hermetica, 11, 13, 35, 42, 70
Hermit, the, 22, 54, 56–57, 62, 65, 72, 79, 83–84, 98, 139, 169–171, 177
Heruka, 118–119, 251
Hills, Christopher, 207
Hinduism, 6, 10, 12–14, 84, 93–94, 101, 107, 126, 166, 174, 206, 233, 247, 266, 284, 301, 305
Holy Roman Empire, 19, 149, 153
horse, 53, 66, 72, 84, 121–123, 144, 159, 163–165, 167, 179, 182, 188, 195, 266, 269, 273

I Ching, 254
I Trionfi, 12, 60–65
Iamblichus, 5, 11, 34, 37, 40–41, 138, 143, 205
immortality, 38, 47, 62, 64, 67, 80
India, 1–2, 4, 6, 9–13, 15, 30, 45, 81–83, 89, 93, 97, 99, 104–105, 131, 134–136, 138, 171, 173, 193, 203, 207, 215, 227, 229, 239, 247, 257, 290, 301, 310
Indra, 144, 191, 233, 247
Islam, 2, 12, 17, 42–45, 49, 54, 94, 174–175
Italy, 4, 6, 9, 13, 16–22, 24, 44, 46–47, 59, 61, 70, 76, 90, 96, 132, 140, 149–150, 159, 163, 170, 185, 200, 211–212, 216–217, 221

Jainism, 85, 93, 97, 99, 219, 303
jewel, 53, 106–107, 117, 121, 129, 180, 222, 231, 240, 244, 252–258, 260, 262–267, 269–270, 300, 313, 318, 324
Japan, 1, 115, 250, 269, 288, 308
Jerusalem, new, 66
Jina, 90, 99, 115–118, 120–123, 131, 133, 182, 210, 213–214, 224–225, 231–232, 235, 237, 250–251, 269, 277, 285, 288, 290, 300, 302–304, 308, 324
jnana yoga. *See under* yoga
Joan, Pope, 145
jongleurs, 46, 56–58, 76
Josaphat, Saint, 2, 58
Judgement, 23, 62, 66–67, 80, 99, 218, 229–230
Jung, C. G., 3, 28, 92, 101, 116, 124–126, 174, 234, 253, 272, 291, 312
Justice, 22, 30–32, 68, 79–80, 92, 165–168, 173–174, 176, 179–180, 225

Kabbalah, 12, 14–15, 23, 55, 175
Kantaka, 84, 144, 159, 165–166, 179, 266
Kapilavastu, 82, 134
karma, 115, 129, 165–166, 174–175, 178, 184–185, 188, 210, 308
karma yoga. *See under* yoga
Kingsley, Peter, 6
knot, 122, 303
Ksatriya, 82, 94
Kuan Yin, 289
Kublai Khan, 2
kundalini, 202–204

ladder, 29, 34–35, 37, 43, 52, 55, 57–58, 104, 136, 204–205, 208, 211

Leadbeater, C. W., 206
lion, 62, 73, 82, 111, 120–121, 144, 181–182, 225, 290
Locana, 118, 121, 214, 248
lotus, 82, 109, 121–122, 129, 144, 200, 207, 219, 225, 231, 237, 244, 248, 252, 271–275, 277–279, 281–282, 284–289, 291, 324
Lovers, the, 20, 22, 56, 62, 78, 98, 145–146, 158–159, 161–162, 215
Lumbini, 143
Lull, Ramon, 12, 42, 53, 58, 72, 76, 78, 133, 135, 155, 158, 165, 169

magic, 14, 25, 42, 99, 101–102, 106, 118, 122, 274
Magician, the, 22–23, 76, 139–140, 142
Mahaprajapati, 83, 143–144
Mahayana Buddhism, 115–116
Mamaki, 118, 121, 214, 267
Mamluk deck, 17, 49
mandala, 7–8, 80, 82, 99, 101–103, 105, 107–109, 111, 113, 115–117, 120, 123, 125, 127, 129, 174, 203, 224–225, 255, 312, 323–325, 327
Mara, xiii, 85–86, 98, 131, 179–180, 190, 194–203, 209, 218–219, 250, 302
maras, 85, 194
Marseilles, Tarot of, 7, 13, 22, 56–57, 62, 72–74, 76, 78–80, 98, 114, 134–135, 139–140, 142, 144, 149–150, 153, 156, 159, 163, 166, 170, 177, 181, 184, 188, 192, 196, 200, 204, 211, 216, 221

Maya, 82–83, 134, 138, 143–144, 146–147
Mecca, 102
meditation, 5–6, 8, 33, 37, 55, 57, 84, 86, 92–94, 99, 101–102, 107, 171, 180, 182, 188, 191, 196, 203, 206–207, 210, 212–213, 218, 220, 224, 237, 248, 255, 260, 267, 287–288, 307, 323
Mercury, 31, 36, 43, 104, 147, 204
Michelangelo, 71, 76
Milan, 18–20, 22, 61, 79, 163
Minchiate, 52, 62, 72, 185, 215, 221, 229
Mo, 310
Moakley, Gertrude, 61
Moon, the, 23, 66, 80, 99, 141, 203, 209, 211–212, 215, 217
Mount Meru, 82, 104–105, 116, 133, 224, 296, 305
Mount Sinai, 103
Mucalinda, 203–204, 207, 305
mudra, 120, 122, 156, 200, 212, 221, 232, 235, 237, 248, 250, 269, 277, 288, 300, 302, 308
music of the spheres, 5, 205
mysticism, xii, xiv, 3, 6–8, 11–12, 15, 20–21, 24–27, 29, 31, 33–35, 37, 39, 41, 43–47, 49, 51, 53–55, 57–59, 61, 63–71, 73, 75–77, 79–80, 85, 96, 101, 104, 111, 126, 145, 150, 175–176, 204, 216, 221, 229, 237, 247, 266, 269, 312
Mysteries, 26, 55, 104

nagas, 203, 305
Necessity, 30–31, 36, 175, 215
Nemesis, 175, 185
Neoplatonism, 11–13, 24–26, 33–35, 40–45, 52–55, 57–59, 61,

68–70, 72–73, 75, 100, 108, 136, 144, 170, 174, 204, 224
Newton, Isaac, 58, 206
Nirvana, 8, 33, 86–87, 93, 131, 180, 219, 230, 306
Nous, 33–34
nude, 13, 66, 71, 73–76, 80, 112, 141, 204, 224

One, the, 3, 5, 21, 27–31, 33–35, 37–38, 41, 45, 65, 68, 77, 93, 97, 104, 108, 127, 133, 140, 167, 177–178, 248, 250, 273, 277, 306, 324
O'Neill, Robert, xii, 19
oracle, 32, 143, 254, 309, 311
Oracle of Delphi, 32, 136, 150
ouroboros, 47, 177

Pali, 81
Pandara, 118, 121, 214, 287
Papa, 98, 228
paper, 11–12, 15–17, 19, 21, 23–24
Papesse, the, 22, 77–78, 144–146, 156
Parinirvana, 131, 227, 229–230, 325
peacock, 121–122, 267, 286, 289
Petrarch, 12, 59–65, 67, 163, 170, 221
Plato, 4–6, 10–11, 25–34, 36–37, 40–44, 52, 54, 56, 59–60, 62–65, 68–71, 79–80, 87–89, 91–93, 96–97, 104, 116, 128, 135–136, 161–163, 167, 174, 176, 178–179, 192, 203–205, 215, 218, 221, 227, 321
Plotinus, 2, 11, 25–26, 33, 35, 70, 93
Poimandres, The, 35–37
poisons, 91, 116, 120, 174, 178, 195, 222, 232, 253, 264, 267, 279, 286, 294
Poliziano, 70

Polo, Marco, 2, 12, 17, 95, 100
Pope, the, xiii, 22, 77–78, 96, 98, 144–146, 156, 159
Porphyry, 11, 33–34
Prudence, 30, 32, 68, 79, 176, 185, 225
Psyche, 27, 33
Pythagoras, 4–7, 9, 11, 26, 28, 30, 34, 40–41, 43, 63, 76–78, 90–91, 97, 138, 140, 143, 160, 174, 205–207, 223, 282, 324

quincunx, 109, 112, 122, 224
quinta essentia, 8, 111–112
Quran, 45

Rahula, 84, 158, 160
raja yoga. *See under* yoga
Ramon the Fool, 57, 155
Ratnasambhava, 117, 121, 214, 252, 265–267, 269–270, 300
reincarnation, 4–5, 7, 9–12, 30, 80, 84, 87, 91, 172, 174–176, 178, 184
Renaissance, xiv, 3, 6–8, 12–13, 17–18, 24–26, 31, 42, 44, 47, 54, 58–59, 61–62, 64–65, 68–72, 76, 79, 96, 140–141, 145–146, 150, 159, 161, 163, 170, 181, 185, 192, 195, 236, 312
Republic, The, 27, 29–31, 79, 88–89, 176, 192, 215
romanticism, 12, 42, 46–47, 53, 56, 58–60, 67, 135, 145, 150, 161
Rome, 2, 33, 35, 61, 155, 216
rosary, 55, 310

sacred center, 8, 52, 82, 97, 99, 103, 122, 133, 150, 191, 199, 213, 215, 222, 224, 233, 324

sadhu, 84–85, 98, 139, 169–171, 173, 180, 184
Sakti, 37, 64, 117–121, 181, 213–217, 224, 231, 248, 267, 287, 303, 306, 308, 324
Sakyamuni, 81
Samson, 181–182
Sanskrit, 30, 81, 101, 116, 246, 252, 265, 318
Saturn, 31, 36, 43, 64, 72, 95, 104, 170, 204
seven planets, 31, 34, 36, 58, 61, 73, 80, 104, 204–205, 211
seven sacraments, 57, 104, 206
seven vices, 34, 36, 56–57, 206
seven virtues, 20, 34, 56–57, 206
Shri Yantra, 107–109
Siddhartha, xi, xiii, 5, 41, 81–86, 94, 96–99, 115–116, 123, 134–136, 139, 143–144, 146, 148–150, 152–160, 162–174, 179–183, 185, 187, 195, 199, 232, 239, 266, 301
snake, 82, 120, 178, 202, 204, 286
Socrates, 31, 37–38, 92, 136, 162, 164, 179, 218, 221, 294
Sogal Rinpoche, 189
Sola-Busca deck, 21
Sorti, Le, 140–141
soul, 4–5, 8, 10–11, 27–31, 33–34, 36–46, 54, 56, 60–61, 63–65, 67–68, 71, 73–74, 77–78, 80, 88–89, 94, 96–97, 111, 135, 152, 163, 167, 175, 187, 203–207, 215, 217–218, 224, 229, 291, 300, 317, 321
Spain, 12, 17, 24, 42, 44–46, 49, 53–54, 94, 175
Sri Lanka, 1, 10, 115
staffs, 78, 95, 121, 231, 271–272
Star, the, 23, 58, 72, 80, 99, 202, 204, 211

Stoicism, 31–32, 97
Strength, 3, 20, 23, 68, 79, 120, 179, 181–182, 225
stupa, 52–53, 78, 105–107, 109, 206, 260
Suddhodhana, 82–83, 98, 134, 139, 148–149, 153, 155–158, 163, 190
Sudra, 94
Sufis, 2, 12, 44–45, 54, 175
suits, 8, 16–18, 20, 22, 24, 77–78, 95, 115, 120, 124, 129, 140, 225, 231
Sujata, 85, 98, 191, 193
Sun, the, 23, 66, 99, 118, 120, 213, 215–216
sutras, 87, 184, 229
Switzerland, 13, 17, 22, 72, 156
swords, 17, 78, 95, 121, 231, 236
Symposium, The, 34, 37, 71, 128, 161

tanha, 88–89, 220
Tantra, 64, 107, 202–203, 206–207, 214, 246, 286, 305
Tara, 118, 121, 214, 223–225, 306–308, 311, 323–324, 327
tarocchi, 18
Temperance, xiii, 23, 29, 68, 79–80, 88–89, 96, 98, 176, 190, 192–193, 225
Themis, 31–32, 167
Tibet, 8, 12, 15, 30, 80, 105–106, 115, 122–123, 131–132, 182, 188–189, 193, 206, 224, 233, 236, 238, 242, 245–246, 250, 257–258, 262, 269, 273–275, 281, 296, 304–305, 308, 310–311
Timaeus, 31, 42, 205
Tower, the, 20, 23, 53, 80, 98, 106, 142, 198, 200–201, 260

Trionpho della Fortuna, 76, 141, 156, 160
triumph, 17, 61–65, 71, 78, 95, 146, 163–164, 170, 173, 188
troubadours, 46–47, 49–53, 60, 128
trumps, xii–xiii, 3, 7–8, 18, 20–22, 24, 31–32, 47, 52, 58, 61–62, 65–66, 68, 72, 76–79, 94, 96, 98–100, 115, 121, 131, 135, 140–142, 144, 146, 150, 156–157, 167, 177, 185, 196, 200, 229, 236, 312–313, 324
Tusita Heaven, 82–83, 133–134, 136, 144, 179, 325

umbrella, 122, 164, 203, 239
Upanishads, 174, 206, 215

Vaisya, 94
vajra, 118, 121–122, 129, 192, 214–216, 224, 231, 233, 235–240, 242, 244–248, 250, 290–294, 296, 298, 300–306, 308, 315, 323–324
Vajradharisvari, 118, 121, 214–216
vegetarians, 5–6, 90
Venice, 2, 17, 140–141, 145
Venus, 13, 31, 36, 43, 71, 104, 145–146, 204
Vairocana, 117, 120–122, 174, 182, 213–216, 221–222, 235, 324
vase, 122, 263
Vedas, 9, 173–174, 215
Vieville, Jacques, 75–76, 159, 192
virtue
    cardinal virtues, 20, 22, 79, 87, 89, 91, 176, 185
    Christian virtues, 20, 176
    ten virtues, 82, 166, 199

Visconti-Sforza deck, 18, 20, 66, 150, 156, 163, 167, 176, 181, 221

Waite-Smith deck, 135, 156, 231, 236, 272
Wesak, 82, 86, 144, 146, 159, 165, 209, 213, 228
wheel
    Wheel of Fortune, 23, 79, 98, 141, 176, 200, 284
    Wheel of Life, 4, 82, 120, 172–174, 177–178, 210, 222, 232, 264, 279, 284, 286, 294, 313
    Wheel of the Law, 87, 174, 176, 220, 222, 235, 266, 284, 290
World, the, 23, 47, 62, 66, 68, 73, 75–76, 80, 99, 114–115, 120, 223–225, 229, 306, 323

yab-yum, 118–119, 216
Yantras, 107
Yasodhara, 83, 98, 144, 148–151, 153–155, 158
yin-yang, 177
Yggdrasill, 97, 103
yoga
    bhakti, 127–129, 174, 210, 272
    jnana, 127–129, 174, 180, 234
    karma, 127, 129, 174, 253
    raja, 128–129, 174, 180, 210, 291

Zen, 57, 296–297

ORDER LLEWELLYN BOOKS TODAY!

Llewellyn publishes hundreds of books on your favorite subjects! To get these exciting books, including the ones on the following pages, check your local bookstore or order them directly from Llewellyn.

Order Online:
Visit our website at www.llewellyn.com, select your books, and order them on our secure server.

Order by Phone:
- Call toll-free within the U.S. at 1-877-NEW-WRLD (1-877-639-9753)
  Call toll-free within Canada at 1-866-NEW-WRLD (1-866-639-9753)
- We accept VISA, MasterCard, and American Express

Order by Mail:
Send the full price of your order (MN residents add 7% sales tax) in U.S. funds, plus postage & handling to:

Llewellyn Worldwide
P.O. Box 64383, Dept. 1-56718-529-0
St. Paul, MN 55164-0383, U.S.A.

Postage & Handling:
Standard (U.S., Mexico, & Canada). If your order is:
Up to $25.00, add $3.50
$25.01–$48.99, add $4.00
$49.00 and over, FREE STANDARD SHIPPING
(Continental U.S. orders ship UPS. AK, HI, PR, & P.O. Boxes ship USPS 1st class. Mex. & Can. ship PMB.)

International Orders:
Surface Mail: For orders of $20.00 or less, add $5 plus $1 per item ordered. For orders of $20.01 and over, add $6 plus $1 per item ordered.

Air Mail:
Books: Postage & Handling is equal to the total retail price of all books in the order.
Non-book items: Add $5 for each item.

Orders are processed within 2 business days. Please allow for normal shipping time. Postage and handling rates subject to change.

The Buddha Tarot

ROBERT M. PLACE

The combination of Buddhism and Tarot might seem strange at first, but the underlying archetypal pattern reveals stunning similarities. The story in the Tarot's major arcana parallels the story of Siddhartha's journey to enlightenment. This sequence of twenty-two cards has been interpreted by many as an allegorical description of the soul's journey to enlightenment, beginning with the naive Fool and culminating in the universal consciousness represented by the World card.

The Buddha Tarot includes a 79-card Tarot deck designed and created by artist Robert M. Place, acclaimed for his distinctive style and artwork with religious and sacred themes. Also included is a booklet exploring the parallels between the Tarot and Buddhism, the life of Buddha, and interpretations for each card.

Perfect for divination, meditation, and unlocking one's inner wisdom, *The Buddha Tarot* awaits you as a gentle guide on your journey toward enlightenment.

0-7387-0441-5

Boxed kit: 79-card deck, black organdy pouch, and 72-pp. instruction booklet $24.95

To order, call 1-877-NEW-WRLD
Prices subject to change without notice